W9-BSC-240

Thinking through

Philosophy

An Introduction

Chris Horner
Cambridge Regional College,
Cambridge, UK

Emrys Westacott
Alfred University, New York,
USA

CAMBRIDGE
UNIVERSITY PRESS

PUBLISHED BY THE PRESS SYNDICATE OF THE UNIVERSITY OF CAMBRIDGE
The Pitt Building, Trumpington Street, Cambridge, United Kingdom

CAMBRIDGE UNIVERSITY PRESS
The Edinburgh Building, Cambridge CB2 2RU, UK
40 West 20th Street, New York, NY 10011–4211, USA
477 Williamstown Road, Melbourne, VIC 3207, Austrailia
Ruiz de Alarcón 13, 28014 Madrid, Spain
Dock House, The Waterfront, Cape Town 8001, South Africa

http://www.cambridge.org

© Cambridge University Press 2000

This book is in copyright. Subject to statutory exception
and to the provisions of relevant collective licensing agreements,
no reproduction of any part may take place without
the written permission of Cambridge University Press.

First published 2000
Reprinted with revisions 2001
Fifth printing 2004

Printed in the United Kingdom at the University Press, Cambridge

Typefaces Rotis Serif and Sans Serif *System* QuarkXPress®

Illustrations by Jerry Ball, Eikon Ltd

A catalogue record for this book is available from the British Library

ISBN 0 521 62657 9 paperback

Contents

In memory of Kathleen Horner (1914–1999)

Preface

Consider these questions:

- When I make what feels like a free choice, am I really acting freely?
- What explains the astonishing progress of science in modern times?
- In the age of science, is it irrational to be religious?
- When we say that racism is morally wrong, are we stating an objective truth or are we just expressing our personal feelings?
- What is it about art that we value, apart from the pleasure it gives?

These are the kinds of questions that philosophers discuss. But almost everyone thinks about philosophical issues from time to time. Who has not, at some point in their life, wondered whether their mind could exist without their body, or whether there is a God, or whether we can ever be absolutely certain that we are not dreaming? Questions like these are enormously interesting. But they are not easy. Trying to think them through by ourselves, unassisted by the insights of others who have addressed the same questions, is a daunting prospect – a bit like setting out to scale a rock face without the benefit of other climbers' experiences and without any special equipment. The chances of getting 'stuck' a few feet off the ground are quite high.

This book is written for people who wish to begin thinking about philosophical issues like these. No previous knowledge of philosophy is assumed. Our primary purpose is to help readers come to grips with some of the most fascinating and important problems of philosophy. The book is not a history of philosophy, though at times we do discuss the ideas of some of the major thinkers in the Western tradition. Nor is it a catalogue of philosophical doctrines, though in the course of our enquiries we do identify, describe and appraise specific doctrines. What we try to do more than anything else is show what it means to *think philosophically*.

The eight chapters by no means represent all the branches of philosophy. It is not possible to do that in a book of this sort. We therefore had to make a selection, but the areas we chose to concentrate on are all areas that have been at the centre of philosophical enquiry for a long time – and they remain very exciting fields of research today.

Each chapter is a more or less self-contained enquiry and can be understood by itself, without any familiarity with the other chapters. However, issues in one branch of philosophy are often closely linked to issues in another area: for example, how we approach questions in political philosophy about the nature of justice is bound to be affected by how we answer questions in ethics concerning the nature of the good and the right. This means that sometimes the discussion of a topic in one context overlaps with what is said elsewhere, but not to the extent of making one chapter dependent on another.

We begin each enquiry by raising a question or positing a thesis that is likely to be familiar to most readers. We then discuss the matter in a way that tries to stay in touch with the thoughts and questions likely to occur to someone who travels this road for the first time. To this end, we punctuate the text here and there with inset queries and assertions that express such thoughts. This approach also helps to give the discussions something of the structure and feel of a philosophical dialogue, which is very often the form that even solitary philosophical reflection takes.

No chapter tries to cover the whole of its field. On the contrary, each chapter generally focuses on a small number of closely related topics. The Metaphysics chapter, for instance, is largely devoted to two controversies: freedom versus determinism, and materialism versus idealism. Similarly, the Philosophy of art chapter is a sustained enquiry into the question of why we value art. This approach accords with our general aim of demonstrating the character of philosophical reflection as opposed to communicating information about the full range of philosophical options available.

However, the history of philosophy is certainly worth knowing about, both for its intrinsic interest and because it has decisively shaped the way in which we today conceive of and address our philosophical problems. We thus supplement our explanations of important philosophical positions with brief sketches of some of the major thinkers whose ideas we discuss. In order not to interrupt the philosophical discussion, these summaries are set apart from the main text. For the same reason, 'think critically!' boxes provide separate explanations of certain basic definitions and distinctions relating to aspects of reasoning referred to in the text, complete with illustrative examples.

While the book is aimed first and foremost at the general reader, it is also eminently suitable for use as a textbook or as a supplement to other readings in introductory courses at the secondary school and college level. But whatever the reason readers have for engaging with the issues discussed here, we hope the book gives them a sense of what it means to 'do philosophy', an appreciation of how absorbing it can be, and a desire to explore further those questions they find most exciting.

Acknowledgements

For various forms of support and assistance, we would like to thank our colleagues at Alfred University and Cambridge Regional College. In addition, we owe special thanks to the following individuals: Howard Caygill, Jim Booker, Alison Ainlie, Bill Dibrell, Neil Gascoigne, Fiona Tolhurst, Phillip Blond and Frances Viggiani for their valuable advice and support; Simon Christmas, an early collaborator on this project who wrote the first draft of the chapter on the Philosophy of mind; Noel Kavanagh, for his encouragement, patience and editorial guidance; and Djuna Thurley and Vicky Westacott, whose contributions as readers, critics, partner and friend have been invaluable.

1 Metaphysics

The term 'metaphysics' was coined by students of the great Greek philosopher Aristotle (384–322 BCE) who were editing his writings after his death. The literal meaning of the word in its original use was 'after the physics', the title that Aristotle's editors gave to the treatise they placed after the one entitled *Physics* in the master's collected writings. But the treatise in question also went *beyond* the physics in a philosophical sense, for it dealt with questions that in some ways lie deeper than physics and most other branches of human enquiry: questions concerning the fundamental assumptions and theoretical foundations of these other enquiries. Consequently, 'metaphysics' came to mean the branch of philosophy that addresses basic questions about the nature of reality. For example:

- Is there a difference between the way things appear to us and the way they really are?
- Does mental or spiritual reality ultimately depend on the physical world, or is it the other way round?
- Is everything that happens predetermined? If so, does this rule out the possibility of our making genuinely free choices?
- What makes something the same thing at two different times?
- What makes a person the same person throughout the course of his or her life?

As even this small sample shows, metaphysics covers quite a range of philosophical topics. But these questions often tend to be bundled together because they all relate directly to the question at the centre of metaphysics: What is the ultimate nature of reality? Particular sciences focus on some part or some aspect of reality. The various branches of philosophy deal with certain parts or aspects of human experience: aesthetics with art, epistemology with knowledge, ethics with moral life and values. But metaphysics takes in the whole – everything that exists in whatever form – and tries to reach conclusions about its basic nature. In this short chapter we cannot hope to cover all the issues that metaphysicians discuss, but we can try to think through a few of the most interesting problems that metaphysics raises and seeks to resolve. Let us begin with the debate over whether everything that happens is predetermined.

Fatalism: whatever will be, will be

To say that everything is predetermined sounds a lot like fatalism. A fatalistic attitude may sometimes be useful – when dealing with misfortune, for example – but is there any reason to suppose that there is a force, 'Fate', that dictates the course of events in the world?

We need to distinguish between fatalism and determinism. **Fatalism**, understood as a doctrine rather than just an attitude, can take more than one form. The idea that there is some sort of metaphysical force controlling our destinies is perhaps the most familiar to us because it is central to many Greek legends. As the Greeks saw it, fate decreed that Patroclus would be killed by Hector, who would be killed by Achilles, who would in turn be killed by Paris, and not even the gods could alter this sequence of events. This doctrine expresses a feeling of helplessness in the face of natural and supernatural forces over which people feel they have little control. It has less currency nowadays, presumably because we feel less helpless.

Fatalism has also been put forward as a doctrine about the timelessness of truth. Take the statement 'On 24 March 1603, Queen Elizabeth I of England died.' This was true on that very day. It has remained true ever since and will continue to be true for ever. By the same token, the statement was true at any time prior to Elizabeth's death. So millions of years before she lived, it was still true that she would die on that particular day. For that matter, it was true on the day Elizabeth died that you would read this sentence at precisely this moment in time. What, if anything, are we to conclude from this? Certainly, we can say that this kind of timelessness seems to be a feature of our concept of truth. But it is hard to see how this entails the dramatic conclusion that our lives are somehow predestined and that nothing we do can alter what has been preordained for us.

Fatalism can also be understood in a very general way as the view that the course of future events cannot be altered from what it is going to be. Our hopes, desires, intentions and actions are powerless to make any difference because they themselves are part of the inevitable sequence. This differs from the first form of fatalism mentioned above in that it does not posit fate as a supernatural force directing natural events. Indeed, it does not posit any explanation at all as to why the future is unalterable. It is thus compatible with, yet different from, determinism, which specifies why the future must be the way it will be.

Determinism: one thing leads to another

According to **determinism**, everything that happens is determined by prior causes. The word 'determined' here denotes a relation between two events or states of affairs. To say that A determines B is to say both that A *causes* B and that A *necessitates* B (that is, given A, B *must* follow). Determinism thus holds that every event is the necessary result of the chain of causes leading up to it, a chain that runs back indefinitely into the past. Put more globally, the state of the universe at any particular moment could not be otherwise, given the state the universe was in at the immediately preceding moment. One implication of this view is that from a given state of the universe there can only be one possible future. Another implication is that all future states of the universe are – in principle at least – completely predictable.

The idea that everything has a cause seems reasonable. But the idea that the entire history of the universe follows a necessary, predetermined path does not obviously follow from this principle and is not obviously true. So why should we believe it?

The principle that every event is caused is known as the **causal principle**. It is presupposed in science (except in some parts of quantum mechanics) and also in everyday life. If you start to feel a pain in your neck you assume that something is causing the pain. If your doctor tried to tell you that the pain was one of those rare occurrences, an event without a cause, you would immediately conclude that you need to change your doctor. It is possible to be a good doctor and not know what is causing a patient's pain; it is not possible to be a good doctor and believe that some pains are uncaused. Such a belief would immediately undermine one's credibility both as a scientist and as a person of common sense.

It is perfectly true that the causal principle by itself does not logically entail determinism. But the route from one to the other is fairly direct. An old version of the causal principle, first proposed by the Greeks, says that 'nothing can come from nothing'. This obviously excludes the possibility of objects suddenly popping into existence from nowhere and for no reason. But it also rules out the possibility that an effect could somehow contain more than was 'in' its cause or causes. For instance, a car cannot weigh more than the sum of its parts; water in a pan cannot get hotter that the burner that is heating it. These considerations lead to what is known as the **principle of sufficient reason** which, in its simplest version, states that everything has a complete explanation. This principle is intended to apply equally to events, things, and states of affairs. If, for simplicity's sake, we just speak of states of affairs (which we will allow to include laws of nature), the principle asserts that for any state of affairs (S), there is some other state or combination of states (C) which is *sufficient* to produce S. Saying that C is 'sufficient' to produce S means that given C, S will necessarily follow. The complete explanation of S is thus an accurate description of C.

Let us illustrate what we have just said with an example. Suppose S to be the sinking of the *Titanic*; C will be all the relevant factors that helped bring this about: the course and speed of the ship; the course and position of the iceberg it hit; the size of the iceberg; the thickness of the ship's hull; the physical structure of the ice and the steel that collided; the laws of physics that account for the fact that the ice broke through the steel rather than bouncing off it or crumbling before it; and so on. It is easy to see that this list could be extended infinitely; there is no limit to the number of things that could be included in the complete explanation. For instance, in a complete explanation we would have to mention the fact that the ship left port exactly when it did, the fact that there is ice at the earth's poles, and the fact that radar had not yet been invented.

Suppose, though, that S is the state of the whole universe at the present moment. According to the principle of sufficient reason, this too has a complete explanation. The explanation will be a description of the way the universe was at all previous times together with the laws of nature that govern the way the universe changes over time. But if this really is a complete explanation, then the way the universe is right now was *necessitated* by its previous states together with the laws of nature. It could not have been otherwise. To say it could have been otherwise would be to say that some features of the universe in its present state cannot be explained; they just happen to be that way for no particular reason. This possibility is precisely what the principle of sufficient reason rules out.

Determinism thus seems to be implied by the principle of sufficient reason, which makes it theoretically very plausible. Its credibility is also bolstered by the fact that it has long been a basic presupposition of modern science. Most of the astounding progress that science has made over the past four centuries has been made on the basis of a mechanistic and deterministic view of the world, a view that treats the universe as a system of objects moving and interacting according to fixed laws, rather like balls on a pool table. This analogy is actually quite helpful, and brings out further implications of what we have said above.

Imagine a pool table without pockets. If I set a ball in motion on this table, it is possible to predict more or less where it will be in ten seconds' time. A well programmed computer, provided with accurate data about the dimensions of the table, the initial position, speed and direction of the ball, the level of friction between it and the table surface, the elasticity of the edge cushion, the presence and type of spin imparted to the ball, etc., could predict the position of the ball at any future time with great accuracy. Should another ball be introduced, also moving around the table, the computer would be able to take account of this added complexity and predict whether the balls would ever collide, and if so, where, when and with what result. In principle, no matter how large the table, and no matter how many balls are set in motion on it, a sufficiently powerful computer provided with accurate enough information should be able to predict where each ball will be and what it will be doing at any given future moment.

The scientific point of view, which has been so spectacularly successful over the last few centuries, sees the difference between the pool table and the actual universe we live in as quantitative not qualitative. The universe may contain many more objects; these objects may be less uniform and their interactions incredibly complex. But for all that, their behaviour is governed by a small number of basic, universal laws. A powerful enough computer, properly programmed and provided with enough information should, in principle, be able to predict with complete accuracy the state of the universe at any future moment.

> *Is this really still the way scientists view the world? What about such discoveries as the indeterminacy principle, or the more recent advent of chaos theory? Haven't they knocked determinism on the head?*

To some extent, quantum mechanics has indeed dented determinism's prestige. According to the indeterminacy principle there are some events – the behaviour of individual electrons in certain circumstances – that are not causally determined and therefore impossible to predict. We can predict that, say, seven out of ten electrons in a given situation will behave in a certain way; but we cannot be sure how any particular electron will behave. The natural response to this is to assume that our inability to predict what the electron will do is due to our ignorance of the causal factors that determine its behaviour. But most quantum physicists explicitly reject this idea. The indeterminacy, they say, is not simply a matter of our own uncertainty; it inheres in nature.

Two points about this claim are worth noting. First, there have always been some physicists who are suspicious of it, most famously Albert Einstein who objected that 'God does not play dice' (to which his fellow physicist Niels Bohr replied, 'Albert, stop telling God what to do!'). Just possibly, we will one day arrive at a different theoretical model that will provide an explanation for events which on our present model appear undetermined and hence inexplicable. Second, the indeterminacy in question only concerns subatomic particles; the behaviour of larger objects, which range in size from the microscopically small to the astronomically huge, is still thought to be thoroughly predictable – at least in principle.

Chaos theory is somewhat different, since it is not incompatible with determinism. It says only that there are some systems and subsystems that are so complex, and in which small variations in the initial conditions can lead to such massively different outcomes, that accurate predictions are impossible. Long-term weather patterns or trends in the global economy offer familiar examples of this kind of unpredictability. But complexity, no matter how great, is not the same as indeterminacy. Die-hard determinists can accept chaos theory because the limits it places on predictability arise from the limitations of our knowledge and reasoning abilities, not from the intrinsic nature of things themselves.

Freedom versus determinism

If we grant that outside the realm of subatomic physics determinism seems to be supported by the success of the sciences that presuppose it, doesn't this imply that human actions are just as predetermined and therefore as predictable as all other events? If so, isn't determinism obviously false, given the fact that we have free will?

Here we arrive at one of the great metaphysical disputes in the history of philosophy: the conflict between determinism and the belief in what is usually called free will. This controversy is actually one of several that arise when the scientific picture of the world conflicts with so-called common sense. As we have seen, the success of the sciences seems to provide a good reason for accepting determinism. But if determinism is true, then human decisions and action must, like all other events, be the necessary effects of prior causes. Yet most of us believe that at least some of the time we are responsible for our actions; we praise and blame ourselves according to what we do, just as we praise and blame others. In holding ourselves responsible, we imply that we are in control of our actions, that we might act otherwise, and that in adopting one course of action over another we make a free choice. But determinism would seem to rule out the very possibility of this sort of freedom.

It is very important to be clear about the kind of freedom that determinism threatens. Let us make a distinction between 'metaphysical freedom' and 'practical freedom'. **Practical freedom** is the freedom to do what one wishes, to realize one's desires. This is the kind of freedom that people can have in differing degrees. Someone in prison has less of it than someone at liberty. Winning the lottery would increase my practical freedom: it would enable me to travel more extensively, attend more concerts and eat at more expensive restaurants. Losing both arms would reduce my practical freedom: it would prevent me from practising the violin, decorating my bedroom or playing tennis.

This kind of practical freedom is quite distinct from **metaphysical freedom**, often referred to as **freedom of the will**. To exercise this kind of freedom means being ultimately responsible for one's choices. I may be tied up in a prison cell, my practical freedom severely limited; but it is still up to me whether I fight against my situation or resign myself to it, whether I fraternize with my jailers or go on hunger strike, whether I spend my time daydreaming or humming my favourite songs or practising mental arithmetic or composing limericks. Although we might allow that young children and mentally impaired people do not have this kind of freedom to the same extent as normal adults, we generally think of it as something that, if we have it at all, we all have to more or less the same degree. However, free will is not usually ascribed to other animals. Compared to practical freedom, it is thus viewed as something that one either has or does not have, depending on one's basic mental capacities. It should be clear that it is this metaphysical notion of freedom – freedom of the will – that is threatened by determinism.

Given that we are committed to making our beliefs consistent with each other, there seem to be three obvious ways in which we can respond to this conflict:

Option 1: Accept determinism and reject the belief in free will.
Option 2: Show how determinism and the idea of free will are compatible.
Option 3: Endorse the idea that we have free will and reject determinism (at least as far as human actions are concerned).

Let us consider these options in turn.

Option 1: Determinism is true, freedom is an illusion

This view is often called **hard determinism**. Its proponents see themselves as taking a hard-headed attitude towards our precious but (as they see it) mistaken belief in freedom and responsibility. We have already seen that determinism is a plausible doctrine, supported by the success of science. An obvious question, then, is whether anything can be said against it by defenders of free will.

One reason for holding that freedom is real and not illusory is simply that this is how it feels. Samuel Johnson articulated this argument when he pronounced, in typically dogmatic fashion, 'Sir, we *know* the will is free, and there's an end of it.' When I make certain choices, whether they be trivial or momentous, it usually seems to me that I could have chosen otherwise and am thus responsible for my decision. When I order a drink I have it in my power to order either tea of coffee. If I give evidence at a trial I can choose to tell the truth or to lie.

This argument is essentially an appeal to intuition. It has the merit of being supremely simple and, for many people, extremely persuasive. But to those who are sceptical about free will it is too simple – even simplistic. What kind of argument consists of nothing more than an appeal to the way things *seem*? The sun *seems* to move across the sky, and for thousands of years the belief that the sun moved while the earth was at rest was common sense; but appearances were deceptive, and common sense was wrong. Feelings, too, can easily be misleading. Millions of people feel that they are being watched over by a divine power, but this hardly constitutes an argument for the existence of God. Hard determinists are thus unlikely to be moved by an appeal to unexamined feelings.

A second reason for upholding the idea that we have free will is that all our moral principles and institutions rest on the assumption that we are free. We routinely praise and blame ourselves and others for what we do. We think that at least some of the people who break the law are justly punished. And we believe that people who are acclaimed and rewarded for significant achievements deserve their laurels. But if determinism is true, the whole idea that anyone *deserves* anything is nonsense, since no one is truly responsible for any of their actions.

How strong is this argument? It certainly shows that determinism conflicts with some of our most deeply entrenched beliefs and practices. But it hardly proves that determinism is false. A determinist can reply: 'So much the worse for those beliefs and practices. It might be nicer if they were well founded; but they are not. The truth is sometimes other than what we would wish.' Moreover, so far as rewards and punishments are concerned, these can perhaps be justified from a deterministic point of view, since they help to determine actions in a beneficial way. Rewards promote good behaviour, punishments discourage bad behaviour. Indeed, the reason we all believe this is precisely because human behaviour is fairly predictable. Determinists could even argue that the sooner we accept the full implications of this idea the better, since we will then be encouraged to set about fine tuning the mechanisms we already use to condition and control people's propensity to act in certain ways. Of course, there may be some social benefits to keeping alive the whole mythology of desert; that is something else the social scientists will have to investigate. But this does not constitute an argument for the truth of the mythology.

These two arguments – from the way things feel and from morality – may help to explain why so many people believe in the reality of free will. But the arguments do little or nothing to *demonstrate* that we are free, and are thus unlikely to impress serious determinists. But determinism may be vulnerable to a different, rather subtle kind of criticism, one that questions determinism's own internal coherence.

If someone espouses a philosophical doctrine we are always entitled to ask why we should believe it. Usually, we are then given reasons for believing this doctrine rather than some alternative theory. The reasons typically consist of empirical evidence, logical arguments, demonstrations that the doctrine in question follows from other beliefs we hold, refutations of rival positions, etc. The discourse in which these reasons are presented – whether it is spoken or written – implicitly presupposes that both the speaker and the audience should be swayed only by rational considerations of this sort (see the 'Reasons and causes' box).

How does all this relate to the debate about determinism? Well, according to the determinist, everything we do is causally determined. But if this really is a universal truth it must cover our acceptance of certain beliefs and our rejection of others. From the determinist perspective, it should be just as possible to predict which philosophical positions a person will embrace as it is to predict what kind of foods they will prefer or what kind of partner they will select. Determinists must

think critically!   Reasons and causes

Always distinguish between reasons and causes when analysing an argument. This is a very important distinction. Suppose I ask someone why they believe abortion to be morally wrong. Here are two possible responses they might give:

1 I believe abortion is wrong because I was brought up as a Catholic.
2 I believe abortion is wrong because I think the foetus has the status of a
  person, and it is wrong to kill an innocent person.

In a sense, response (1) offers a reason for their belief; but it is not the kind of reason that has any persuasive power. With (1) they have, in fact, cited a *cause* of their belief as opposed to providing a rational justification for it. I can accept that what they say is true – their being raised as a Catholic did lead them to condemn abortion – while still rejecting the belief in question. If, on the other hand, they respond to my question with (2), then they have given a genuine reason for their belief in the sense of providing it with a *rational justification*. In this case, I cannot consistently accept what they say while still disagreeing with their conclusion.

This distinction between reasons and causes correlates to a distinction between justification and explanation. Our actions and beliefs can perhaps be *explained* by identifying their causes; but they cannot be *justified* in this way. Only reasons can justify. And only reasons are to be respected as having legitimate persuasive force.

therefore concede that although they play the game of supporting their deterministic philosophy with rational arguments, these arguments are not necessarily what led them to embrace determinism; their opinions, like all their other preferences, are merely the effects of causes over which they have no control. Moreover, similar considerations apply to their attempts to persuade other people to adopt their point of view. Whether or not their arguments are persuasive may have nothing to do with their intrinsic soundness. It is not even clear why determinists should care about whether their arguments are sound. Offering sound arguments is one method of persuasion; producing effective rhetoric is another. Does a determinist have any reason to prefer the former to the latter?

Determinists may try to wriggle out of this difficulty by claiming that rational justifications are still important in their eyes because good evidence and sound arguments have greater causal efficacy than weak evidence or invalid reasoning; our brains are so wired as to be more readily affected by rational considerations. But this response is weak in two ways. First, it just is not true that the stronger argument always – or even usually – defeats the weaker. Distressingly, good evidence and sound reasoning can easily be overwhelmed by effective rhetoric. Secondly, and more importantly, the response fails to recognize the depth of the problem. Causal influence and rational persuasion are two entirely different kinds of operation; the corresponding concepts belong to different spheres of discourse. The critical question that determinists must answer is: Why should we respect anyone's belief in determinism if their holding this belief is, ultimately, only the predetermined outcome of a long causal chain? Why should we take their arguments seriously if they themselves conceive of rational persuasion as just a form of causation?

Determinism thus seems to undermine a basic presupposition of rational discussion: ideally, at least, we ought to arrive at our theoretical beliefs solely on the basis of evidence and argumentation.

Option 2: Freedom and determinism are compatible

> *Why must determinism and the idea that we are free be viewed as incompatible? Doesn't the whole debate over freedom and determinism arise because freedom is being thought of as something mysterious, some weird breach in the natural order? But to be free simply means being able to do what one wants. And if we stick with this common sense notion of freedom there need be no problem, since it is perfectly compatible with determinism.*

This attempt to reconcile the two positions is commonly called **soft determinism**. It has attracted many adherents, among them Thomas Hobbes, John Locke and David Hume. Soft determinism is, as its name indicates, a form of determinism; it does not allow for uncaused events. But it sees no need to, since it holds that even if all events are causally determined there is still a clear difference between free and unfree actions. I am free at this moment to leave my desk and go for a walk, but I am not free to fly like a bird. I am free to go down to the basement, but if armed robbers burst into my room and forced me into the basement at gunpoint I would not be acting freely. According to the soft determinist, then, I am free to perform an action as long as I am not forced to do it or prevented from doing it. If, however, I am constrained or coerced, then I am not free.

Soft determinism certainly has a superficial plausibility. But for many philosophers its claim to dissolve the conflict between free will and determinism turns out to be a conjuring trick, a piece of metaphysical sleight of hand. Recall the distinction we made earlier between practical freedom (the freedom to do what one wishes) and metaphysical freedom (being ultimately responsible for one's choices). The problem we are discussing is how to reconcile determinism and the idea of metaphysical freedom (also known as free will). Soft determinism claims to be able to do this, but it only does it by switching the concept of freedom that is at issue.

To see this, consider the following scenario. Suppose you hypnotized twenty people, and while they were under hypnosis you told them that when next offered a choice between vanilla ice cream and strawberry ice cream they are to choose vanilla. A little while after being woken they are given this choice and, predictably, they all choose vanilla. Now let us ask this question: When they choose vanilla, is their choice free? Well, there are no external constraints: both kinds of ice cream are available, both are affordable, and no risk accompanies either choice. Nor is there any external coercion. No one is putting a gun to anyone's head and forcing them to choose vanilla. Moreover, if you asked them why they chose vanilla they would probably simply say that they preferred this kind of ice cream on this particular occasion. In other words, they were just doing what they wanted to do, fulfilling their desires. Since this is precisely how we defined *practical* freedom, we must conclude that, at least in this sense, they are acting freely.

Yet there is something odd about describing this sort of choice as free. In every case the choice followed from a particular desire; but the desire was not something for which the person was responsible, nor something over which she had any control. There may have been no external coercion, but there was a kind of internal coercion. Through your suggestions you, the hypnotist, determined each person's choice. Their choices were thus perfectly predictable; and while they may have been free in one sense of the term, they were not free in the metaphysical sense. In short, at the moment of choice they were not exercising free will.

Soft determinism may well show that the concept of *practical freedom* is compatible with determinism. But no one ever really doubted this. The problem had to do with the metaphysical notion of freedom, and soft determinism does nothing to show that *this* concept of freedom can be reconciled with determinism. By identifying freedom with practical freedom, soft determinism effectively collapses into hard determinism. Confronted with the question of whether we are ultimately responsible for any of our choices, soft determinists must say no. Like hard determinists, they are completely sceptical about the possibility that human beings can influence the course of events by exercising something called free will.

This failure of soft determinism to advance beyond hard determinism comes out most clearly when we consider actions and choices that are morally significant. Suppose I decide to drive my car even though I have been drinking. If I cause an accident, should I be penalized? Common sense says yes, and the reason is simple: I ought not to have driven while intoxicated. But according to a well known formula first stated by Immanuel Kant, 'ought implies can'. That is, it only makes sense to say that I *ought* to do something if it is *possible* for me to do it. Conversely, if an action lies beyond my powers I cannot be under any obligation to perform it. This is why it makes no sense for me to tell you that you ought to cure cancer, but it is reasonable of me to tell you that you should keep your promises.

Whether I should be penalized for driving while intoxicated thus hinges on whether I could have chosen not to drive. According to the defenders of free will I could have made this choice. According to hard determinists my choice was inevitable, given all the antecedent circumstances. And according to the soft determinists? Soft determinists will perhaps say that I could have not driven if I had made a different choice; and I could have made a different choice if certain other things had been different: for instance, the configuration of my brain at the moment of choice, my genetic inheritance, my upbringing, or particular moments in my life history. But answering the question in this way is surely a cop out. The issue is not whether I could have chosen otherwise *under different circumstances*, but whether I could have made a different choice in that particular situation. And the soft determinists, when it comes right down to it, have to say that I could not.

Option 3: Freedom is real; determinism is false

It is one thing to identify problems in hard and soft determinism; it is another thing entirely to provide positive grounds for believing that human beings really do have the remarkable capacity known as freedom of the will: the capacity to make choices that are not predetermined and that somehow initiate new causal chains. Determinism may have its difficulties; but the idea that each of us is the site of a strange kind of fault in the natural order of things – a place where the sequence of causes and effects can be halted, broken and then given a new beginning – is undeniably problematic. The central problem facing all those who defend free will even though they see it as incompatible with determinism can be stated simply: How is free will possible?

One way of answering this question is just to identify freedom with the absence of causal determination, a view sometimes referred to as **indeterminism**. On this view, an act of will (what philosophers call a 'volition') is free simply in virtue of being uncaused. The model of free action to which this gives rise is something like this. I am continually subject to all sorts of causal influences, both physical and psychological. These determine many of my characteristics, preferences, desires and actions. But at least some of the time I can summon up a volition that is not an effect of anything; it just occurs. However, although it is not caused, the volition itself can be a cause; it causes me to act in a certain way. For example, when faced with a choice between tea or coffee, the volition is the mental act through which I choose one or the other. I then act accordingly, and since my action flows from an undetermined volition we describe it as free.

There is an obvious problem with this sort of indeterminism. If the volition is something I 'summon up', then it does not just occur: it is the effect of my act of summoning. If, on the other hand, it really does just occur in an uncaused way, then it is something that just happens to me. But in that case it seems to be more like a spasmodic twitch than a deliberate action, so it can hardly be the basis for what we think of as a free, responsible choice. Nor does it help to relocate the undetermined event by supposing that while the volition is caused by my act of summoning it up, this latter act is undetermined. This simply pushes the difficulty back one step. Exactly the same objection can now be raised against the undetermined act of summoning or producing a volition. If it is uncaused, then it is something that happens to me, not something I choose or make happen; it is not, therefore, something for which I can be held responsible.

The roots of responsibility: an indeterminist view

Clearly, simple indeterminism will not do. Yet many philosophers who wish to defend the idea of free will believe that indeterminacy of some kind must play a role in any positive account of how this kind of freedom is possible. After all, if it does not, then we seem to be left only with sequences of fully determined events, and it is hard to see how any of these could be called free acts. In recent times, philosophers have therefore offered more sophisticated attempts to view some of the anti-deterministic developments in science mentioned above – notably quantum mechanics and chaos theory – as providing us, as agents, with the opportunity to make occasional creative interventions in the causal sequences that influence our lives. Let us consider an account of this sort. (The account that follows is loosely based on the defence of free will put forward by the American philosopher Robert Kane.)

The key idea to be defended is that we are, in some way and to some extent, responsible for our actions. For this to be so it is not necessary that every act we perform be perfectly free. It might be enough for us to be responsible for a relatively small number of choices we make – those choices that are especially significant in establishing patterns of behaviour, moral character, and the trajectory of our lives. For example, if I am a smoker I may not be free simply to give up smoking at any time. I may resolve this morning to go though the day without a cigarette, but the physical and psychological dependencies may prove too great, amounting to an irresistibly strong causal determination of my actions. But there will have been times in the past, before I was hopelessly addicted, when I was better able to avoid lighting up and chose not to.

Having free will, on this view, is a matter of being responsible for at least some key life-shaping and character-shaping decisions. For this to be possible it seems I must be able, by means of a mental act (a volition), to affect the physical sequences of events that take place in my brain. Exactly how I do this is not clear; perhaps I determine by my decision what would otherwise be an undetermined event at the subatomic level. And this influence which my volition brings to bear on subatomic events in my brain – taking advantage, as it were, of the chink in determinism offered by subatomic indeterminacy – can ultimately be quite profound; for chaos theory tells us that in enormously complex systems (and the brain is certainly such a system), minute variations at one point in a sequence can result in massive differences later on.

This account of how freedom is possible contains at least two important ideas. First, the fact that the contemporary scientific picture of the world is not perfectly deterministic does weaken the case against free will; something like the principle of indeterminacy may indeed provide one of freedom's necessary conditions. Second, I can be ultimately responsible for my behaviour even though many, perhaps the great majority, of my individual actions are fully determined by past events. But it also runs up against two serious objections. One of these has to do with the moment of volitional influence. The brain is a physical system and, like other physical systems, operates according to laws of cause and effect. These laws govern the way *physical* things interact. Whether we are talking about planetary motions, chemical reactions, photosynthesis, cell reproduction, electromagnetism or quantum mechanics, we are always talking about physical things and forces. The principle of indeterminacy is similarly a theory about physical entities, forces and processes. But according to the above account of freedom, a decision or volition by me, an event we commonly understand as a *mental* event, somehow affects *physical* processes in my brain; electrons that might have done one thing do something else as a result of my decision.

How this is possible, though, remains a mystery. If the volition or decision for which I am responsible is itself simply a physical event in my brain, then it is presumably determined by causal laws like almost all other physical events, in which case it cannot be free. If, on the other hand, it is not a physical event, how can it exercise an influence on physical events? The fact that the purported effect of this influence may be tiny, nothing more than a minute alteration in the behaviour of an electron, does not lessen the mystery one jot. To be fair, this problem – how any kind of mental causation is possible – has troubled philosophers for centuries and is one of the central controversies in the philosophy of mind. Nevertheless, it is a problem that any attempt to link free will to physical indeterminacy has to confront.

There is a second objection to the indeterministic account of free will we have been discussing. We saw how, according to this theory, I can be held responsible for my actions even though most of them of them are causally determined and therefore, considered in themselves, not free. All that responsibility requires is that my actions flow from behaviour patterns or aspects of my character for which I am ultimately responsible. In this way, the theory avoids supposing that the kind of indeterminacy that free will requires is continually present and that we continually take advantage of it, somehow influencing the otherwise undetermined behaviour of electrons in our brain every time we make any kind of decision. But here the theory loses touch with some of the common sense intuitions that prompt us to believe we have free will in the first place. What common sense tells us is not that we exercise free will *occasionally*, at the crucial crossroads of our lives, but that we do in fact exercise it all the time. I am now sitting down. If I wished to, I could now stand up. Indeed, at each and every moment during the time that it takes me to write this sentence I could, if I chose, stop writing and stand up. *That* is what having free will feels like. An adequate account of free will needs to accommodate and, if possible, explain this basic intuition. But it is not clear how an indeterministic theory like the one discussed can do this.

The feeling of freedom

Why keep worrying about how to reconcile the idea of freedom with determinism? Isn't this basic sense we all have – that we are free – at least as important and as credible as any philosophical theory?

Boldly asserting the reality of freedom is one way of cutting the Gordian knot in the tangled controversy over free will and determinism. This is, in effect, the step taken by one of the twentieth century's best-known champions of metaphysical freedom, the French philosopher Jean-Paul Sartre (see the box). According to Sartre, the fact that we are free is a, or rather *the*, fundamental truth about the kind of beings we are. It is a truth we are continually aware of, even if only dimly at times. Sartre does not try to show how freedom is possible in a deterministic world. Rather, he takes the experience of what it is like to be a human being – which involves, at its centre, the experience of freedom – as unshakeable evidence that determinism does not hold sway here.

However, Sartre does try to explain how freedom is possible in another sense. In his view, our freedom arises out of the peculiar nature of consciousness. When I attend to something, as when I listen to a piece of music, my consciousness is filled, so to speak, by what it is attending to. Similarly, when I fully engage in an activity – say, dancing – I 'give myself over' almost entirely to that activity. But however immersed or engaged I am, however much I lose myself in the subject or activity, I never lose myself entirely. There is a always a residual kind of self-consciousness present, a background awareness that whatever is happening is happening to me. Because of this, I can at any moment become fully self-conscious about my situation and what I am doing. The residual self-consciousness serves as a kind of pilot light, always there to fire up a more fully fledged self-consciousness under certain circumstances. And with full self-consciousness comes the possibility of withdrawal, of disengagement from what occupies me now and a turning to some alternative object or activity.

This ability to disengage from one activity and engage instead in something else is precisely what we mean by freedom, though I express my freedom just as much

Jean-Paul Sartre (1905–1980)

Jean-Paul Sartre was born in Paris and lived most of his life there. A prolific writer, he gained renown as a philosopher, novelist, playwright, literary critic and journalist. He was also a well-known political activist, though he was never affiliated to any political party. His best known works include the novel *Nausea*, the plays *No Exit* and *The Flies*, and two huge philosophical treatises, *Being and Nothingness* and *Critique of Dialectical Reason*. Sartre's earlier writings are representative of the philosophical movement known as **existentialism**, which emphasizes the importance of lived experience (rather than abstract theoretical principles) as the starting point and proper subject matter for philosophical reflection.

Like other thinkers whose names are often linked to existentialism (such as Kierkegaard, Dostoevsky, Nietzsche, Heidegger, Kafka and Camus), Sartre focuses on the situation of the individual who feels essentially alone in a world which is, at best, indifferent to his or her wishes. What is most striking about Sartre's account of this situation is his emphasis on and conception of human freedom. Sartre rejects most traditional accounts of human nature, arguing that in the case of human beings 'existence precedes essence'. What this means is that we have no fixed nature that determines what we will do, the way a rock, a tree or a dog has; nor were we designed with a definite purpose which it is our job to fulfil, as is the case with any human artefact. Instead, we have to choose for ourselves what actions to perform, what values to embrace, what lifestyle to adopt, what goals to pursue. And in the contemporary world we make our choices without the guidance, comfort or security of the metaphysical and religious doctrines that people leaned on in an earlier time. I may try to follow the Ten Commandments; but it is still my decision to view them as objective moral or religious truths. I may join a political movement and fight for social justice; but I can offer no absolute proof that my ideals are better than any others, or that the cause I adopt will necessarily triumph in the long run. Thus, while Sartre holds that we are radically free – free at every moment to break with what we have been in the past and with what is expected of us – he also sees this freedom as a burden. We are, in his words, 'condemned to be free', and we make our choices 'in anguish, abandonment, and despair'.

when I continue doing what I am doing as when I switch activities. Both courses of action are equally the result of a choice I make. The choices may be trivial or life altering; the freedom they express is essentially the same. While teaching a class, I may be thoroughly immersed in the issues being discussed and in my role as teacher. But if I notice through the window the warm air, the green grass, the smell of lilac and other signs of spring, I have the option of instantaneously ending the class, discarding my professorial persona, and heading off for the great outdoors. By the same token, I am free not to show up for class tomorrow, or ever again for that matter, abandoning my job in order to pursue some other goal or experiment with a different lifestyle. Of course, most of us do not do this kind of thing; our behaviour, on the whole, is actually rather predictable. And some choices are certainly much easier than others: for example, it is easier to choose to have another cigarette if one is addicted to nicotine than it is to give up smoking on the spot. But this does not alter the fact that, if Sartre is right, throughout our lives as conscious adults every moment is a moment of choice.

What conclusions can we draw from our discussion of the problem of freedom and determinism? We have shown that the middle way offered by soft determinism does not resolve the dilemma. We are thus left with the original sharp opposition between two apparently irreconcilable views. Determinism has behind it the weight and authority of traditional science; but it is unclear how determinists can defend the rationality of their own position if they agree that their acceptance of it is causally determined. Moreover, the indeterminism that has appeared in certain branches of contemporary physics perhaps offers a loophole for defenders of free will, and both common sense and our moral interests encourage us to try to climb through it. Unfortunately, we are not sure how to do this. One reason is that science, in addition to being largely deterministic, is also materialistic: it takes reality to be entirely physical. If this is true, then every so-called mental event, whether it be a sense-perception, an idea or a volition, must manifest itself in physical terms. Every thought, every wish, every choice must not just have a physical correlate in the brain but must somehow be identical to some event in the brain. Whether or not this is the case is a question much discussed in the philosophy of mind. What concerns us here, though, is the fact that once again we find the scientific account of the world apparently shutting out the possibility of free will. For free will to be exercised it seems that it must be possible for a mental event to determine a physical process: for instance, my *thought* that drunken driving is wrong and my decision to act on this conviction must cause me to hand over my car keys to a friend. Exactly how this is possible if reality is essentially and entirely physical remains a mystery.

Materialism

As so often happens in philosophy, one problem leads to another. The question of whether we have free will turns out to be linked to the question of how mind and body are related. And this central issue in the philosophy of mind relates to still broader metaphysical questions: Is the universe a purely physical entity? Or do we have good reason for supposing that there is more to reality than that?

> *Why assume that the universe is ultimately material, or, for that matter, ultimately any one type of thing? We witness tremendous variety in the world around us – compare a pebble, a glass of water, a snake, the human brain and the sun – and this all occurs only in the tiny nook of the universe that we happen to inhabit.*

Given the variety of phenomena we encounter, it is rather remarkable how readily philosophers have asserted that all reality belongs, ultimately, to a single category. This view is called **monism**, and the most popular form of monism in the history of Western philosophy has been **materialism**. The philosophical doctrine of materialism should not be confused with the kind of materialism that involves placing great value on the acquisition and possession of wealth and consumer goods. Materialism in metaphysics is simply the view that reality is essentially material.

Materialism is certainly a venerable doctrine. Some of the earliest Greek philosophers were materialists, most notably the atomists who held that reality is made up of indivisible material particles (atoms) which move around in a void and combine together to form all the different kinds of things to be found in the world. In this bold speculation the atomists were following in the footsteps of earlier thinkers who had posited the key idea that underlying the apparent diversity of the world we inhabit there is a fundamental unity. Thales of Miletus, for instance, who is generally credited with being the first philosopher in the Western tradition, believed that this unity consisted in the fact that everything came from or was in some sense made from water. Although this idea is likely to strike us as bizarre at first, a little reflection may lessen our incredulity. What probably struck Thales about water, apart from it being necessary for all life, is that it can take the form of a liquid, a solid or a gas depending on its temperature. Underlying these variations there is just one substance that is able to appear in different forms. Admittedly, it is still a bit of a leap to conclude that water is the basic component of everything in the world. But Thales' speculation is noteworthy for being one of the earliest versions of the general principle that reality is, at bottom, one. This means that when we observe change we are not observing the disappearance of one thing and the creation of another but, rather, the transformation of a single thing from one of its forms to another. It also means that all the marvellous variety we encounter in the world is, from a metaphysical point of view, superficial; the deeper reality that gives rise to it has a single, uniform nature. On this view, the deepest understanding of phenomena involves gaining insight into the unity that underlies difference and change.

The Presocratic Philosophers

Western philosophy usually traces its origins back to a group of remarkable men who lived roughly between 600 and 400 BCE, mainly in the eastern part of the Greek world. They are often referred to as the Presocratics because they preceded Socrates (469–399 BCE), the Athenian thinker who decisively influenced the direction of Western philosophy through his brilliant student Plato. Only fragments of their writings have survived, but we have enough to reconstruct at least some of their thinking (though some of their pronouncements remain enigmatic). Working before there had been any serious attempt to demarcate the different areas of human enquiry, the Presocratics combined scientific investigations and metaphysical speculations, often expressing their ideas in poetic or figurative language.

Thales of Miletus was one of the first of these thinkers. He achieved renown in his day for, among other things, successfully predicting a solar eclipse. But his contribution to philosophy lies in his hypothesis that a uniform reality underlies the many ways things appear to us. Thales identifies this reality with water, which was understood to be one of the four primary elements (the other three being earth, air and fire).

Anaximander of Miletus moved away from thinking of ultimate reality as essentially like some particular substance that we encounter in experience. He conceived of it more abstractly – a crucial step in the development of science – as what he called the 'boundless', something without spatial or temporal limits. Out of this source come opposites like hot and cold, wet and dry, which interact to produce the phenomena with which we are familiar. The 'boundless' also serves to maintain an overall balance between the opposites, ensuring that no one element becomes predominant.

Parmenides of Elea also avoided identifying ultimate reality with any particular substance. But he does argue that the only way to comprehend its true nature is through reflection rather than through sense perception. And such reflection, he claims, reveals that reality must be essentially one, unmoving, indivisible, unchanging and perfect. This position was ingeniously supported by his follower Zeno, who constructed a number of paradoxes aimed at showing that such things as change, motion and divisibility, which common sense believes in, cannot be real.

Heraclitus of Ephesus shares with Parmenides a somewhat enigmatic style. Indeed, his obscure utterances may have been responsible for his alleged sobriquet 'the Dark One'. But unlike Parmenides he is not inclined to view diversity and change as illusory. On the contrary, he takes them to belong to the very essence of reality, which he conceives of as a process rather than a vast substance. This idea is captured in two of his best known metaphorical sayings. One, highlighting the continuous and irreversible character of temporal change, asserts the impossibility of ever stepping into the same river twice. The other likens reality to fire in the way its continual, incessant alterations in themselves constitute a kind of regularity and stability; continuous change thus provides us with a fundamental constant.

This search for the unity that underlies difference and change has been characteristic of Western philosophy and science right up to the present day: indeed, it is often precisely what novel theories seek to establish. Part of Newton's great achievement in physics was his demonstration that the same basic force – gravity – governed the orbits of the planets, the ocean tides and the falling of an apple. The fundamental idea behind atomic theory is that the different elements are composed of the same stuff, namely, neutrons, protons, electrons and so on; differences between the elements are thus not absolute but can be explained in terms of the number and arrangement of subatomic particles. According to materialism, the fundamental stuff of the universe is matter, so all explanations must ultimately be descriptions of material entities and processes. This was certainly one of the key metaphysical presuppositions that supported the rise of modern science. Nowadays, though, many scientists and philosophers prefer the term **physicalism** to materialism. This is because according to relativity theory matter and energy are interchangeable, which means that energy is just as fundamental as matter. Physicalism, which asserts that ultimate reality is physical – a notion that covers matter and energy – is therefore seen as a more precise label.

It is not too difficult to see how the kind of explanatory reductions illustrated by the theory of gravity or atomic theory could eventually lead to a monistic picture of the universe as a physical system operating according to a small number of basic laws. But there is at least one aspect of our experience that seems to pose a problem for this picture: namely, consciousness. My awareness of the world around me, and my experience of sights, sounds, pains and delights, seem to belong to another dimension. They are subjective or mental. They are *had* by me – suffered or enjoyed as the case may be. They may be correlated with or caused by events in the physical realm; but that does not make them physical. To many philosophers, this difference between the physical and the mental is not one that can be overcome or reduced to some underlying unity. They therefore propose a dualistic account of reality according to which the physical and the mental are both equally fundamental categories, and everything that exists falls into either one or the other. (For further discussion of dualism, see the chapter on Philosophy of mind.)

Materialism versus idealism

Mind and body, the mental and the physical, do seem to be qualitatively different. But isn't the physical more fundamental? It presumably came first and gave rise to the mental.

Here we encounter another of the great debates, one that has been at the centre of modern metaphysics. Which is prior or more basic, the physical or the mental? Physicalism obviously views the physical as primary. The opposite view, which gives priority to mind, traditionally goes by the name of **idealism**. (This use of the term 'idealism' to denote a metaphysical position should not be confused with the other common meaning of the word, according to which 'idealists' are people who hold lofty ideals, resist worldly cynicism and refuse to compromise their principles.) Naturally, much depends here on what we mean by expressions like 'prior' or 'more fundamental'. One kind of priority is *temporal* priority. Here the question is which came first in time. According to many traditional religious views, God, who is conceived to be pure spirit, existed prior to the material world which he created at a certain point in time. Any metaphysics informed by one of these religions will thus grant temporal priority to mind. By contrast, the modern scientific view is that the physical universe existed before there were any beings endowed with sentience or consciousness; on this view, matter existed before minds, the latter only appearing on the scene when certain physical conditions were satisfied.

There is also another, less familiar notion of priority: *ontological* priority. (The term 'ontological' comes from **ontology**, which is the branch of metaphysics that deals with the nature of existence and the kinds of thing that exist.) Here, too, modern science tends to grant ontological priority to the physical world, since it views minds as dependent on bodies but not vice versa. Historically, this view was unacceptable to most Western philosophers until modern times for a simple reason: it undermines the idea that the mind or soul – the spiritual part of a person – can exist independently of the body. It is thus incompatible with the traditional Christian doctrine that one's soul survives the death of one's body. It is also at odds with the religious idea that the physical universe is dependent on God for its continued existence from moment to moment. On both counts, anyone who accepts religious teachings in which God or human beings are conceived in essentially spiritual terms is likely to reject physicalism completely.

Now, since a religious outlook predisposes one towards some sort of idealism while the modern scientific viewpoint tends to be physicalistic, we may expect modern philosophy to have drifted away from idealism. Surprisingly, though, even among contemporary professional philosophers there are many who continue to endorse a form of idealism. They do not, in most cases, follow Bishop Berkeley and deny that matter even exists (see the discussion of phenomenalism in the Theory of knowledge chapter). Nor is their position based on any assumptions about how the universe was created. The kind of idealism that continues to appear persuasive to many today rests on the idea that the world that we inhabit and that science describes has the character it does, at least in part, *because it is known by us*. Mind does not *create* the world, but it does *shape* it at a very deep level. This position was first developed systematically by the great German philosopher Immanuel Kant (see the box). To distinguish his view from that of Berkeley and other idealists whom he regarded as naive or extreme, he called it 'transcendental idealism'. Because of both its intrinsic interest and its huge influence on subsequent thought, it is worth examining more closely.

How the mind shapes the world

Kant does not, like some thinkers, entertain doubts about whether the human mind is capable of attaining knowledge. Instead, he assumes from the outset that we do have knowledge of the world around us and that the natural sciences represent one of humankind's highest intellectual achievements. He then proceeds to classify the main types of knowledge by introducing two key distinctions: (1) the distinction between analytic and synthetic statements; and (2) the distinction between a priori and a posteriori knowledge. Let us consider these in turn.

All statements through which we express our knowledge, says Kant, are either analytic or synthetic. **Analytic** truths are statements whose denial would lead to a contradiction, such as 'All fathers are male.' Since 'father' can be defined as 'male parent', this sentence asserts that all male parents are male. To deny this is to assert that not all male parents are male. This implies that there is at least one parent who is both male and not male, which is contradictory. Kant called such statements 'analytic' on the grounds that the predicate (in this case, 'male') is 'contained within' the subject ('father'); we thus arrive at this sort of knowledge simply by *analysing* the subject term in the statement. It would be absurd to try to establish that all fathers are male by conducting a survey or carefully examining the census statistics. To know that this statement is true we only need to know the meanings of the words it contains.

Synthetic truths, by contrast, are statements that are true but that one could deny without falling into a contradiction, such as 'All human fathers are over two years old.' Kant calls such statements 'synthetic' because they bring together or *synthesize* two quite different concepts: in this case, the concept of being a human father and the concept of being over two years old. The latter is not 'contained within' the former. We know the statement is true on the basis of experience, not simply by virtue of understanding the meanings of words. If one of the sensationalist tabloids ran the headline 'One-year-old boy fathers twins!' we would undoubtedly dismiss the claim as absurd. We would even say that such an event is impossible. But we view it as impossible only because of our knowledge of the laws of nature and because of our assumption that these laws do not allow exceptions. It is not impossible in the way that 'Four-sided triangle found in Argentina!' is impossible. A one-year-old father is conceivable; a four-sided triangle is not.

Immanuel Kant (1724–1804)

Immanuel Kant was the son of a saddler who lived his entire life in Königsberg, a university town and an important port in East Prussia. A church minister recognized his abilities when Kant was still a child and helped him continue his education until he was able to attend the university. Apart from a brief period as a house tutor, Kant supported himself throughout his life by teaching at the university. Although he published several works in the 1750s and 1760s, including a theory of how the solar system formed, it was not until the 1780s (after a 'silent decade' of intense reflection) that he published the works for which he is now remembered. The most important of these were: *Critique of Pure Reason, Groundwork to the Metaphysics of Morals, Critique of Practical Reason* and *Critique of Judgement*. By the time he died, the saddler's son had become the most renowned thinker in Europe, and he is now generally reckoned to be one of the greatest philosophers of all time.

Kant's most significant achievements were in metaphysics, ethics and aesthetics. The fundamental problem that he faced was how to reconcile the claims of natural science with the claims of morality and religion. Kant had the greatest respect for all three (religion here being understood in a very individualistic way as an aid to personal virtue), but he saw the determinism and the materialism of science as threatening the moral-religious dimension of human existence. His solution, in his own phrase, was 'to deny knowledge in order to make room for faith'.

The *Critique of Pure Reason* thus contains a profound critique of what Kant calls speculative or transcendent metaphysics, the kind that aims at proving claims about the nature of God, the soul, free will or the reality that lies behind the world we experience. The empiricists were right, Kant says; we cannot have knowledge of such things. Knowledge is what science gives us, and that relates only to the world we perceive with our senses. However, Kant argues also that this world cannot be thought of as 'ultimate reality'. It is the world *as it appears to us*, and therefore a world of appearances only. So neither science nor metaphysics can give us *knowledge* of ultimate reality. This leaves a space open for us to have *faith* that those beliefs that provide the underpinnings to morality – such as the belief that we are free and responsible, or the belief that there is some sort of cosmic justice to ensure that virtue will eventually be rewarded – are true.

Let us now look at the distinction between a priori and a posteriori knowledge. A **priori** knowledge consists of statements that we can know to be true without consulting experience ('a priori' means 'independent of experience'). Empirical evidence, observations, experiments, surveys and the like are not needed here. According to Kant, a priori truths are always both necessarily true and universally true. Necessity here is to be contrasted with contingency. A statement is **contingently true** if things just happen to be the way the statement says they are. For instance, it just happens to be the case that human beings have two eyes; it is easy to imagine that we might have evolved differently. By contrast, a statement is **necessarily true** if we cannot conceive of any possible world in which it would be false. For instance, '2 + 3 = 5' seems to be necessarily true in this sense. *Universality* is to be contrasted with *particularity*. Kant's claim is that a priori truths never refer to some specific entity; rather, they always express law-like generalities that hold without any exceptions – for example, 'All fathers are male.' This is why there is no point in conducting empirical investigations to establish their truth.

The great majority of our true beliefs, however, are not arrived at independently of experience but are based on experience. These constitute **a posteriori** knowledge. 'The earth is round', 'Snakes are cold blooded', and 'Napoleon invaded Russia' are examples of such truths. The only way to decide whether such statements are true is to make observations, collect evidence, perform experiments, read reports, conduct interviews and so on. These, then, are the main ways of classifying our knowledge according to Kant.

	Analytic	Synthetic
A priori	Example: 'All fathers are male'	Example: . . .?
A posteriori	No examples possible	Example: ' Jupiter is bigger than Mars'

As the table shows, statements can be both analytic and a priori; they can also be synthetic and a posteriori. Indeed, most philosophers would agree that *all* analytic truths are known to be true a priori and that all a posterior truths are synthetic. There is also general agreement that a statement cannot be *both* an analytic *and* an a posteriori truth (if a posteriori means can *only* be known on the basis of experience). The category that most interested Kant, however, and about which there has been the greatest philosophical controversy, is that of synthetic a priori truths.

Empiricist philosophers hold that all our knowledge of the world is derived from experience. They therefore insist that there are no statements that are both synthetic and yet known to be true a priori. In their view, the only kind of a priori knowledge we can have consists of analytic truths that are, in effect, tautologies that are merely true by definition. According to Kant, however, some of our a priori knowledge is synthetic: it is about the way the world is, not just about the meanings of terms. He held mathematical knowledge to be of this sort. In his view, axioms of Euclidean geometry (such as 'Two straight lines cannot enclose a space') along with all the theorems that can be deduced from these axioms constitute a body of synthetic a priori knowledge. So too does the knowledge contained in other branches of mathematics. Kant also claimed that certain very general principles that underlie the natural sciences embody synthetic a priori truths: for example, the causal principle, which states that every event is caused, and the conservation principle, which states that matter (in contemporary science, matter or energy) can be neither created not destroyed.

Whether or not these do constitute synthetic a priori knowledge is still a matter of controversy. Strict empiricists see mathematical statements as complicated tautologies, and hence as merely analytic truths. And the statement that every event is caused they see as merely an empirical generalization, and hence as a synthetic a posteriori truth – on a level with statements such as 'All men are mortal' or 'All planets move in ellipses.' However, defenders of Kant's view argue that our belief in the causal principle cannot be derived from experience. If it was, then we would have no difficulty accepting the possibility that it might be false. Yet we never allow anything to count against this principle. Faced with what looks like an uncaused event we always assume that we do not know the cause, not that there was no cause at all. Similarly, confronted with an apparent instance of something popping out of existence, we would assume that it had gone somewhere or been converted into some other form; we think we know in advance that it could not just cease to exist.

Suppose, then, we accept Kant's claim that truths such as the causal principle are necessary and universal without being analytic. The question now arises: How is this to be explained? How can we know something *about* the world without having simply derived this knowledge from observing the world. As Kant famously puts it: How is synthetic a priori knowledge possible? This is the profound question upon which he spent years meditating and which eventually led him to a radically new view of the way mind and world are related.

Kant argues that there is only one way of explaining how we can have this kind of knowledge: if the world has certain necessary features, it must be because we have put them there. In our experience of things there is much that is perfectly contingent: the fact that an object is round rather than square, smooth rather than rough, red rather than blue and so on. These properties are contingent because they could easily be otherwise. But some properties of objects are not like this. For instance, all physical objects that we encounter exist in space and time; moreover, we cannot even imagine a physical entity that did not have a spatio-temporal location. Existence in space and existence in time thus appear to be necessary features of objects. According to Kant, this is because they are 'forms' that our mind imposes on the content of our sensory experiences. This is why a discipline like geometry – which Kant calls 'the science of space' – yields a priori knowledge of the way the world is.

In a somewhat similar way, he claims, our mind imposes the form of causality on the world. This is why we automatically view every object as participating in chains of cause and effect, and why we cannot conceive of any object that is not subject to causal laws or any event that was not the effect of some cause. Another 'category' (to use Kant's term) that our mind imposes on things is that of substance. Every object we experience is thus viewed as being more than just a collection of sensible properties (colours, tastes, etc.); we always assume that there is something underlying these that binds them together, something that persists over time and cannot cease to exist in any absolute sense.

Why does our mind organize experience under these forms? Put simply, it does it in order to make experience intelligible. Kant's argument for this point is famously complex and difficult to follow, and we need not go into it here. His main point is that unless we organized the content of our experiences by imposing form on it, we would have nothing that we could call intelligible experience at all, let alone a scientific knowledge of nature. At best there would only be – to use William James's phrase – 'a blooming, buzzing confusion'.

A much used but still illuminating analogy to explain Kant's fundamental idea is that of a person who is only able to see the world through tinted spectacles. Suppose that prior to birth you had a surgical procedure performed that fixed some kind of green tinted contact lens over each eye so that everything you saw would be some shade of green. One consequence of this would obviously be that you could predict with perfect confidence that any object you encountered would be green. And if you were given to philosophizing along Kantian lines, you might eventually conclude that this perfect predictability indicated that the greenness of things was not an inherent property of the things themselves but a property they had *in virtue of being known by you*. This analogy captures the essence of Kant's argument. It also brings out its radical implications: if some of the fundamental features of the things we cognize are present only because they are known by us, then these things, as we know them, are in some sense *mind dependent*. This is why Kant's metaphysical position is a form of idealism.

Kant described his way of thinking as a 'Copernican revolution in metaphysics'. Copernicus had provided a better explanation for the motions of heavenly bodies by assuming that the earth is not stationary (which is how it feels) but is actually turning on its axis and moving around the sun. Similarly, Kant believed he had provided a better explanation for the way things appear to us by assuming that instead of the mind passively receiving an impression of the way things are (which is how it feels), it actively determines their nature in so far as they are objects of our experience. The inescapable upshot of this, though, is that the world we experience every day, which is also the natural world investigated by science – the world of space, time and causal relations – is the world as it *appears* to us, not reality as it is in itself. Kant does not deny the reality of this world; on the contrary, he insists that it is 'empirically real', meaning that from the standpoint of everyday experience and natural science it exists objectively and exhibits objective properties that we have to discover through investigation. But from a philosophical point of view, this world is 'transcendentally ideal', since its existence depends on the human mind. Kant uses the phrase 'things in themselves' to refer to reality as it is independent of any relation that we might have to it (which includes, of course, any cognitive relation). And it clearly follows from his general metaphysical position that we can have no knowledge whatsoever of this reality.

The 'thing in itself': a limit to understanding

If we can have no knowledge whatsoever of any reality that exists independently of our experience of it, how can we even know that it exists?

This question was immediately posed by some of Kant's successors. And some of them pressed Kant's idealism to its logical conclusion. If we can know nothing at all about reality as it is in itself, then the very concept of the so-called 'thing in itself' is empty. According to Kant, our knowledge is limited to the things that form part of what we might possibly experience. The key word here is 'possible'. Thus, although human beings may never *actually* know whether there is life in the Andromeda galaxy, we can easily imagine the kind of experience that would confirm our speculative belief that there is. But things in themselves, by definition, are not possible objects of experience, so we are not really entitled to say anything about them. Even calling them 'things' implies that the concept of plurality applies here; but we cannot even know that. Nor should we assume, as Kant seems to, that things in themselves somehow give rise to our experience by providing the 'content' of our sense-perceptions, which our mind then renders intelligible through the imposition of form. This hypothesis illegitimately extends the notion of causality beyond possible experience. So the only reasonable thing to do with Kant's notion of 'things in themselves', according to his critics, is to reject it.

But if we throw out the concept of things as they are in themselves, then we are forced to the conclusion that *all* of reality is entirely mind dependent – the content of our experience just as much as its form. As espoused by German idealists like Johann Fichte (1762–1814), this view became known as 'absolute idealism'. Most people automatically reject it as inherently implausible. Are we supposed to take seriously the idea that the world around us, everything from our own bodies to the most distant galaxies, is continually being spun out of our own subjectivity? On the face of it, this does sound like the kind of metaphysical speculation that can give philosophy a bad name. To be fair to idealists, though, it is always important to keep in mind that they are not trying to *redescribe* our experience; they are only trying to *explain* why it is the way it is. Moreover, while someone like Fichte describes the process whereby the objective world emanates from a spiritual subject as the 'ego positing a non-ego', he does not actually think that each individual human being is responsible for the world's existence. Rather, the 'ego' that 'posits' the objective world, on his view, has to be thought of as an impersonal or suprapersonal force which, to speak metaphorically, flows through us rather than out of us.

Kant, however, like most other modern idealists, is not ready to embrace this extreme form of idealism. In his view, there is one fundamental fact about our experience that philosophy has to respect: namely, the fact that we continually feel as if we are encountering something that is other than ourselves. Put bluntly, we bump into things! Put philosophically, there is a dimension to our experience that seems to have its source outside ourselves, and this source he calls the realm of things in themselves. It is tempting, but mistaken, to conceive of the thing in itself as a material substance that we cannot ever really know because we only perceive the way it appears to us through our senses (a problematic view that is discussed more fully in the next chapter, on the Theory of knowledge). Material substances, on Kant's view, belong to the world we know and inhabit, the world of space, time and causal relations. The concept of the thing in itself has to be understood more abstractly. It denotes the limit to what we can hope to know, the mystery that is present in every experience we have and that cannot be dissolved by either philosophy or science, no matter how advanced, sophisticated and successful they become.

Perfect understanding, Kant sometimes suggests, would require subject and object to be identical; the object could then be known from the inside, so to speak. But we are not identical to the world we try to understand; even though our minds impose order on it and thereby render it somewhat intelligible, there is forever something about it that is alien and defies comprehension. Science may discover the fundamental laws that describe how our universe operates; but it cannot answer every question that we wish to ask. And even if we arrive eventually at one law from which all the others can be deduced, we are still left with the question: Why this law rather than some other? Interpreted broadly in this way, Kant's notion of the thing in itself identifies one reason why, as he often says, it is part of our human condition to ask ourselves questions that we are not capable of answering.

Whether we should try to stop asking such questions is another matter. The sensible view, of course, is that there really is no point in wracking our brains over problems we can not hope to ever finally resolve. Some would even say that unanswerable questions should not be thought of as genuinely intelligible or meaningful, especially if they use terms like 'God', 'Being', 'ultimate reality', or 'cosmic purpose' that do not correspond to anything we are acquainted with in ordinary experience. But sometimes the value of a thing does not lie in its avowed purpose. The metaphysical impulse, as it has been called, perhaps does lead us to seek knowledge where none can be had. But it does not follow that we should try to purge ourselves of this tendency. Metaphysical speculation may not have produced a body of knowledge to place alongside biology or physics; but there are forms of insight and understanding other than those that bear the scientific stamp of approval. Furthermore, a willingness to speculate has produced philosophical systems of great beauty; it has helped to expand our intellectual horizons; it has enabled deeply felt needs and desires to find a means of expression; and perhaps most importantly of all, it keeps alive a sense for the mystery of things. Martin Heidegger once proposed that the fundamental question of philosophy is: Why is there something rather than nothing? This is not a question that has an answer. But pondering it may renew and deepen the sense of wonder that Aristotle says is the beginning of philosophy.

2 Theory of knowledge

Metaphysics asks about the fundamental nature of reality, as we saw in the previous chapter. From the time of the ancient Greeks to the end of the middle ages, this was usually the central area of enquiry around which the rest of philosophy was organized. But in the seventeenth century, under the impact of events such as Columbus's discoveries, the Renaissance, the Reformation and the rise of the new science, philosophy took what has been called an 'epistemological turn'. Leading philosophers began to argue that before we can even address questions about the nature of reality, we need to ask some other questions. In particular, we need to ask questions like:

- What are human beings capable of knowing?
- How can we justify our claims to knowledge?
- Are there limits to human knowledge?
- If there are limits, what are they, and what fixes them?

And, perhaps most fundamental of all:

- What is knowledge?
- What is it to know something?

Epistemology, or the theory of knowledge, is the branch of philosophy that deals with these and related questions. (The word 'epistemology' is derived from two Greek words, *epistēmē*, meaning knowledge, and *logos*, meaning rational account.) As should be evident already, some issues in epistemology overlap with some issues in metaphysics. Thus, at the end of the last chapter a discussion of the way the mind shapes the reality it cognizes led into a discussion of the limits of human knowledge. But it is not difficult to see how epistemology came to occupy a central place in modern philosophy. Every other area of enquiry – both inside and outside philosophy – makes knowledge claims, and hence presupposes answers to questions such as those mentioned above, or at least presupposes that they can be answered.

The challenge of scepticism

To really know something means that you cannot possibly be mistaken. But so often we think we know something and it turns out we were mistaken. Given such experiences, how can we ever be sure that we know anything?

Calling into question our ability to know anything at all is the attitude of a sceptic. All of us are sceptical about some of the knowledge claims we encounter. Perhaps the person making them has a record of being mistaken. Or perhaps the claims belong to a discipline like astrology whose methods we do not respect. **Philosophical scepticism**, however, is more global than this. It challenges our claim to know anything at all. As a species we pride ourselves on our knowledge (*Homo sapiens* means 'knowing man'), and as individuals we usually have great faith in our own common sense and wisdom, so scepticism represents a disagreeable threat – the pin that might just pop our balloon. It is thus a good idea to begin our enquiry by trying to decide how serious a threat it is.

Like many other 'isms', scepticism comes in more than one form. For our purposes, let us identify just three: extreme scepticism, moderate scepticism and methodological scepticism. The most extreme kind of scepticism holds that knowledge is impossible, at least for human beings. Few serious philosophers have held this view, but apparently there have been some. One Greek philosopher is supposed to have said something like: 'We cannot know the truth. Even if we could know it, we couldn't communicate it. And even if we could communicate it, we wouldn't be understood' – which is about as sceptical as one can get. But there is a good reason why few philosophers have embraced this kind of scepticism (quite apart from a self-interested concern for their own employment prospects). If I say that knowledge is impossible, then either my claim constitutes a piece of knowledge or it does not. If it does, then knowledge must be possible after all, in which case my original claim was false. If it does not, then I have no business making the assertion; neither I nor anyone else has any reason to believe it. Perhaps it was to avoid falling into this trap that one ancient Greek sceptic would respond to anyone who tried to engage him in disputation by simply smiling and wagging his finger at them.

However, scepticism does not have to be so extreme. A more moderate sceptical position does not deny that knowledge may be possible, or even that some of our beliefs may in fact be true. It merely holds that we cannot be *sure* that any of our beliefs are true. This view is not obviously self-refuting: after all, one can present it deferentially, admitting all the while that one may be mistaken. Moreover, it is a view that can be supported with cogent arguments. For instance, in order to decide whether or not to believe something we need some sort of criterion for deciding which statements we should believe. But there are many criteria we could adopt:

- Is the belief supported by evidence from sense-perception?
- Can it be deduced from self-evident premises?
- Does it conform to the Bible?
- Is it accepted by the majority of people?
- Can it be confirmed by repeatable experiments?

Obviously, we need to decide which criteria we should employ and which we should reject. But this decision requires us to use a further criterion – a criterion for distinguishing between good and bad criteria. If we cannot provide one, then we are admitting that our beliefs cannot ultimately be justified in rational terms. If we simply use the same criterion as before, then we are using a criterion to justify itself, which is circular reasoning. And if we introduce a further criterion, then the same question can be asked once again – What justifies this criterion rather than some other? – and we have begun an infinite regress.

Practical certainty and theoretical certainty

Surely, though, there must be something misguided – or at least pointless – about even this more moderate kind of scepticism. After all, we don't spend our lives racked with doubt, unable to decide what to believe. We are actually pretty certain about many things.

We are indeed quite certain that many of our beliefs are true. Do I know for sure that heating the kettle will result in the water inside the kettle getting hotter? Of course I know that! Proof of this is the fact that I would never agree to pour that water over my hand after it had been on the stove for a few minutes. Am I certain that the little girl who just entered the room is my daughter and not Ghengis Khan come back to life and in disguise? Yes I am, and I would be quite willing to stake everything I have on my belief being true. But what do these considerations really prove? They prove that in everyday life we go about our everyday business with enormous confidence in our everyday beliefs. Unfortunately, this fact does not provide us with a quick and easy refutation of scepticism. The problem is that as an argument against scepticism it misses the point; more precisely, it misunderstands the nature of the doctrine it is supposed to refute. Let us agree that with respect to many of our beliefs we enjoy what has been called 'practical certainty'. From a practical point of view I am absolutely certain that if you push me off the roof of a skyscraper I will plummet to my death; that is why I will resist so fiercely. This kind of certainty is roughly equivalent to complete confidence. But philosophers, or at least some of them, being the strange species that they are, ask whether another, higher kind of certainty is possible – call it 'theoretical' or 'metaphysical' certainty. What they want to know is not how *confident* most people are about the truth of their beliefs but whether that confidence is ever fully *justified*.

Our confidence in the truth of most of our beliefs is justified by the fact that they work. We cope with the world pretty well from day to day, and that in itself shows that most of our beliefs are true. If they were not we would never survive.

This looks like a perfectly sensible argument. Our ability to do even simple things rests on a great many beliefs. For instance, just to make a cup of tea I must have beliefs about where the tea is, what will happen when I turn on the tap, how to boil the water, what condition the cup is in, and so on. If enough of these beliefs turned out to be false I probably could not complete the task. However, there are two problems with this line of reasoning. First, it does not prove any *particular* belief to be true; at best it only shows that a fair percentage of our beliefs must be true. To illustrate this point, imagine you were predicting the outcome of an election. You take into account numerous factors: the appeal of candidates to different groups within the electorate; the popularity of their positions on various issues; the quality of their advisors; how much money they are able to spend on advertising, and so on. If your predictions are correct, it is reasonable to infer that your information on these matters is accurate and that you are factoring it into your calculations correctly. All the same, it remains quite possible that any particular piece of information you are working with is false, and that your interpretation of the importance of the data is mistaken. In that case, your accurate prediction is due in part to luck. Some of your beliefs are actually false, but these errors cancel each other out. The general point here is that practical success, while it is explained most simply as resulting from correct beliefs, does not guarantee the truth of any particular belief.

The second objection to the 'argument from practical success' actually presses this point a little deeper. From a theoretical point of view, our practical success in dealing with the world is compatible with *none* of our beliefs being true – in the sense of accurately describing the way things are. Our beliefs form a system that functions as a model of reality. We generally trust this model because it works   – in the sense of allowing us to make accurate predictions and manipulate things (as when we make a cup of tea). But we have no way of proving that this model accurately maps the way things are other than by appealing to its practical success; and this success only proves the model's *usefulness*; it does not prove its *truth*. Again, an example may help. The geocentric model of the solar system that was generally accepted before Copernicus was quite successful from a pragmatic point of view. It enabled astronomers to predict accurately the paths of the planets and stars, eclipses of the sun and moon, and other such occurrences. But we now think that this model, although useful, was not a true representation of reality. It seems, then, that while the success of our belief system may well be the main reason why we enjoy so much practical certainty, this success does not give us the theoretical certainty that the sceptic demands and non-sceptical philosophers desire.

Moderate scepticism is thus not as easy to refute as extreme scepticism. What is needed, it seems, is a demonstration that at least *some* of our beliefs are unquestionably true. But how are we supposed to proceed? Any ordinary proof will rest on premises, and the conclusion can only be as certain as those premises. But how can we know that the premises are true? If we try to prove they are true with an argument then we have only pushed the problem back a step; this argument must also rest on premises that need to be justified. Alternatively, we can perhaps try to show that there are some statements that we can know to be true without any proof, statements whose truth is so obvious that it simply 'shines forth'. In the jargon of philosophy, such statements are said to be 'self-evident'.

Descartes's methodological doubt

By far the most famous attempt in the history of philosophy to tackle this problem, to refute scepticism by showing that we can be absolutely certain about some things, was made by the French philosopher René Descartes (1596–1650). In the early seventeenth century, when Descartes was developing his ideas, scepticism was very much in the air. The new science pioneered by people like Copernicus, Bacon and Galileo encouraged people to challenge accepted authorities and traditional ways of thinking. Naturally enough, scholastic theologians and philosophers who were rooted in the older, religion based philosophy felt threatened by the new scientific outlook, and one defensive reaction to this threat was a turning towards scepticism. This might seem odd, but it is actually quite understandable. In effect, these theologians were saying: 'This new science may look very impressive, but actually all claims to knowledge by human beings are vain. So science does not represent a superior method or a more secure body of knowledge than religion has to offer; on the contrary, it is just the latest futile attempt to escape our inescapable ignorance.'

Descartes's response to this sceptical attitude was to execute a kind of philosophical judo move. Instead of opposing it head-on he carried it to an extreme, embracing what is usually referred to as 'methodological scepticism'. It is important to keep in mind that methodological scepticism is not a philosophical position; it is not a view that some people defend and others attack. Rather, as its name suggests, it is a *method*. It consists in adopting the most radically sceptical attitude possible to see if there are any beliefs that are impervious to doubt. In his *Meditations*, Descartes undertakes a thought experiment to help him pursue this methodological scepticism. He imagines that there is a being who, like God, is all-powerful but who, unlike God, is a malicious deceiver. Moreover, this evil demon's main purpose is to deceive Descartes into holding false beliefs: he can make him think he is awake when in fact he is dreaming; he can make him think there is a material world of objects in space when in fact there is no such world; he can even make him think that 2 + 2 = 4 when in truth it does not.

Obviously, this is a rather bizarre hypothesis. But it has the merit, as Descartes points out, of being global. It does not call into question only certain categories of belief, such as beliefs about physical objects or beliefs about other people's minds. It calls into question, 'in one fell swoop', every single belief that I hold. Descartes compares his quest for certainty to someone trying to make sure that there are no rotten apples in a barrel (a rotten apple here standing for a false belief). The method of rummaging through the barrel and throwing out any rotten apples one finds has an obvious flaw: it is quite possible to miss one and, to continue the analogy, this remaining rotten apple could infect the rest. Therefore a much better method is to empty out the barrel completely and then put back only those apples that one is sure are healthy. This is how methodological doubt works. It forces me to take nothing for granted, to take a fresh look at even those beliefs that I have held longest, or are most widely accepted, or are supported by the most respected authorities. The question is: Will I able to affirm any beliefs at all in the face of such radical doubt? Or will the medicine turn out to be more dangerous than the disease it is supposed to cure?

A belief that cannot be doubted

According to Descartes, if I try to doubt all of my beliefs I will find that there is at least one whose truth I cannot doubt. Even if there is an evil demon deceiving me at every turn, making me entertain any number of falsehoods, I can still be certain about one thing – I exist. After all, if I did not exist, I could not doubt or even be deceived about anything. Descartes expresses this insight in one of the most famous propositions in the history of philosophy: 'I think, therefore I am.' This, he claims, is an indubitable certainty that can serve as a foundation upon which he can build the rest of his philosophical system and thereby lay to rest the spectre of scepticism.

On the face of it, the claim that we cannot doubt our own existence does look very plausible, and most philosophers will grant that we have here a belief that it does not make much sense to doubt. Nevertheless, Descartes's famous first certainty, and the means by which he establishes it, are not quite as straightforward as one might think. First of all, it is not entirely clear what this first certainty is supposed to be. Is it 'I think', or is it 'I exist'? Descartes seems to say it is the latter. Yet if we take the statement 'I think, *therefore* I am' at face value, he seems to be *inferring* his existence from the fact that he is thinking, which implies that 'I think' is actually his first certainty.

If we interpret Descartes along these lines a further problem arises. It begins to look as if 'I think, therefore I am' is an abbreviated form of a full-blown syllogism – that is, a logical argument with premises and a conclusion along the following lines:

Premise 1:   Whatever thinks, exists.
Premise 2:   I think.
Conclusion: I exist.

Now, the premises of this argument appear uncontroversial, and the logic cannot be faulted. We would therefore normally conclude that the argument is sound and the conclusion true. But we are not normally imagining that there is an evil demon deceiving us at every turn! If we *are* working under this hypothesis, and we want to establish the truth of a belief in the face of this radical doubt, then there are problems in proceeding by means of this argument. First of all, we have no right to assume that the major premise – 'Whatever thinks, exists' – is true; however plausible it sounds, this could be something we have been deceived into believing. Second, we cannot be sure that the conclusion really does follow from the premises.

Our belief that it does rests on assumptions about logical validity that have been called into question along with everything else.

Perhaps, then, Descartes is not offering an argument at all. Perhaps when he says 'I think', or 'I exist', he is simply making assertions whose truth is immediately evident at the time they are asserted to the person who asserts them. On this view, no proof of their truth is necessary; their truth is self-evident. This is certainly a plausible interpretation of what Descartes means. It also sounds eminently reasonable. What could be more self-evident than the fact that I, who right now am considering these matters, exist? Once again, though, it is not clear whether this suffices to foil the evil demon. If the demon can deceive me about whether $2 + 2 = 4$, could he not equally well deceive me into thinking a statement is self-evident when in fact it is not? If so, then the appeal to self-evidence is no better than the simple syllogism. Neither can extricate Descartes from the corner into which he has painted himself.

> *Suppose we forget about the evil demon. Perhaps Descartes asks too much when he demands that our first certainties be proof against a doubt so radical. The point is, while I may be hopelessly wrong about many things, I cannot seriously doubt that I am now thinking and that I now exist. To all intents and purposes, this is certain.*

This seems to be correct. In fact, the point can be made more general. As a sentient, thinking being, from moment to moment I am having all kinds of experiences: thoughts, desires, fears, sense-perceptions, daydreams, pains, etc. Some of these may be misguided or mistaken: my fear that I am about to lose my job may be unfounded; my belief that someone just called my name may be false. But that I am having these subjective experiences is something about which I cannot be mistaken. The statement 'Someone just called my name' may be false; but the statement 'It *seemed to me* that someone just called my name' can still be true. And if I am being sincere, it is hard to see how I could be mistaken in a case like this. First person reports of subjective experiences are thus peculiarly reliable. Of course, we may sometimes lie about our subjective states, as when we pretend to have a pain to elicit sympathy. It is also possible to have false memories of what we experienced in the past: thousands who actively or passively supported racist practices in days gone by now recall how disgusted and appalled they were at the time. Just conceivably, there may even be occasions where we manage to fool ourselves about what we are presently experiencing: perhaps the dentist's drill is not really hurting us as much as we think it is. In general, though, as long as we are merely describing our own present experiences we cannot easily be mistaken.

Rationalism and empiricism

If we accept the conclusion just drawn, then the kind of scepticism that says we cannot be sure if *any* of our beliefs are true must be rejected. Our beliefs about our own subjective states are indubitable, and these beliefs constitute knowledge. However, this is hardly a complete or satisfactory victory over scepticism. Most of what we think of as knowledge concerns not our subjective states but the way things are in the objective world – the world of physical objects existing in space and time. This is the world we talk about all the time, the world investigated by the natural and social sciences. Unless we can justify our claims to have some knowledge of this world, we can hardly pronounce scepticism defeated.

This was certainly Descartes's view. In his *Meditations*, once he establishes that he thinks, that he exists, and that he can be certain about the character of his subjective experiences, he sets about the task of proving the existence of a world beyond his own consciousness. His argument is fairly convoluted. Briefly, he argues from the fact that he has an idea of God (that is, an infinite, perfect being) in his mind to the conclusion that God must exist (since only God could have caused him to have such an idea). Descartes then argues that we can trust our natural inclination to believe that our sensations are caused by physical objects acting on our bodies; for God has implanted this inclination in us and, being perfect, he would not deceive us. We will not follow Descartes down this path. Most critics agree that the proofs of God's existence upon which his argument hinges are flawed; and this way of resolving the problem has little appeal nowadays.

What is noteworthy about Descartes's approach, though, is that he tries to lay the foundations of all philosophical and scientific knowledge entirely by a priori reasoning (that is, by reasoning that does not appeal to sense-experience or observation). This is characteristic of **rationalism**. Rationalists do not deny that detailed knowledge of the world around has to be based on observation. How far the earth is from the sun; how many people live in Moscow; at what temperature iron becomes molten; such things obviously cannot be discovered by pure rational reflection. But rationalism holds that at least *some* things about the world around us can be known by reason working on its own, unaided by sense-experience. Moreover, it typically claims that this a priori knowledge constitutes a foundation for the rest of human knowledge. Descartes, for instance, believes he can demonstrate a priori that God exists, that God is infinite and perfect, that every other being depends on God for its existence, that mind and body are distinct substances that can exist independently of one another, that every event has a cause, and many other such far-reaching propositions about the general character of the world. Pure reason draws the outlines, and reason combined with sense-experience colours in the details.

> How can we know anything about the way the world is except on the basis of experience? We can speculate, perhaps; but genuine knowledge must surely rest on observation.

The view that all knowledge has to be based on empirical observation – which for human beings always takes the form of either sense-perception or introspection – is known as **empiricism**. In standard histories of philosophy, empiricism and rationalism are usually presented as rival philosophical schools confronting each other through the seventeenth and eighteenth centuries, with empiricism stressing the importance of experience and rationalism the importance of reason in the construction of knowledge. Yet this is an oversimplified and in some ways misleading picture. Rationalists like Descartes never deny the need for empirical study; and empiricists like John Locke (1632–1704) usually recognize that some fundamental principles, as well as branches of knowledge like mathematics and logic, are not based on mere generalizations from experience. It is probably fair to say that since the eighteenth century empiricism has had the best of it. Kant, whose views we discussed in the previous chapter, is sometimes credited with reconciling rationalism and empiricism. As we saw, Kant argued that our experience of the world is shaped in some ways by our minds; this allows us to have some a priori knowledge, and to this extent the rationalists were correct. However, he also insisted that this a priori knowledge is always about the spatio-temporal world we experience; it never goes beyond it. In this respect the empiricists were right.

Going beyond subjectivity

The philosophical problem that still concerns us is scepticism. We saw that Descartes's approach justifies our claim to have knowledge of our own subjective states but runs into difficulties when the task is to justify our beliefs about the external world. Empiricism places great weight on sense-experience. But does it provide a way of dispelling the sceptical doubts surrounding the move from describing my subjective states to describing an objective world?

Let us take a simple belief about the world that I hold to be true: There is a tree in the garden. Why do I believe this? The obvious answer is that I believe it because I can see a tree in the garden. In other words, I am having certain sensations, and from this I infer that there is a material object of a certain kind causing me to have them. How can I confirm that this inference is correct? The obvious answer is to go out into the garden and put my hands against the tree. Feeling its solidity will confirm that what I have seen is not a hallucination, a mirage or a hologram. But while this answer may be obvious, it is not philosophically satisfactory. The problem is that the sense of touch does not 'put us in touch' with what lies behind our sensations; it only gives us another kind of sensation. It is not privileged over the other four senses, somehow providing us with direct access to reality itself.

When I experience a tactile sensation I make an inference from the sensation to its cause just as I do in the case of visual sensations. I can just as easily imagine – especially with the advent of virtual reality – having certain tactile sensations and then using my other senses to check whether the cause is what I assume it to be. For example, I can imagine being blindfold with my nose blocked while having the sensation of holding segments of an orange in my hand. In this case, to confirm that the tactile sensations are not being artificially induced by some highly sophisticated machine, I could take off the blindfold, unblock my nose, and use sight and smell (and perhaps taste too) to verify my initial inference. The general point here is that, from a philosophical point of view, the information furnished by the different senses is all on the same level. True, we normally rely much more heavily on sight and touch than on smell or taste to inform us about our environment. But this does not mean that either sight or touch provides us with a guarantee that our other sense-impressions are *veridical* (that us, tell us the truth about the way things are).

Direct realism: in touch with reality

> *Why, when I perceive a tree in the garden, is there a need to confirm anything? In this situation, most of the time, I don't make a dubious inference that there is a tree out there. The tree is what I see, hear, smell or touch; and that, in itself, is sufficient to prove its reality.*

This is certainly the way we normally think and talk about sense-experience, at least before we have studied any philosophy. For this reason, the position stated here is called 'naive realism' or, alternatively and less condescendingly, **direct realism**. It is a kind of **realism** because it holds that our claims about the world are made true or false simply by the way the world *is*, independently of our cognition of it. If I say that the tree is a conifer, what determines whether or not I am right is the objective character of the tree. This kind of realism is 'naive' or 'direct' because it holds that our senses put us in immediate contact with the physical world.

Direct realism has two appealing features: it accords with common sense; and it denies a foothold to sceptical doubts about the match between our subjective experiences and objective reality. For these reasons many philosophers are drawn towards it. But appealing features are not the same thing as convincing arguments, and these apparent advantages of the theory dissolve under critical scrutiny. As far as common sense is concerned, why should we consider it a virtue of a theory that it be close to common sense? After all, common sense once told people that the earth was flat and that the sun moved around the earth; and in the twentieth century, relativity theory and quantum mechanics have stood common sense on its head. If by common sense one means sound practical wisdom, then it is undeniably a good thing. But if by common sense is meant the relatively unreflective and theoretically uninformed opinions that support our day-to-day interactions with the world, there is no particular reason why philosophers should try to make their theories conform to it, any more than scientists, social scientists or artists should. The most that can be expected, in some cases, is that a theory should be able to *explain* common sense: that is, the theory may need to account for the fact that a certain way of thinking comes to us naturally (just as Copernicus's heliocentric theory also explained why it *looks* as if the sun moves around the earth).

The second supposed advantage of direct realism – the fact that it shuts out a certain kind of scepticism – perhaps deserves to be taken more seriously. But however much we might like to dispose of the sceptical threat in this way, there is an obvious problem with the theory that prevents us from doing so. Direct realism says that we directly and immediately perceive physical objects themselves. But we know that this is not always true. In the case of illusions, hallucinations and dreams, we have sense-impressions that we often mistake for perceptions of real things. The reason we are fooled in such cases is obvious but important. It is because there are no *intrinsic* differences between the two kinds of experience. Having a vivid visual hallucination of a tree (or seeing a hologram of a tree, for that matter) is exactly like seeing a real tree. We are only able to distinguish them by reference to other, supplementary experiences such as what happens when we try to touch the tree or walk around it. The well-known phenomenon of 'phantom limbs' provides a dramatic illustration of the same point: people who have had an arm or a leg amputated usually continue to feel sensations for a few days afterwards 'in' the limb that they have lost. Even though they no longer have a right wrist, they may still experience aches, itches or other sensations that are exactly like those they had prior to the amputation.

These familiar observations are the basis for a seemingly irrefutable argument. Clearly, when I have a hallucination I cannot be directly perceiving any physical object since there is no object present. The sense-experience must therefore be entirely 'within' me, and I am fooled by the hallucination only if I judge that it is caused by a corresponding physical object of a certain kind. But if veridical sense-perceptions are *intrinsically indistinguishable* from hallucinations, then I cannot be in unmediated contact with physical reality in either case. Tree-like sensations caused by a tree and tree-like sensations caused by hallucinogenic drugs are of the same kind. So even a non-hallucinatory sense-experience is essentially subjective, and I *infer* the existence and character of its physical cause. Obviously, this does not mean that I am continuously and consciously making such inferences. I do not actually think: 'Aha! I seem to be seeing a tree, so there probably is a tree out there.' From the youngest age we think and talk and act as if we perceive the things themselves, unless we have a good reason to think otherwise. To say that I infer the existence of things from my subjective sense-impressions does not imply that certain thought processes are actually taking place in my mind. Rather, it expresses a philosophical recognition of three things:

1 There is a difference between the subjective claim that I am having certain sense-experiences and the objective claim that a material object exists independently of these experiences.
2 The objective claim rests on the subjective claim – that is, if the objective claim were to be challenged, the subjective claim would usually constitute its main justification.
3 It can happen that the subjective claim is true while the objective claim is false.

The same general point – that what we immediately perceive is 'within us' rather than 'out there' – can be supported by another quite simple argument. We all know that light travels at a certain speed. This means that when we look at the stars we see them not as they are now but as they were many years ago. So if, one night, we see a star become a nova, what we are witnessing is an event that has already happened. While we were seeing what looked like an ordinary star, the star itself had already exploded. It is thus possible to see something that no longer exists, simply because of the time lag between the thing's sending out light and our registering this information. But what is true for a distant star is true for the television across the room or the book in your hand. Strictly speaking, you see even these things as they were a fraction of a second ago. A similar argument holds for the other senses too, since it takes time for messages to be conveyed from the sense organs to the part of the brain where they are registered and enter consciousness. But if it is possible for me to have a sense-impression of something that no longer exists, we have to conclude that the sense-impression is distinct from the thing of which it is an impression.

The veil of perception

For these reasons, direct realism has to be rejected. We are then left with a theory of knowledge according to which the immediate objects of cognition are our own subjective sense-impressions, from which we make inferences about the existence and nature of things in the material world. Our sensations represent this world to us, but we have no access to it except through sense-perception. This account of our cognitive situation is commonly called the **representative theory of perception**. It was widely accepted during the seventeenth and eighteenth centuries, and remains, in spite of numerous attacks on it, a powerful and persuasive theory from which even its critics have difficulty distancing themselves.

> *Doesn't the representative theory of perception lead us back into scepticism? How do we know that our sense-perceptions represent anything at all? And even if they do represent something, how can we know whether or not they represent it accurately?*

This is without doubt one of the most serious drawbacks to the theory. Our situation, as the theory portrays it, might be likened to that of a person sitting alone inside their own private cinema, watching films that purport to depict the world beyond the cinema but unable to go outside and check whether what they see on the screen corresponds to anything at all. We noted earlier that Descartes's way of escaping from this prison of subjectivity by invoking God's benevolence is not open to us. But is there any other way to avoid the sceptical implications of the representative theory of perception? Or should we perhaps conclude that since it entails scepticism the theory itself has to go? Let us examine this problem in more detail.

There are two questions here:

- Do our sense-perceptions entitle us to infer anything about the *nature* of the material world?
- Do our sense-perceptions entitle us to infer that a material world exists?

The second question is, in an obvious way, the more fundamental; but there are advantages to addressing the other question first.

The pre-philosophical answer to the first question is fairly simple: what you see (or otherwise sense) is what there is. When I examine a tomato, I perceive a more or less spherical red thing with a certain smell and a certain taste. From this I infer that the thing itself has these properties, and its possession of these properties explains why I have the corresponding sensations. Like direct realism, this way of thinking serves us well most of the time in everyday life. But, again like direct realism, it runs up against some devastating objections. To understand one of these objections, try the following experiment. Place your left hand in a bowl of hot water and your right hand in a bowl of cold water and leave them there for 30 seconds. Then place both hands in a bowl of tepid water. You can probably predict the result: the tepid water feels cool to your left hand and warm to your right hand. If what you feel is what there is, then the same water must be simultaneously warm and cool, which makes no sense. Clearly, the intrinsic temperature of the water is one thing, and how it feels to a perceiving subject is another. A similar experiment can be performed with foods. A strawberry will taste somewhat sharp if eaten after something very sweet, but quite sweet if it follows something bitter; and both its taste and its smell will be fainter if I am suffering from a cold.

What do these observations prove? They prove that the character of our sense-perceptions are significantly affected by our situation and condition. Two different subjects can perceive an object very differently, and the same subject may perceive it differently at different times. In both cases, though, the variations are entirely due to subjective differences, not alterations in the object. This means that at least some of the qualities that we ascribe to things on the basis of our sense-perceptions do not actually inhere in the things themselves. We may assume, if we wish, that our sense-impressions are normally caused by material objects affecting our sense-organs. But the sense-impressions themselves, being the result of an interaction between subject and object, are determined by subjective factors such as the nature and condition of our faculties. We may not, therefore, infer from the fact that a thing looks red, tastes sweet, feels cold or produces other similar sense-impressions in us that it actually possesses these qualities.

One could, perhaps, try to defend the naive or pre-philosophical view by arguing that the variations in perception described above should not be granted equal status. We regularly distinguish between true and false, accurate and inaccurate, distorted and undistorted perceptions. A strawberry may look orange to a person with jaundice while appearing red to a healthy observer. But why conclude from this that it has no inherent colour? The strawberry is red; the person with jaundice has faulty vision. Similarly, someone with a cold has an abnormal sense of taste, just as a person under the influence of drugs may suffer from distorted perception generally. Distorted perception means not perceiving things the way they really are. How they really are is the way they appear to normal, healthy subjects. If we recognize this, then we can allow for variations in perception without denying that things really do possess properties like those we perceive.

This defence of the naive view is not sufficient, however. Certainly, we describe perception as 'correct', 'faulty', 'impaired', 'normal' and so on. But our use of such terms does not imply that correct or normal perception gives us impressions that correspond to similar qualities within the things perceived; for we can define concepts like 'normal' or 'faulty' in an entirely conventional way. For example, we might well say that someone who perceives as orange what most observers describe as red has faulty vision. But this really does not mean anything other than that this person's colour sensations are different from those of the great majority. We may even say that the 'true' colour of a ripe tomato is red. But this can be explicated as follows: red is the colour that the overwhelming majority of observers who are not known to be sick, under the influence of drugs, looking through tinted lenses or in some other unusual condition, will report seeing when they look at a ripe tomato under white light. The concept of truth in perception, like the other concepts mentioned, can thus be defined – and perhaps, in the end, has to be defined – in relation to our community's perceptual experiences and expectations rather than in relation to the intrinsic nature of the things perceived.

Representative realism

Granted that properties like colours, smells and tastes are not actually in the objects we perceive, surely some other properties are. For instance, if I see and feel two oranges on a table, there really are two of them, and they really are spherical.

This seems plausible. Indeed, it was precisely for this reason that Descartes and other leading thinkers of his time like Galileo and Locke drew a distinction between a thing's primary and secondary qualities. According to them, an object's **primary qualities** really do belong to the thing itself. The most important ones are usually taken to be:

- extension in space
- shape
- quantity
- motion (whether or not it is in motion, and if so what kind of motion)
- impenetrability (not allowing anything else to occupy the space it occupies)

Not coincidentally, these are the properties of things with which physics is concerned, and which can described mathematically. They can also typically be apprehended by more than one sense: I can both see and feel that the orange on the table is single, spherical, about eight centimetres in diameter and stationary. And our perceptual representation of these properties is held to resemble or in some sense match the properties themselves: I see a small round shape moving slowly from left to right, and believe that corresponding to my sense-impressions there is a round object moving slowly through space in the same direction.

The term **secondary qualities** has been used in two ways. It is sometimes used to refer to subject-dependent, sensible properties such as colour, taste, smell and the like. Although we are naturally tempted to think of these properties as inhering in things, we have already seen that there are good reasons for rejecting this idea. In this first sense, then, secondary qualities are not 'in' things at all; rather, they are sense-impressions that exist or occur only in the mind of the perceiving subject. Nor is there anything in the perceived object that resembles them; the flavour of the orange is no more within the orange than is the pleasure I derive from tasting it.

In the other sense of the term, secondary qualities *do* belong to things, because they are independent of our perception of them. They are those qualities a thing possesses that cause us to have sensations of colour, taste, smell and so on when we encounter it. In other words, secondary qualities in this second sense are the intrinsic properties of objects that give rise to secondary qualities in the first sense. These properties do not resemble the sense-impressions for which they are responsible. What causes us to taste sugar as sweet is not itself sweet; it is a property that can ultimately be described by physical science in terms of the microphysical structure of sugar crystals and their component parts. Similarly, what causes us to see a rose petal as red is its capacity for reflecting light photons of a certain energy while absorbing others – a capacity it has in virtue of the kind of atoms that constitute it and the way they are connected.

Representative realism is one name for the view that our sense-impressions are caused by independently existing physical entities possessed of basic physical properties describable in the language of mathematical physics, and that these properties can be inferred from our sense-impressions. Like direct realism, it holds that what makes our beliefs true or false is the way things are, independently of our cognition of them; this is what makes it a form of realism. Representative realism does not hold that we are in direct perceptual contact with these independently existing things, but it does maintain that:

- there is a resemblance between my impressions of primary qualities and the primary qualities of objects; and
- there is also a correspondence between the similarities and differences among my sense-impressions and similarities and differences in the external world.

For instance, if a tomato and a red pepper appear the same shade of red to me, that is because of some similarity in their physical make-up which causes them both to reflect light in a similar way. By the same token, from the fact that a lemon looks yellow and a lime looks green I can infer that there is a corresponding objective dissimilarity in the two objects, which is responsible for the difference in my sense-impressions.

Let us take stock of the route we have travelled so far. We began by considering the threat of scepticism, and saw that Descartes's insight into the certainty I enjoy regarding my present subjective experiences refutes the suggestion that I can have no knowledge whatsoever. But it leaves intact scepticism regarding any knowledge I might claim to have of the world beyond my own mind. *Empiricism* teaches us that the royal road to such knowledge is through sense-perception, but this plausible view immediately throws up difficulties and complexities. *Direct realism*, the view that we directly perceive physical objects themselves, is unable to handle the distinction between veridical perception and illusions. We are thus led to embrace some form of the *representative theory of perception*, a theory that leads us to distinguish between qualities possessed by things themselves and qualities that only exist in the mind of the perceiver. *Representative realism* provides one fairly plausible account of the relation between what we perceive and what exists independently of us.

Before we pronounce scepticism defeated, however, or assume that representative realism offers the only plausible account of our cognitive relation to the external world, let us consider again the two questions we posed earlier:

- Do our sense-perceptions entitle us to infer anything about the *nature* of the material world?
- Do our sense-perceptions entitle us to infer that a material world exists?

We have seen how representative realism answers the first question. But this answer presupposes an affirmative response to the second question, and so far nothing has been said to justify such a response. Clearly, we need to tackle this question directly.

One way of trying to justify our belief that our perceptions are caused by material objects external to our minds would be to set up some technologically sophisticated apparatus to detect the presence of these objects. But it should be obvious what is wrong with this procedure. For one thing, the apparatus itself is assumed to be a material object, and this is precisely the kind of belief we are trying to justify. For another thing, whatever results the apparatus provides, we can only register these by means of our sense-perceptions; so using the apparatus cannot possibly confirm that things exist independently of our perceptions. In fact, I already have a sophisticated apparatus that I believe helps me to detect material objects – my own body, equipped with its sense organs. An additional piece of equipment that is supposed to mediate between myself and these objects cannot possibly provide any further reason for believing that the objects exist. For exactly the same reasons, taking a photograph of something does not prove it exists independently of my perception of it.

Another possible way of trying to justify my belief in the external world is to appeal to the testimony of other people. What proves that my perceptions are not merely subjective but relate to things beyond my own mind, according to this argument, is that other people report having similar sensations when they are placed in the same situation as myself. Obviously, though, this argument commits the same kind of fallacy as the one just considered. Other people, from my vantage point, are part of the external world. On the basis of their behaviour, including their linguistic behaviour, I infer that they, like me, are subjects of experience. But if my aim is to justify my belief in a world *beyond* my own mind, I can hardly introduce as evidence the behaviour of certain things *within* that world. Once again, I would be 'begging the question' – that is, assuming what I am trying to prove (see the box).

Clearly, it is not such an easy matter to prove the reality of a world that exists beyond my subjective experiences and gives rise to them. The natural first move is to appeal to sense-experience. But, on reflection, it is hard to see how *any sense-*experience can suffice. According to the representative theory of perception, I am never in direct contact with independently existing reality. I perceive only my own sense-impressions. Material objects are posited in order to explain why I have the

---

think critically!   Begging the question

The expression 'begging the question' does not mean 'raising the question' or 'implying the question', although this is how it is sometimes used these days. Rather, to beg the question is to commit a certain, very common, kind of fallacy. Here is an example:

> All criminals come from families with problems. Where this isn't obvious, and the criminal seems to come from a happy, stable, loving family, we just don't know about the problem. But we can be sure there must have been one, since if there hadn't been any problems the person would never have become a criminal.

The main thesis here is that all criminals come from families with problems. An obvious objection to this thesis is that there seem to be counterexamples – criminals who grew up in wholesome domestic circumstances. This objection is met, and the main thesis is thus indirectly supported, by the claim that a person's criminality constitutes evidence that there must have been some problematic feature of their early family life that caused them to go off the rails. But this latter claim actually does nothing to support the main thesis, for it is only true if the main thesis is true. Someone who claims that criminality is sure evidence of a problem in the family is already assuming that all criminals come from families with problems. Their argument thus 'begs the question' because it assumes what it is supposed to prove.

sense-experiences I do. But between me and them there is always a 'veil of perception', and I can never apprehend the world except from behind this veil. I can never look at things 'sideways on', so to speak, to see if my sense-impressions actually relate to material objects and, if they do, what that relation is.

> *Within this theoretical framework, then, it seems impossible to use my sense-experience in any direct way to prove the existence of anything beyond sense-experience.*

This is a powerful argument. One possible response to it is simply to embrace scepticism regarding our knowledge of the external world. If we cannot even prove that such a world exists, then, surely, none of our beliefs about this world can constitute knowledge. Another response, however, is to take this apparent sceptical impasse as evidence that something must be misguided about the reasoning that led up to it. This is the position taken by George Berkeley, an Irish philosopher of the early eighteenth century who became famous for his radical critique of the materialism which prevailed in his day (see the box). Taking a closer look at Berkeley's arguments against the representative realism described above, and at the remarkable alternative position which he put forward in its place, should help us to deepen our understanding of the issues involved.

Berkeley's idealism: 'to be is to be perceived'

In Berkeley's view, once you have accepted the basic tenets of the representative theory of perception you cannot avoid being sucked into scepticism. This is because the theory's main thesis is that reality – the realm of what Descartes and Locke called material substance – lies hidden behind a veil of sense-impressions. As we can never peek around the veil, we are condemned to remain completely ignorant about this supposed reality. To avoid this conclusion, Berkeley argues that we should take a harder look at what we think an object is. The truth is, everything we know about an object we learn through sense-perception. So instead of thinking that the real object is something mysterious that lies behind and hidden from our perceptions, why not entertain the idea that an object is nothing over and above our perception of it? In Berkeley's view, this is actually in line with common sense. After all, if I was asked to describe an apple, all I would ever think of doing is to list its sensible properties: its size, shape, weight, colour, texture, smell, taste and so on. It would not occur to me to add to the end of this list the mysterious, indiscernible property of being a material thing. Thus, to all intents and purposes, the apple is nothing over and above a collection of sensible properties.

Thinking of objects in this way certainly puts paid to some of the sceptical doubts thrown up by the 'veil of perception' view. We don't have to worry about whether or not our sense-impressions correspond to or resemble material reality; and we don't have to wrestle any longer with the problem of how to justify our

George Berkeley (1685–1753)

George Berkeley was born in Kilkenny, Ireland, and educated at Trinity College, Dublin. After the failure of a scheme to found a missionary college in the Bermudas, he eventually became Bishop of Cloyne. Throughout his life his guiding intellectual purpose was to defend religion from what he saw as the threat posed by the materialism of the new sciences which, in his view, encouraged scepticism and atheism.

Berkeley's most important philosophical work is his *Principles of Human Knowledge*, published when he was 25. In this book Berkeley attacks various aspects of the 'representative realism' of Descartes and Locke – in particular the doctrine that our sensations are caused by material substances existing independently of us in space. Against this view, he argued that the very idea of objects existing unperceived was unintelligible. One of his arguments for this thesis was very simple. Try to form an idea of an object existing unperceived by anyone. Inevitably, what you will do is imagine the object as it would appear if you were perceiving it. To think of it existing unperceived would involve thinking of it without thinking of any of its sensible properties, which cannot be done. Therefore, the whole idea of matter existing unperceived is literally unthinkable.

Berkeley's philosophy was not well received. Most people assumed he was saying that the world we think of as the 'real' world is an illusion and has no real existence. In an effort to correct this misunderstanding, Berkeley wrote his other main philosophical work, *Three Dialogues between Hylas and Philonous*. These dialogues present his ideas in a marvellously readable form, but most intellectuals continued to regard Berkeley's philosophy as too bizarre to be taken seriously, even though few knew how to refute his arguments. As David Hume put it, Berkeley 'often astounds, but rarely can convince'. Gradually, however, and partly thanks to Hume, his contribution to philosophy came to be increasingly appreciated. His work contains many remarkable insights; and it significantly advanced our understanding of the tasks and difficulties facing anyone trying to construct a fully fledged empiricist account of knowledge and reality.

belief that there is such a reality. On Berkeley's view, the whole idea that objective reality is material and exists independently of any perceiving subject is mistaken. This follows from his revised concept of an object as nothing more than the totality of its sensible properties. It further follows that since these properties, as everyone admits, are essentially subjective – that is, they exist only in the mind of the perceiving subject – what we call objects are also mind dependent. In fact, says Berkeley, their being consists in their being perceived, and thus they can exist only 'in' the mind.

> *This looks like another case where the cure is worse than the sickness. The doctrine that objects only exist in so far as they are perceived is absurd. It implies that if I am alone in my room and close my eyes, most of the contents of the room suddenly cease to exist, only to pop back into existence when I reopen my eyes.*

This certainly appears to be a serious objection to Berkeley's brand of idealism. (It should be obvious from our discussion of idealism in the previous chapter that Berkeley is an idealist, though his kind of idealism differs from Kant's in important ways.) There is actually nothing self-contradictory about the idea that trees, cars, mountains, oceans, planets and galaxies continually come into being, then cease to exist, then come back into being again. It is also consistent with the data furnished by our sense-experience. But it strikes us as a fantastically unlikely hypothesis. The world we experience seems to exhibit a great deal of regularity and order, and we generally believe that all, or almost all, that happens can be explained in terms of universal causal laws. On the hypothesis in question, both the orderliness of our experiences and the explanation for the coming and going of things would be quite mysterious.

Berkeley recognizes this, but he believes he can overcome the problem without reverting back to a belief in material objects. His argument is very simple. If we accept that:

- representative realism and the representative theory of perception are untenable,
- objects cannot exist without being perceived, and
- objects continue to exist even when I am not perceiving them,

we are forced to conclude that objects must be perceived by some other mind when I am not perceiving them. Naturally, being a bishop, Berkeley identifies this other mind with God. The philosophical picture that results is something like this: The universe consists of minds and their contents (which includes sensations, thoughts and various other mental entities). What we call things or objects are ideas in God's mind. These ideas have no causal power themselves (unlike material objects on the materialist view); they thus do not cause us to have sensations. The cause of our sensations is God himself, acting directly on all our minds simultaneously. This explains why my sensations cohere with yours. God affects our mind in similar ways, rather as a TV transmitter causes different television sets to show the same picture. It also explains why our sense-experiences are so orderly – why whenever I look at a certain spot in the garden I see a tree, and why this tree exhibits regular and predictable seasonal changes over the years. God ensures that the sense-perceptions he causes us to have will exhibit this orderliness so that we can cope with the world (that is, with the succession of sensations we experience), investigate it systematically, and eventually come to understand it.

One response to this explanation of our sense-experience is to view it as a reasonable alternative to representative realism – an alternative that avoids the sceptical dangers of positing mysterious unknowable material substances and that offers a novel proof of God's existence as well. This was Berkeley's view. Another response is to condemn it as bizarre and implausible, a classic example of the folly into which philosophers fall when they fail to temper their abstract arguments with a hefty dose of common sense. This was the view of most of Berkeley's contemporaries. But we should not dismiss theories simply because they are strange or contrary to customary thinking. If we decide that Berkeley's position is unacceptable we must be able to justify this negative verdict by pointing to errors in his reasoning, internal contradictions, or other theoretical failings.

The most famous 'refutation' of Berkeley was offered by his contemporary Samuel Johnson who, asked what he thought of Berkeley's ideas, dramatically kicked a stone and declared 'I refute Berkeley thus!' But a little reflection makes it clear that this is actually a very poor objection, since it is based on a misinterpretation – or, at least, an extremely unsympathetic interpretation – of what Berkeley is saying. Johnson's 'refutation' rests on the assumption that Berkeley's philosophy either implies that stones will not appear solid to the touch or cannot explain why they do so. But, as we noted earlier, tactile sensations such as Johnson received from kicking the stone are still only sense-impressions – they are not essentially different from other sensations – and there is no reason to suppose that Berkeley has a special problem explaining why things feel solid as opposed to appearing blue or tasting salty. In fact, Johnson's mistake is quite common among readers of Berkeley, both then and now. The mistake is to suppose that Berkeley is offering a novel description of what our experiences are like, and one that is evidently false. But he is not doing this at all. What Berkeley is offering is not a *redescription* of what we actually experience but a novel *explanation* of why our experience has the character it does. The question is whether it really is, as he claims, a superior explanation to those that posit material objects existing in space.

When we put the problem this way, some of the problems with the Berkeleian view start to emerge. For instance, he dispenses with the concept of material substance in part because we cannot perceive it; positing it as the cause of our sensations is condemned as a piece of dubious metaphysical speculation. But Berkeley himself does exactly the same with the idea of God. God is the imperceptible cause of our sense-perceptions, and his power and intelligence account for their orderliness. In fact, Berkeley goes still further and proposes that

God's mind is full of ideas, which is what permits him to say that the things I am perceiving do not cease to exist when I no longer perceive them. But the place in his theory of these ideas in God's mind is very problematic. First, like God – and like the material objects posited by representative realism – these entities cannot be perceived by us, since all we ever perceive are our *own* ideas. It is thus hard to see how Berkeley, on his strict empiricist principles, can justify positing them. Second, Berkeley is adamant that the only kind of causal action he recognizes is *willing*, something we are familiar with because we perform acts of will. For this reason, he rejects the idea that 'inert' material objects could cause us to have sensations. But, by the same token, what he calls ideas are also 'inert' and have no causal power. It follows from this, as he frankly admits, that God's ideas play no causal role in his theory. They are not what we perceive; nor are they the cause of our sense-impressions, since God is said to act on our mind directly, without any mediating mechanism. In one place, Berkeley says they are the 'occasion' for God to affect our minds in certain ways; but God should hardly need reminders of what he has to do! It seems, then, that the only reason for supposing that God has these ideas is to avoid the implication that trees, trains, moons and stars continually pop in and out of existence.

Phenomenalism

The objections we have raised are not the only problems with Berkeley's position, and very few philosophers have been willing to defend his positive doctrine. But his critique of the representative theory of perception and the realist accounts of how sense-perception gives us knowledge of the external world cannot be ignored. The basic problem he identifies is that if we posit imperceptible causes of our sensations that exist independently of us, then we are abandoning a true empiricism. Instead of restricting our knowledge claims to the world of possible experience, we are indulging in a form of speculation that lacks a philosophical justification, even though it may accord with common sense. Convinced by this reasoning, a number of thinkers have followed Berkeley's lead and adopted a position known as **phenomenalism**. (The label 'phenomenalism' derives from the way this school tries to interpret all knowledge claims about the world solely in terms of claims about 'phenomena' – that is, actual and possible sense-experience.) This way of thinking was especially influential in the first half of the twentieth century.

Phenomenalists do not call on us to eschew all talk about material objects existing independently of us. Such talk in everyday conversation or in scientific discourse is unobjectionable. But from a philosophical point of view it has to be understood as a kind of shorthand for talk about subjective sense-experience. Thus, the statement 'I see a tree' can be translated into 'I am having tree-like visual sensations.' The statement 'There is a tree in the garden' can be translated into 'If you look at the garden or go walking in the garden you will experience tree-like sensations' (the kind of sensations one normally associates with trees).

It might be thought that phenomenalism has trouble differentiating between veridical sense-perception and hallucinations or illusions. If all talk about an external world ultimately reduces to talk about my sense-experience, how is this distinction to be drawn? What is the difference between really seeing a tree and having a hallucination of a tree? In fact, though, phenomenalists can deal with this objection quite easily. The distinction can still be drawn, but it is drawn entirely in terms of actual and possible sense-perceptions. To say that I am seeing a 'real' tree is to imply that my visual sense-impression of a tree is, or could be, correlated with other sense-impressions. If I were to walk towards what I see, I would find that it gradually takes up more of my visual field; I would begin to smell the blossoms; I would hear the leaves rustling in the wind; finally, I would receive the expected tactile sensations when I stretch my hand out to it. To describe what I see as illusory is to say that my initial perceptions would not cohere in this way with the rest of my sense-experience.

Of course, it is not always possible for practical reasons to corroborate our perceptions in this manner. This is especially true in the case of distant objects. What matters for the phenomenalist, though, is whether such corroboration is possible *in principle*. So long as it is, our statements about the world can be translated into conditional statements about what our sense-perceptions *would be*, if we were to put ourselves in a certain position or perform certain actions. Whereas Berkeley said 'to be is to be perceived', which makes objects mind dependent, his phenomenalist successor John Stuart Mill described objects as 'permanent possibilities of sensation'. This definition of an object aims to maintain a rigorous empiricism, refusing to talk about anything that lies beyond possible experience, while avoiding some of the pitfalls of Berkeley's idealism.

> *Even in its more modern form, phenomenalism is still a hard doctrine to swallow. After all, there must be some reason why we have the sensations we have. But phenomenalism doesn't seem to offer any explanation at all. This has to be a serious liability.*

This question – What is responsible for our sensations? – does indeed present a major difficulty for phenomenalism. In fact, it leads to several telling objections. The most basic problem is that in the absence of the material substances of representative realism, or Berkeley's God, or some other cause, the fact that we have any sense-experience at all remains completely unexplained: a brute mystery. Why do we experience something rather than nothing? Surely, there must be a reason. A second problem is that phenomenalism cannot explain the fact that our experiences are *coherent*. They are actually coherent in several ways. First, the impressions received by the different senses cohere with one another; I hear the dog bark at the same moment that I see it open its mouth. Second, my experiences from one moment to the next fit together; every time I look up from my desk and out over the garden, I see more or less the same scene. Third, my experiences over longer periods of time fit into a coherent and predictable narrative. I see infants turn into children, then into teenagers and then into adults; the stages never occur in any other order. Fourth, what I experience coheres with what other people say they experience. If I ask a friend to describe the Eiffel Tower, their description matches mine; and two descriptions of the tower offered from different vantage points agree and disagree in just the ways one would expect. What accounts for all this coherence? To pronounce it inexplicable or to refuse to attempt an explanation is completely unsatisfactory. Yet phenomenalists appear willing to forgo any possibility of an explanation rather than violate their principle of not talking about things that cannot be perceived.

Phenomenalism, or something like it, may be the position we arrive at if we insist on sticking to this principle. But if so, then we have to wonder whether the principle is worth sticking to, and why. One reason for doubting its soundness is that if I take it seriously I ought to refrain from assuming that other people have minds like my own. After all, I cannot perceive another person's mind; all I ever perceive is his or her bodily behaviour. Phenomenalists are thus presented with an uncomfortable choice. They must either concede that it is reasonable to posit other minds in order to explain the observed behaviour of other people – in which case it becomes unclear why they will not posit material objects in order to explain the rest of our sense-experience – or they must refuse to posit the existence of other minds. This latter option need not imply that all mention of other people and their mental attributes should be eliminated from ordinary conversation. Rather, it means that from a philosophical point of view whatever I say about other people's minds can be converted into talk about their observable behaviour, and whatever I say about their observable behaviour can be translated into reports about my actual and possible sense-experience. Talk about other minds is thus viewed as a 'logical construct' out of talk about my sense-experience. But now we really do seem to be on the brink of absurdity. If I hold that other people are logical constructs out of my own sense-experience, then I am refusing to grant them any independent existence.

Phenomenalism thus seems to be a slippery slope leading ultimately to the view that, to the best of my knowledge, the world consists entirely of my own mind and its contents. Whatever knowledge I may claim to have about the world really extends no further than this. And whatever I say about the world – its character or its contents – is really just a shorthand way of talking about my own sensations. This view is known as **solipsism**. Few philosophers take it seriously. Most would say that any philosophical view that leads to solipsism is thereby proved to be misguided. For although solipsism may not be self-contradictory, it is hard to believe that any sane person could sincerely believe it. Its absurdity is nicely illustrated by an anecdote told by Bertrand Russell who reported that he received a letter one day from an aspiring philosopher which began as follows: 'Dear Professor Russell, I am a solipsist. Why isn't everyone else?'

The insight of idealism

We suggested above that phenomenalism is unable to provide a satisfactory explanation of why we have sense-experience and of why it exhibits so much coherence. Representative realism, on the other hand, does seem able to meet this demand. It holds that we have sensations because our bodies interact with other physical entities and forces; and their coherence is due to the fact that these physical entities exist in space, independently of any particular perceiving subject, part of an objective realm governed by universal causal laws. This looks like a strong reason for preferring representative realism over phenomenalism. In choosing between the two theories we make an 'inference to the best explanation'. Of course, there is room for plenty of debate over just what counts as the 'best' explanation of any given phenomenon. Berkeley, for instance, would argue that his explanation of our sense-experience as the result of God's direct action on our minds is better than an explanation that requires material substances, existing unperceived, to affect our senses. But it is precisely because Berkeley's explanation seems rather far fetched that most people feel unable to take it seriously.

Can we conclude, then, that representative realism is the best philosophical account of how sense-experience serves as a foundation for knowledge of the external world – or at least the best of the theories we have considered? Certainly, something like this view is fairly popular among contemporary philosophers. However, many others believe that Berkeley's idealism, for all its drawbacks, contains an important insight; and this insight uncovers a fundamental problem with most forms of realism, representative realism included. The point in question is one we have already touched upon. Almost any form of realism conceives of knowledge as involving beliefs that are true because they correspond to an independently existing reality. But this notion of an independently existing reality is philosophically suspect. While it makes sense in everyday life and everyday discourse to talk about how well our beliefs correspond to the facts, it does not make much sense when we are reflecting philosophically and in very general terms about what constitutes knowledge. In everyday life I can compare my beliefs with the facts: I believe the library is open; my friend thinks it is closed; we settle the dispute by walking over to the library and trying the door. But from a philosophical point of view, what we call the 'facts' in such cases are really nothing more than those beliefs that are not in dispute. We can never really compare our beliefs to the facts as they are, independent of our sense-perceptions, our assumptions, our theories and all our other beliefs. For this reason, say realism's critics, the realist conception of knowledge is vacuous. If we accept it, we may be forced to conclude that it is impossible to say whether or not any of our beliefs constitute knowledge.

The alternative view, which insists that any reality we seek to know must ultimately be reality as experienced, interpreted and shaped by us, is nowadays usually called **non-realism** (or occasionally anti-realism). The debate between realists and non-realists arises where several branches of philosophy intersect – notably epistemology, metaphysics and philosophy of science. Since we will discuss it further in the chapter on Philosophy of science, we will not pursue it in detail here. Instead, we will turn our attention to an even more radical and controversial view of knowledge and truth that many think is entailed by non-realism – namely, relativism.

Relativism

Let us take stock once again. Scepticism challenges us to justify our claim to have empirical knowledge of anything beyond our own subjective experiences. The natural response is to argue that our sense-perceptions indicate that a material world exists and also that they reveal at least something about its nature. We saw that there are a surprising number of difficulties that can be raised regarding this view, but that overall it seems to be a more reasonable view than the phenomenalist alternative. However, the phenomenalist critique of realism indicates the problematic nature of the realist concept of an independently existing reality and, with it, the realist conception of knowledge and truth. For this reason, some philosophers have been led to reconstruct these concepts in surprising ways. To see how and why this is so, let us first clarify the conventional understanding of these notions.

'What is truth?', as Pontius Pilate is supposed to have asked. Probably most people would say something along these lines:

> *A statement is true if it corresponds to the facts.*

This is the natural, commonsensical way we all think of truth most of the time. A statement like 'Napoleon spoke French' is true simply because Napoleon did, as a matter of fact, speak French. And if he had not, the statement would be false. This conception of truth is known, for obvious reasons, as the **correspondence theory of truth**. It tends to be favoured by realists, since they believe in the possibility of a correspondence between our descriptions of reality and reality as it is in itself. But because non-realists deny the legitimacy of this realist notion of reality, they are also inclined to reject the correspondence theory of truth. To be sure, they say, in ordinary speech when we say a statement is true we mean that it corresponds to the facts. But that only tells us about the everyday meaning of the term 'truth'; it does not provide an adequate philosophical analysis of the concept.

The interesting question, say non-realists, is not 'What do we mean when we use the word "true"?' but 'How do we decide whether or not a statement is true?' Since, according to the non-realist's argument, we cannot directly compare our beliefs or statements with an independent reality, correspondence to reality cannot, ultimately, be our criterion for deciding which statements are true. We must therefore use some other criterion, and the most widely touted alternative to correspondence is *coherence.* On this view, we decide whether a belief is true by seeing how well it coheres with our other beliefs. These other beliefs include, for example, beliefs about what we are perceiving right now, general assumptions about the reliability of sense-perception, memories, items of general knowledge, scientific laws and basic principles of reasoning. Thus, I believe that Napoleon spoke French because this fits in with countless other beliefs I hold about France, about the veracity of the reports given by people who knew him, about the reliability of historians and so on.

Now, it is possible to hold that the *meaning* of truth is correspondence to reality while the *criterion* of truth is coherence with one's other beliefs. And perhaps this does describe how things are in everyday life. But the **coherence theory of truth** does not just say that coherence is how we test for truth; it maintains that the truth of a statement *consists in* its coherence with other statements. To realists this makes no sense; they view truth as a relation between a statement and a non-linguistic state of affairs we call a fact. But to the coherentists, what we call facts are really nothing more than beliefs about which there is virtual unanimity. From this perspective, comparing a belief to 'the facts' is, at bottom, a matter of seeing how a somewhat doubtful belief coheres with beliefs that are utterly uncontroversial.

> *If truth is a matter of coherence, doesn't this imply that the same statement can be both true and false? It could cohere with one system of beliefs while being inconsistent with another system of beliefs.*

This seems to be correct. Another way of putting the point would be to say that truth is *relative to* a system of beliefs (sometimes referred to as a conceptual scheme or theoretical framework) – a view called **cognitive relativism.** Cognitive relativists see themselves as merely working out the implications of non-realism. Realists, on the other hand, usually view this kind of relativism as a *reductio ad absurdum* of non-realism – that is, they argue that since it is obviously false, any view that entails it must also be false. Before seeing why the realists think the relativists are so misguided, let us get a clearer idea what the relativists are saying.

Relativism is a view that is more commonly held about moral values than about truth. According to moral relativism, right and wrong can only be defined relative to some particular culture; there is no objective, universally valid moral code; nor are there any neutral, transcultural criteria by which we can rank different moral codes. This view of morality has become increasingly popular over the past hundred years or so, primarily because of the difficulty of proving that one moral code is superior to another. (For a discussion of moral relativism, see the chapter on Ethics.) Relativism regarding truth is less common because we tend to think that questions of fact can be settled once and for all in a way that questions of value cannot. However, in recent times an increasing number of philosophers have found themselves drawn towards some form of cognitive relativism.

Cognitive relativists make two claims:

- The truth or falsity of any statement is relative to some particular standpoint (often called a conceptual scheme, or a theoretical framework).
- No standpoint can be proved to be superior to all others.

Let us see what this means in the case of a simple example. Take the statement 'The earth orbits the sun.' If any of our beliefs are objectively true, surely this one is. But according to the relativist, it is only true relative to a particular theoretical framework – that is, a certain set of assumptions, beliefs, accepted theories and methodological principles, such as the set that is characteristic of post-Copernican astronomy. Relative to the Ptolemaic conceptual scheme the statement is false.

One difficulty for this view has already been voiced: it seems to imply that the same statement can be both true and false, which on the face of it is absurd. But relativists believe they can meet this objection by arguing that the expression 'relative to' introduces a qualification that gets them off the hook. We are all familiar with the way hidden qualifications can affect the truth value of a statement. 'I am French' is true when some people say it and false when other people say it: the speaker here constitutes the 'standpoint' relative to which the statement is either true or false. In a somewhat analogous way, claim the relativists, the truth value of any statement must always be relative to a standpoint because it can only be assessed in relation to some standpoint. If we accept the coherence theory of truth, we decide whether or not a statement is true by seeing how it coheres with other statements that constitute our theoretical framework. Thus if we are pre-Copernican astronomers, 'The earth orbits the sun' will seem false; if we are Copernicans it will appear true.

> There is a difference between a statement appearing to be true and its being true. 'The sun orbits the earth' may have appeared true to Ptolemaic astronomers, but we now know that they were wrong. This statement is false. 'The earth orbits the sun' is true, and relativists, like the rest of us, believe this to be the case. So how can they seriously say that in some sense the Ptolemaic view is also true?

This objection makes an important point. Clearly, contemporary relativists, if they wish to be taken seriously, have to admit that they regard the Copernican view as true and the Ptolemaic view as false. The question is whether, as relativists, they can consistently take sides in this way. Obviously, they think they can. 'The earth orbits the sun', they will argue, is true; but like all other truths, its truth is relative to a standpoint – in this case that of Copernican astronomy. Since contemporary relativists share this standpoint with the rest of us, they naturally affirm the truth of the statement. But they also deny that the superiority of this standpoint over alternative standpoints can be conclusively demonstrated (the second of the two claims we identified above as constituting relativism). Any attempt to demonstrate its superiority will have to make use of certain premises. Those who accept these premises already share the standpoint; and if there are some who do not accept these premises, they obviously will not be convinced by an argument that rests on these premises.

Critics of relativism will still insist, however, that the relativists are trying to have their cake and eat it too. On the one hand, relativists seem to be saying that all standpoints, all conceptual schemes or theoretical frameworks, are on the same level since none can be proved better than all the rest. But, on the other hand, they choose to adopt one standpoint rather than another. Indeed, they cannot avoid doing so. First of all, life itself requires that we view the world from a particular perspective; no one can really remain neutral between all possible belief systems. Second, when they defend relativism against its critics they are asserting a preference for one point of view over others. But how can they justify doing this? How can they deny that any standpoint is privileged and yet, by adopting one rather than another, implicitly affirm its superiority? This is one of the most common objections to relativism. In essence, the criticism is that relativists necessarily fall into a 'performative contradiction' – a situation where one's actions imply that one holds a belief that contradicts one's stated views.

Many see this as a devastating objection to relativism. However, relativists believe they can deal with it. Everyone agrees that according to relativism no standpoint is privileged over all others in the sense of being demonstrably superior. But relativists insist that this does not mean that there are no reasons for ever preferring one standpoint to another. There are. But these reasons cannot be advanced from a neutral vantage point. They themselves constitute a standpoint. Thus, relativists judge the Copernican conceptual scheme to be better than that of Ptolemy. They do so because they accept criteria for evaluating theories that have become generally accepted, especially in modern science: criteria such as coherence with other beliefs, predictive power, simplicity and so on. They believe that according to these criteria the Copernican theory is superior. They also hold that these criteria are themselves superior to other possible criteria (such as conformity to scripture, for example). But they do not see how it is possible to justify this last belief from a neutral standpoint. At some point, the justification of one's standpoint will become circular. What do we say to someone who insists that Ptolemy's system is better than Copernicus's because it accords better with a literal interpretation of the Bible? It would obviously be misguided to argue about what the Bible really says or how it should be understood. After all, it is entirely possible that our opponent is right on that score. No, the only sensible approach would be to argue that conformity to scripture is not the best criterion for assessing the truth of a scientific theory. But how do we set about constructing an argument to support this conclusion? The argument will need premises, and it is quite likely that these will be unacceptable to the person we are trying to persuade who, after all, takes it as a given that the Bible is infallible.

Aren't relativists being inconsistent when they affirm the truth of relativism? After all, if all truth is relative, then the truth of relativism must also be relative. But how can they accept this limitation on their theory?

Confronted with this argument, relativists have two choices. One option is to say that all truth is relative, except for the truth that all truth is relative. This position is not self-contradictory; but it is unappealing, since the question arises as to why this one statement is an exception to the general rule. The second, and better, option is to accept that relativism is in the same boat as all other theories. It is not true in some special, absolute sense; rather, it is true relative to a particular standpoint. But this standpoint is one that is shared by an increasing number of contemporary theorists. It includes – or, more accurately, is largely constituted by – a non-realist view of the relation between mind and reality, a coherence view of truth, and a recognition of the interpenetration of empirical data and theoretical principles. Given philosophical assumptions of this sort, the argument goes, a relativistic view of truth and knowledge is the most coherent position available. Moreover, it may carry certain practical advantages, such as fostering open-mindedness and tolerance: if we recognize the relativity of truth and the impossibility of proving that our perspective is superior to all others, we will be less inclined to assert opinions dogmatically. Thus, one can believe there are good reasons for being a relativist without holding that relativism is true in some special sense that is denied to all other theories.

Normative and naturalized epistemology

Isn't relativism really another form of scepticism? Scepticism denies all or most of our claims to knowledge. Relativism seems to say that any belief can, in some sense, be true and believed for good reasons. But that implies that more or less any belief can count as knowledge – which surely undermines the whole distinction between knowledge and error, and utterly devalues the concept of knowledge.

Certainly, this is the conclusion that critics of relativism often draw. But relativists see the implications of their position in a different light. Traditionally, the response to scepticism has been to try to justify our claims to knowledge. A fundamental question underlying this kind of epistemology is: Do those beliefs of ours that we think constitute knowledge *really* constitute knowledge? The attempt to show that they do is a *justificatory* project; it is sometimes called **normative epistemology**. (The term 'normative' indicates that it is concerned with an 'ought' question, a question of what it would be right to do. In this case, the key questions are: Ought we to call some of our beliefs 'knowledge'? If so, which ones?)

Descartes's project of trying to provide a platform of certainty upon which to base the rest of scientific knowledge is a paradigmatic example of normative epistemology. His goal is to justify calling a particular set of beliefs knowledge. His method of going about this is an example of what is called **foundationalism**. As the name implies, this approach involves establishing a secure foundation by showing how a particular set of beliefs can withstand sceptical doubts, and then justifying further beliefs by relating them to these foundational beliefs. Most foundationalists follow Descartes in taking beliefs about our subjective states to offer the kind of immunity from doubt that they seek. As we saw, though, there are very difficult problems associated with moving from the subjective to the objective, with trying to provide a sound rational justification for thinking that our subjective states yield information about the existence and nature of the external world.

To many, these problems have seemed insuperable. One response to this among some epistemologists has been to develop alternative normative epistemologies, that is, to try to justify our claims to knowledge along other lines. For example, **coherentism**, building on the coherence theory of truth, holds that a belief constitutes knowledge when it coheres satisfactorily with the rest of one's beliefs. A more recently developed theory, **reliabilism**, holds that a belief constitutes knowledge when we have arrived at it through a process that we have good reason to regard as a reliable method for acquiring true beliefs.

All theses theories – foundationalism, coherentism and reliabilism – take seriously the normative question: What entitles us to say that a given belief is an item of knowledge? But a more radical response to the difficulties encountered by the traditional efforts to rebut scepticism is to abandon normative epistemology entirely: to give up trying to *justify* our claims to knowledge altogether. This is the approach that relativists tend to favour. Let us see why.

Normative epistemology tries to lay down norms or criteria that, if met, supposedly justify our calling a belief knowledge. But whichever norms we prefer, we still have to ask about their status? What guarantees their validity? What justifies us in appealing to one set of norms rather than another? These are the questions that relativists are inclined to ask. Traditional normative epistemology has to be able to support its claim that certain norms are the 'right' ones, the ones that deserve to be given a privileged status. But how can this kind of claim be justified? For example, consider the following normative principles:

- A belief counts as knowledge if it coheres with our existing network of beliefs.
- A belief counts as knowledge if it can be deduced from premises that the majority of people would accept as obviously true.
- A belief counts as knowledge if it entails statements that be confirmed experimentally.

How is one to set about justifying these claims? How can one justify the claim that coherence with an existing network of beliefs gives us more right to classify a belief as knowledge than our deducing it from premises that the majority of people would accept as obviously true?

Relativists avoid these difficulties by refusing to grant any set of epistemic norms a special, privileged status. They give up trying to decide which epistemic norms are the 'right' ones, and engage in a different kind of project altogether. This alternative project is viewed as primarily – or even wholly – descriptive. The main task is to identify and describe the epistemic norms that different communities, including our own, actually use. Because it eschews the attempt to justify knowledge claims or to evaluate epistemic norms, this approach to the theory of knowledge is sometimes called **naturalized epistemology**. The term 'naturalized' here refers to the way in which the theory is intended to be nothing more than a description of the way people behave, without any normative intention or force.

The naturalization of epistemology carries with it the naturalization (and the relativization) of all our central epistemic concepts. Knowledge is understood as whatever a particular community considers to be knowledge. Beliefs are true when their truth is entailed by the other beliefs and the justificatory procedures that constitute the theoretical framework of the community. Rationality is identified with whatever epistemic norms and justificatory procedures happen to be accepted within the community. This approach will appeal to anyone who thinks that the traditional epistemological quest – the quest for universally valid principles that can tell us what knowledge 'really' is while simultaneously providing the means to refute scepticism – is a futile enterprise.

Needless to say, there are still plenty of epistemologists who do not think this traditional project is futile. From their point of view, relativistic and naturalistic epistemology simply concedes the field to the sceptic. They argue that relativists are effectively saying: 'We cannot answer the sceptical challenge to show that our beliefs about the world constitute knowledge, so we should stop trying. Instead, we should think of the word "knowledge" as just a label for those beliefs that satisfy the prevailing epistemic norms within a society.' But this position undermines the distinction between what we *do* believe and what we *should* believe. It also seems to allow what we think of as errors to count as knowledge – relative to some other theoretical framework – which undermines the whole distinction between knowledge and error. Surely, this outlook is to be viewed as just another form of scepticism?

The attempt to naturalize epistemology is also open to a further, serious objection. In identifying knowledge with whatever our currently prevailing epistemic norms say should count as knowledge, it seems to undermine any motive for taking a critical attitude towards these epistemic norms. A critical attitude involves asking questions like:

- Are the norms we currently employ the best available?
- Could they be improved in any way?
- Would other norms, or a modification of these norms, direct us more reliably towards truth?

These are admittedly abstract questions. But some of the most important advances in human knowledge have come from asking questions of just this sort. For example, the intellectual pioneers of the scientific revolution – thinkers like Bacon, Galileo and Descartes – made that revolution possible by challenging the epistemic norms that had prevailed throughout the middle ages, arguing that reason, experiment and observation should take the place of scripture and other textual authorities. But if relativism is correct, in what sense can the scientific revolution be seen as an *advance* in human knowledge? The medievals had their beliefs, and relative to their conceptual scheme (which included certain epistemic norms) these beliefs were largely true. So what would be the point in criticizing them? Why try to develop new ways of thinking or introduce new epistemic norms? The only conceivable motive would be the thought that the new ways of thinking were somehow better than the old. But in what sense, and by what criteria, could they be deemed 'better'?

For many, this is a decisive objection to epistemological relativism. In the words of the American philosopher Hilary Putnam, trying to eliminate the normative dimension of philosophy is 'attempted mental suicide', since it means giving up the attempt to improve our thinking. However, relativists do have ways of responding to this charge. For instance, they could accept the value of criticizing existing norms but point out that all such criticism must invoke other norms and values. Some of these may be part of our current way of thinking – perhaps a part we are not living up to. Others may be introduced from outside. But in every case, the norms and values in question cannot be proved to have some special superior or privileged status. Of course we view the scientific revolution as representing progress. But we base this judgement on criteria that we employ because we are the heirs of this revolution: for example, we value theories with great predictive power and technological potential. From the standpoint of certain medieval theologians who might place a much higher value on conformity with tradition, reverence for scripture, social stability and the fostering of an otherworldly attitude, the scientific revolution was a disaster.

Relativism does not say we cannot take sides here; it only insists that we be fully aware of what we are doing when we do take sides. We are not aligning ourselves with epistemic norms and values that are demonstrably superior. Rather, we are passing judgements according to the norms that we currently think are best; and the judgement that these norms are best can also only be justified in the same way. Thus, the scientific revolution certainly looks like epistemic progress from the standpoint that it helped to construct. But to justify the claim that it represents progress in a more objective sense we would have to be able to compare different belief systems and different sets of epistemic norms by reference to neutral criteria that are transculturally valid. It is *this* idea about which relativists are sceptical.

It may be helpful to conclude by casting a backward glance over the philosophical path we have followed in the course of this chapter. We began with the challenge of scepticism. We argued that we can be certain about at least some of our subjective states, which refutes the sceptic who denies we have any knowledge at all. We examined in some depth the problem of trying to justify using our sense-impressions as the basis for knowledge claims about a reality existing outside the mind. Berkeleian idealism and phenomenalism try to avoid making the leap beyond what we immediately perceive; but the price they pay for this is too high. Ultimately, it is hard to see how they can avoid solipsism. Nevertheless, their objections to the more orthodox representative realism contain some insights that make a non-realist account of truth and knowledge attractive.

Non-realism leads us away from the idea that knowledge consists of beliefs that correspond to an independently existing reality. This line of thinking, pursued further, leads to relativism, which holds truth and knowledge to be always relative to some theoretical standpoint. Although relativists can consistently affirm their commitment to a particular standpoint, they do not think it possible conclusively to prove that any standpoint is superior to all others. Relativism typically abandons the traditional epistemological search for norms that tell us when a belief 'really' constitutes knowledge. Instead, it is inclined to concentrate on describing the epistemic norms used by particular communities. Whether this is an intellectually coherent or desirable approach to epistemology remains a hotly debated issue in contemporary philosophy.

3 Philosophy of mind

The mysteriousness of consciousness

Think about what happens when someone looks at a bright light. The light entering the eye causes a chemical reaction in the cells of the retina on which it falls; the chemical reaction causes an electrical current in neighbouring nerve cells; this current stimulates a succession of nerve cells in the brain and elsewhere in the nervous system. Some of the nerve cells stimulated may be connected to muscles, for instance the muscles of the iris, and the current in them may cause these muscles to contract. And so it goes on, a chain of cause and effect, with each event being the cause of further events. The cells of the retina, nervous system, muscles and so forth are like components in a very complex machine. They enable that machine – the human body – to respond in more or less sophisticated ways to stimuli. In fact, machines can be built that mimic some of the things the human body does: some cameras, for instance, can automatically match the size of their aperture to the intensity of the surrounding light.

But something else happens when a person looks at a bright light, something that we have not mentioned yet. Provided their sight is not impaired in some way, the person *sees* the light. They have something we might call a visual experience. We all know what such experiences are like, just as we know what it is like to hear, smell, taste, touch and 'feel' (as in 'I feel angry'); we have such experiences all the time. We are all *conscious* of our surroundings.

Now, machines and computers can already mimic some of the workings of the human body. We have just considered a simple example – a camera that matches the size of its aperture to the intensity of light in the surroundings. As technology advances, we may expect further achievements on this front. After all, the human body is itself a very complicated biological machine whose workings we now understand better than ever before, thanks to the labours of anatomists, biochemists and neurologists. The heart, for instance, is a sort of pump; the kidneys very sophisticated filters; the brain not unlike a super-computer. Suppose, then, that a highly sophisticated machine were developed which mimicked a human body so well that we could not actually tell from the way it behaved and interacted with us whether it was a human being or not – an idea explored in numerous science fiction stories about androids. Would such a machine have conscious experiences? If it fell over and damaged itself, would you believe it actually *felt* pain as you or I do? Suppose it had been cleverly wired up to produce small drops of water from the corners of its 'eyes' at such a time: would this convince you?

What, if anything, would convince you?

There is in principle no limit to the degree of accuracy with which such a machine might mimic human beings. But many people would still deny that the machine had any conscious experiences. Their view would be something like this:

> *However sophisticated, a machine is still just a machine, and a mere machine cannot see, or taste, or feel pain or anger, or fall in love. It may perform all sorts of actions, but there is nothing going on 'inside'.*

But if we agree with this, we have a problem. For we said just a moment ago that the human body was a very complicated biological machine. How is it that *this* machine can see, hear, taste and so forth while other machines cannot? Here is one possible answer:

> *A human being isn't just a body. A human being also has a mind. And it is the mind that has conscious experiences – sees lights, feels pain etc.*

This is a very natural response, but does it really explain anything? After all, why can we not build a machine that also has a mind? Once we have a machine that mimics the workings of the human body, why can't we construct an additional bit that mimics the human mind, stick it onto our machine and, hey presto, produce a machine that has conscious experiences?

Mind–body dualism

Someone who insists that machines have no subjective experiences (no 'inscape', to borrow a term from the poet Gerald Manley Hopkins), will quite possibly justify this claim by arguing that a machine, whether it is a camera, an android or a human body, is a purely *physical* system. It is as a physical system that the human body is studied by science. But conscious experiences are not like neural discharges and muscular contractions: they are not physical events. And the mind is not a physical thing. That is why a machine, which is a purely physical thing, cannot have conscious experiences; and it also why we cannot simply build a mind and add it on to a machine.

On this view, then, a human being has both a physical body and a non-physical mind. The mind certainly appears to interact with the body: the stimulation of nerve cells by a bright light results in a conscious experience in the non-physical mind; the thought of looking over a cliff can make the ends of my fingers tingle. But the two things, mind and body, are nevertheless distinct entities.

This view of a human being as consisting of two separate things, a physical body and a non-physical mind, is known as **dualism** (or, more specifically, mind–body dualism). It is a popular view. Many people have a natural sympathy for dualism, though sometimes for reasons other than those just mentioned. But popularity does not prove that a theory is right, and we need to take a closer look to see whether or not dualism is a good way of thinking about the mind.

Dualists are going to have to answer some pretty awkward questions in order to make their theory work. When in the development of a human embryo does a mind become attached to the body? How does this happen? Where does the mind come from? Does it ever happen that the mind fails to attach itself? At what point in evolution did minds first appear? How, and why, did this come about? Obviously, the list of difficult questions could be extended. But these questions seem easy when compared to the main problem faced by the dualist: How can we square the supposed interaction of mind and body with the general outlook of the physical sciences?

Suppose the dualist says, as we might expect them to, that non-physical mental events have some sort of influence on what takes place in the body. I do not just see a cream bun: I see it, decide I want to eat it, wrestle briefly with my conscience, then reach out for the bun. The last of these events is clearly a physical one. The problem is that this goes against a basic assumption of the physical sciences: that physical events only have physical causes, and physical causes only have physical effects.

When scientists set out to understand and explain some phenomenon, they all work on the assumption that it will be possible to do this in purely physical terms. So if we were to accept that some physical events have non-physical causes, as the dualist wants us to do, we might also have to accept that it is impossible to provide a purely physical explanation of many phenomena. The physical sciences would offer, at best, a very partial picture of the world, and science's confidence that everything happens in accordance with physical laws would be shattered. No predictions could be made with any confidence any more, nor could any machines be built and guaranteed to work. Who would know whether the influence of a non-physical event, to which the physical sciences must by definition be blind, could throw a proverbial spanner in the works? From a scientific point of view, a world in which non-physical events influenced the physical world would be strange and full of surprises, and not at all like our world.

Note, however, that the main problem here arises from the supposed influence of the non-physical upon physical events. If we were to deny that there was any causal influence in this direction and admit influences in the opposite direction only – physical causes having non-physical effects, but not vice-versa – the consequences for the physical sciences would be much less disruptive. The subject matter of the physical sciences, the physical world, would be totally unaffected by non-physical events, and could thus be completely understood without reference to anything non-physical (which is what present day physical sciences assume). We might therefore try to get round the problem of squaring the dualist account of mind–body interaction with the physical sciences by limiting mind–body interaction to causal influence in one direction – body to mind. This yields the following position:

Conscious experiences are non-physical events, which are caused by physical events (light hitting retinal cells, nerve cell discharge etc.) but which themselves have no consequences for the physical world.

This variation of dualism is called **epiphenomenalism** because it sees consciousness as an 'epiphenomenon', something that is caused but itself causes nothing, like a cog in a machine that is turned but that does not itself turn any other cogs. Epiphenomenalism helps us to avoid the worst of the problems faced by the original version of dualism. But the picture that emerges is decidedly odd. According to epiphenomenalism, we are conscious of the things going on around us and in our bodies but unable to consciously influence them. More worrying still, if consciousness makes no difference to the workings of the physical world, how are we to tell whether any particular bit of the physical world actually has it? Take a look at the person nearest to you. How do you know that they are not just a sophisticated automaton, a fully functioning human body-machine, but without any conscious experiences? For that matter, how do you know that a desktop computer is not equipped with a rich and varied conscious life? If the epiphenomenalist is right, consciousness makes no difference to what actually happens: so how do we know whether it is there or not?

The problem of other minds

This problem just raised is commonly known as the problem of other minds. It has long been a central problem in the philosophy of mind. (We already encountered it in our discussion of phenomenalism in the Theory of knowledge chapter). The two key questions here are:

- What things other than myself have conscious experiences?
- How do I know that they do?

These are questions that we need to ask in connection with each of the theories of mind we shall be considering in this chapter. For the epiphenomenalist (some would say for any kind of dualist), the problem of other minds represents a serious difficulty – which is somewhat ironic, since one of the reasons we were first inclined to dualism was that it accorded with our 'natural' belief that a machine could not be conscious but that a person could be. Far from supporting that belief, epiphenomenalism seems to imply that we have no way of knowing whether it is right.

Why can't the epiphenomenalist say this: I know that other people feel things much as I do because they are so similar to me in so many other respects. If I pinch somebody else, they behave in similar ways to the ways in which I behave when somebody pinches me. Presumably, then, they also feel pain in a similar way to me.

This sort of argument is called an **argument from analogy**. We make use of analogies in our arguments all the time, and arguments from analogy are to be found elsewhere in philosophy. (See the Philosophy of religion chapter, for instance, for an argument from analogy aimed at proving the existence of God). But philosophers tend to be rather cautious about arguments from analogy, which often turn out to be a bit slippery when closely examined.

think critically!   Arguments from analogy

An *analogy* is a similarity between two things or situations: for instance, a teenager going away to college is analogous to a young bird being pushed out of the nest. In an argument from analogy, the fact that two things are similar in one respect is taken to support the conclusion that they are similar in some other respect. Here is an example:

> Digital computers and human beings are both physically complex systems that can process information.
> Digital computers do not have non-physical minds.
> Therefore, human beings do not have non-physical minds.

The form of the argument is:

> A and B are similar in respect R.
> A also has feature F.
> Therefore, B has feature F.

In general, the stronger the similarity between A and B, the more plausible the argument will appear. But even the strongest analogy cannot prove the conclusion being drawn from it. The reason is fairly obvious. Just because two things are alike in one respect does not mean they are necessarily alike in some other respect. Consider this argument, for instance:

> Digital computers and human beings are both physically complex systems that can process information.
> Digital computers never fall in love.
> Therefore, human beings never fall in love.

The conclusion is obviously false, which indicates that the argument is formally *invalid* (that is, it is possible for the premises to be true and the conclusion false). Nevertheless, arguments from analogy can be very persuasive; they force those who do not accept the conclusion to explain exactly where the analogy breaks down, and that can be hard to do.

How does this analogy between myself and other people fare? First, we need to be clear that an analogy can only ever make a conclusion *probable*, never certain (see the box). The fact that two things share one property does not prove that they share a second property, unless it can be shown that anything with the first property *must* have the second (in which case, we are no longer looking at an argument from analogy). Eggs all have a similar shape and external appearance, on the basis of which we might argue, by analogy, that the egg before us will also taste like all the other eggs we have eaten. Analogies notwithstanding, however, the egg may still turn out to be bad. In the case where I argue that other people are conscious like me because they look and act more or less as I do, the argument seems to be weaker still; I only have one case (myself) with which to make comparisons.

Furthermore, the similarity between myself and others is not always that marked. If I compare myself to a six week old baby, for instance, it is at least as easy to think of differences between our appearance and behaviour as to observe similarities. All the same, if the baby pinches its finger and screams, I do not seriously doubt that it also feels pain. This brings us to a third point. If we demand that the similarity be too great before we attribute consciousness to other beings, we risk ruling out cases such as very young babies; and this runs completely contrary to our instincts in this case. Yet if we allow that the similarity may be quite weak, we risk being trapped into admitting that all sorts of other things – for instance, sophisticated computers – also have conscious experiences. And this was precisely the conclusion we wanted to avoid at the outset; for our natural inclination is to think that however closely a digital computer might model human behaviour, and even human physiology, it would still not have consciousness.

Any analogy I draw between myself and other people, animals, machines or whatever must be based upon features about them that I can observe, such as their behaviour or anatomy. It is only on the basis of such features that I can form opinions about what conscious experiences other people (and any other things I take to be conscious) are having. The actual experiences themselves are private to the person having them. I can guess, listen, sympathise or imagine, but I cannot feel that very same feeling that you are feeling, because anything I feel is my feeling, not your feeling. When it comes to my own conscious experience, by contrast, I do not need to examine my behaviour to find out what experiences I am having: I just have the experiences. There is an asymmetry between the way I find out about other people's mental lives and the way I find out about my own. In fact, I do not 'find out' what I am experiencing: I just know. I *infer* you that you have toothache because I see you in the dentist's waiting room, ice pack clutched to jaw, grimacing in pain. But if I have a toothache I do not come to realize this through inferential reasoning: I feel the pain, and that is sufficient.

Dualism accords very well with one side of this asymmetry – my knowledge of my own mind – but in consequence faces great difficulties in explaining how I can also come to know something about the minds of others. Unfortunately, the argument from analogy is just not strong enough to fill the gap.

What does dualism explain?

That is all very well; but whatever problems dualism faces in accounting for our knowledge of other minds, or in squaring mind–body interaction with the physical sciences, it remains the only way of explaining the experience I have of what is going on in my own mind. There is no way of denying the existence of consciousness – try denying your own! And dualism is the only way of explaining the phenomena of consciousness. Like it or not, we have to be dualists.

This argument rather jumps the gun; for until we have actually looked to see whether there are any alternative explanations of consciousness, we cannot really assess the claim that dualism is the only such explanation. But we can ask whether dualism is an explanation of consciousness at all.

An *explanation* is meant to make something that was mysterious a little less so. For instance, we can explain lightning by giving a detailed account of the way that electrical charges build up in rain clouds and of the circumstances under which a discharge occurs. We can also explain lightning by telling a story about an angry God hurling thunderbolts at the earth. For various reasons, one might prefer explanations like the former to the picturesque explanations of myth and folklore. But both explanations have something in common: they explain a mysterious phenomenon (lightning) by relating it to something less mysterious (electrical discharge, anger).

Consciousness is mysterious in that it does not seem to fit into any of the physical stories we tell about what goes on in the body (such as the story about nerve cells stimulating one another). But saying that conscious experiences occur in some place or some thing called 'the mind' hardly removes the mystery. As yet, all we know about this mind is that it is non-physical, and to that extent it is as mysterious as the phenomena that it is meant to explain. We still have not said anything about what the mind *is* (as opposed to what it is not), or about how it interacts with the body. But these questions appear to raise real difficulties.

However, dualists could respond to this in the following way:

Granted, dualism does not offer a quick and complete explanation of consciousness. But it still makes it less mysterious than it must seem from a purely physicalist point of view. Moreover, consciousness is not the only phenomenon that dualism allows us to explain. It is only if the mind is separate from the body – even if in a living human being the two interact – that we can explain out-of-body experiences, reincarnation and life after death.

This is a contentious argument, to say the least. Many people would deny that reincarnation and the other phenomena mentioned actually occur. So it seems that in order to establish how strong an argument for dualism this is, we have to assess the evidence for out-of-body experiences and so forth. But we can criticize arguments in two ways. One way is to *question the truth of the premises*. In this case it means asking whether out-of-body experiences and the like actually occur. The other way is to *question the argument's logic*: Do the premises really support the conclusion? Here that means asking whether accepting the reality of out-of-body experiences requires us to also accept dualism. Is dualism the only way of explaining these phenomena? If it is not, we can reject the argument without having to wonder whether or not such phenomena occur.

Let us take out-of-body experiences first. Remember that we are not trying to establish whether people actually have such experiences, but whether, if they do, dualism is the only way of explaining that fact. All we have to do to discredit the argument is to offer some other possible explanations that do not appeal to a non-physical mind. And this is not difficult at all. An out-of-body experience is an experience of perceiving the world as if from some point outside one's body, perhaps even of seeing one's own body as if from such a point. But the words 'as if' are crucial here. Why can we not explain such experiences as a variety of hallucination? Is there any reason why such an explanation would not be adequate?

Not only do there seem to be alternative explanations to dualism, it is not even clear that dualism itself provides an explanation. How exactly does the dualist account for an out-of-body experience? Presumably, by suggesting that the mind slips out of its too, too, solid flesh and goes wandering about, taking a look from elsewhere. But, if we are going to be thorough, we ought to point out that for people to have visual experiences (other than dreams and hallucinations) they must have open and functioning eyes. Vision is wholly dependent upon the eyes, which the wandering mind appears to have left behind. So how does the mind see anything? Alternatively, if the mind can see without eyes, why can't blind people see? And why can't the mind feel without fingers? What is it about this second suggestion that makes it sound so bizarre to us?

Regarding the idea of life after death, everything depends on what one means by the words 'life after death'. If one means the survival of some non-physical component of a human, then the possibility of life after death does entail some sort of dualism. But is this the only way to think about life after death? Many medieval Christian thinkers thought of life after death as the resurrection of the body. There are plenty of amusing medieval paintings that show wild animals and birds regurgitating human limbs that they have eaten, those limbs being essential to the resurrection of the unfortunates consumed; and some people are terrified of cremation, because they believe that the destruction of their body in this way may prevent them from enjoying an afterlife. There would be no need to invoke dualism to explain this sort of life after death, were it actually to occur.

We have to be very careful that we do not prove our point by illicitly defining our terms in such a way as to make the proof cast iron, yet hollow. But the life after death argument for dualism seems to do just that. We surreptitiously took life after death to mean the survival of a non-physical element of a human being, thus making dualism a precondition of the possibility of life after death.

A similar worry arises when we turn to the question of reincarnation. If people really are able to 'remember' things that happened to them in 'previous lives', why can this not be explained in purely physical terms? We are familiar with the thought that people may have mistaken memories and remember doing things that they did not in fact do. Why should we not say that this is a case of mistaken memory too? The only obvious difference is that someone else did in fact do whatever is remembered. Are we obliged to conclude from this that that someone else and the person remembering are in fact one person? It is only if we define reincarnation as the transmission from one body to another of some peculiar non-physical thing, a soul, that we are going to commit ourselves to dualism. If, instead, we think of reincarnation as one person remembering doing what someone else in fact did, then, while we may have trouble explaining the phenomenon, we are not obliged to be dualists in order to do so.

Living without a body

> But this all misses the point. What is important is not whether such things as reincarnation do in fact happen, but that they are conceptually possible. I can imagine, say, waking up in someone else's body, or surviving the destruction of my body. If I were just my body and nothing more, then such things would be inconceivable.

This is a different sort of argument from the one we have been looking at. It relies on the notion of *conceptual possibility*. Something is conceptually possible if we can conceive of its happening, whether or not it actually can happen in the real world. For instance, it is conceptually possible, even though it is not physically possible, that a human being should run the 100 metres in 1 second; we can imagine this event occurring. By contrast, it is conceptually impossible that a square should also be a triangle. We cannot even imagine what this might mean.

This may seem like a fairly simple distinction, but in recent decades philosophers have become more and more suspicious of the idea of conceptual possibility and of the claim that one can neatly divide the conceptually possible from the conceptually impossible. Can you really conceive of a person surviving the destruction of her or his body? We know that people can survive the absence or loss of quite large pieces of their bodies. But can you conceive of losing your whole body? Imagine you have lost everything except your head, which is kept alive on a life support machine. That is perhaps conceivable. Now imagine some malicious surgeons decide to take your brain out and keep it in a tub of nutrient fluid, wired up to a powerful computer to keep it alive. Well, you might survive even that in some form. But if the surgeons now throw the brain away . . .? Can you really imagine surviving that? Sometimes it is not at all clear whether something is conceptually possible or not.

A much better argument for the conceptual possibility of my existing without my body is to be found in Descartes's *Meditations*. As we saw in the Theory of

René Descartes (1596–1650)

René Descartes is frequently referred to as the 'father of modern philosophy'. He achieved fame in his day as a mathematician (he invented analytic geometry), as a scientist (he contributed to various fields including physics, optics and meteorology), and as a philosopher. In his *Discourse on Method* and *Meditations on First Philosophy*, he proposed and defended a new approach to science and philosophy. He emphasized the analysis of complex problems into simple tasks, and the importance of guaranteeing the truth of one's solutions by relying only on reason and firm evidence (instead of scripture, tradition, authority figures, received opinion, previous beliefs and so on).

In the *Meditations*, Descartes's goal is to provide human knowledge with a secure foundation. To this end, he tries to doubt all his beliefs by imagining that an evil demon is deceiving him about everything at every moment. He concludes, however, that even if this were true he, Descartes, still cannot doubt that he is thinking and that he exists. Working from this platform of indubitable certainty, he then tries to construct a system that can serve as a foundation for the rest of human knowledge, particularly the natural sciences.

A key feature of this system is its dualistic character. Descartes makes a very sharp distinction between the mind and the body. His basic argument for doing so is that the two concepts are so completely different. Bodies are physical objects, and like all other physical objects they exist in space, are extended and can be divided into parts. The mind, by contrast, is unextended, has no location in space and is indivisible. Body and mind thus have different essential, defining properties: bodies are extended but do not think; minds think but are not extended. He then appeals to God's veracity (which he establishes elsewhere in the *Meditations*) to justify his right to infer from this sharp conceptual distinction an equally sharp distinction in reality.

Knowledge chapter, Descartes here conducts the thought experiment of imagining that a malicious demon is deceiving him about everything it is possible to be deceived about to see if there are any beliefs that are absolutely certain. In the course of his doubt, he decides that it is possible he has no body. The body could be some kind of hallucination foisted on him by the malicious demon. But Descartes argues that the same cannot be said about his very existence. For even if the demon is deceiving him, he must still exist in order to be deceived.

One reason why this argument is important is that it seems to establish clearly that my concept of myself is distinct from my concept of my body. It is fundamental to my overall view of things that I think of myself as being more than just a body. But does Descartes's argument prove that we really are more than just a body? Set out more formally, the argument looks like this:

- I can doubt the existence of my body, but I cannot doubt my own existence.
- If I were just my body and nothing more, it would be impossible to doubt the existence of one and not the other.
- Therefore, I must be more than just my body.

The problem with this argument is that it relies on a questionable assumption. (If you look back, you will see that the earlier argument based on the conceptual possibility of life after death faces the same problem.) Why does my ability or inability to doubt something reveal anything about the way things are in the world?

Descartes's argument moves from the fact that we are naturally inclined to think in a certain way to a conclusion about the relation between himself and his body (they are not identical). But this move rests on the assumption that our 'natural' ways of thinking about the world are fundamentally reliable, that they mirror the way the world really is. But why should we believe this? After all, we naturally think of space as having three dimensions, alongside which we place the fourth dimension of time. Theoretical scientists, however, have advanced very different pictures of the universe in which time is treated as much more like space than we tend to think, and in which extra dimensions of space are postulated – as many as eight in some cases – though these dimensions are 'rolled up very small', which is why we don't notice them! Our everyday ways of thinking about the universe do not seem to countenance such multidimensionality. In fact, only a tiny fraction of the world's population could possibly be said to have any idea of what people are talking about when they speak of eight dimensions. Yet most of us would probably be willing to accept in this case that our everyday way of looking at the world may be faulty. We accept, that is, that *the mere fact we cannot conceive of something does not mean that it cannot be, or that it cannot occur.* Conversely, we must also accept that the mere fact that we can conceive of something does not mean it can exist or occur. So the mere fact that we can imagine existing without our bodies does not prove that we can.

We have arrived, once again, at a very deep philosophical question, one that also arose in the Metaphysics and Theory of Knowledge chapters: How do the ways in which we think about the world – be they our everyday ways of thinking or more sophisticated scientific or philosophical ways of thinking – relate to the way that the world really is? Descartes himself seems to have recognized the need for some guarantee that our natural inclination to think of ourselves as being distinct from our body provides a reliable guide to the way things really are; he spends some time in his *Meditations* trying (and most people would say failing) to find one. Without that guarantee, however, we seem to be left only with the conclusion that we are bound to think of ourselves as more than just our bodies, without any reasons for believing we are right to think this.

Logical behaviourism (getting rid of the mind)

On closer examination, dualism is not as appealing as it first seemed. We have not found any real arguments in support of it, while against it there remains the very strong objection that interaction between a non-physical mind and a physical body runs contrary to a basic assumption of the physical sciences. And science apart, the kind of interaction being posited is extremely hard to understand or explain in theoretical terms. But if the mind is not a non-physical thing, what is it? And if sensations, thoughts, beliefs, intentions, desires and so forth are not events in or states of such a non-physical entity, what are they? We may deny that a human being is anything more than a body, but we still have to say what the mind is, and what mental phenomena are.

At least, it would seem so. But, surprising as it may seem, some philosophers have claimed that we do not have to say what minds or mental phenomena are. In fact, they argue, if we do try to say what they are, we are bound to end up talking philosophical nonsense. According to these philosophers, questions like 'What is the mind?' and 'What are sensations?' are pseudo-questions that should never have been asked in the first place. It is the question that dualists try to answer that leads to all the problems, not the particular answer they give. Let us look at the reasons behind this view.

Imagine you are talking to a friend – perhaps one whose English is not very good – about the British constitution. 'The vote was given to many British women in 1918', you observe, to which your friend responds: 'What was the vote made of? Was it made of iron? Gold? Something else?' What would you say? Certainly you cannot give an answer to your friend. Although grammatically well formed, the question simply does not make sense. It represents a complete misunderstanding of what you said. We can appreciate the exact nature of that misunderstanding a little better if we consider the superficial similarity between the sentence 'The vote was given to many British women in 1918' and the sentence 'The medal was given to the soldier in 1918'. What your friend has done is assume that the job being done by the phrase 'the vote was given' is the same as that being done by the phrase 'the medal was given' in the second? Having made this mistake, it is perfectly natural to then go on to ask the meaningless question 'What is the vote made of?'

By the middle of the twentieth century a number of philosophers, the most famous being Gilbert Ryle, were arguing that a similar state of affairs holds with respect to questions like 'What is the mind?' and 'What are sensations?' It is only because we mistake in a wholesale fashion the jobs that are being done by elements of mental language – words like 'mind', 'sensation' and so forth – that we come to pose such questions in the first place. Once we see our mistake, we will see that these are in fact meaningless pseudo-questions. The philosopher's job is not to answer these questions – no meaningful answers can be given to a meaningless question – but to show where we went wrong in the first place, and to establish what we are really saying (and doing) when we use mental language.

How might you show your misguided friend the error of their ways? One thing you could do is to explain that the expression you have used is just a manner of speaking, a short way of saying something much longer and more complicated. And you might then try to say what that longer, more complicated way of putting things is: for example, 'In 1918 the British Constitution was changed in such a way that in subsequent elections women over the age of 30 who satisfied certain criteria would be allowed to register their choice of candidate in exactly the same way as men had done in previous elections.' In the paraphrase, you may ask your friend to note, there is no mention of anything called a 'vote' being given to anyone. The misleading parallel with the presentation of a medal disappears when we look at the paraphrase.

If you were more thorough, you might do more than just give your friend an appropriate paraphrase of this particular sentence; you might also try to show them how to paraphrase any sentence in which the phrase 'the vote' occurs in a way that completely captures the meaning of the original but which makes no use of the phrase 'the vote'. In this way, you could show your friend how we could do altogether without talking of 'votes'. In philosophers' parlance, you would have given an analysis of the term 'vote'. Note that you would not have offered a dictionary definition of the term 'vote', or a synonymous phrase that may replace it – though in many other cases these might be satisfactory analyses of a word (as, for instance, 'unmarried man' is an analysis of 'bachelor'). What you have done is show him or her how to paraphrase whole sentences in which 'the vote' occurs.

Ryle and like-minded philosophers attempted to deal with mental language in an analogous fashion. They set out to analyse mental language: that is, to develop a theory that would allow one to paraphrase *any* sentence that made mention of a mind or a mental event, state or process in a way that completely captures the meaning of the original but makes no use of mental language. Such a theory would enable us to completely eliminate mental language, and with it the pseudo-questions that arise from a mistaken understanding of the function of such language.

Of course, no one actually thought we should then try to speak without using mental language. Just as talk of the vote is an economical way of expressing a point that would otherwise use up many more words, so expressions that use mental language are much shorter and more convenient than the paraphrases offered for them. In fact, as we shall see shortly, the paraphrases are probably infinite in length. The paraphrases are not offered as serious alternatives for mental language in everyday parlance but as reminders of the work that such language is really doing; this helps us to avoid asking the bogus questions we are otherwise inclined to ask.

So how did Ryle propose to analyse mental language? If such language does not really refer to minds and mental events, states and processes, what does it do? Ryle's answer is that it is in fact a way of talking about *behaviour*. For this reason, this approach to philosophy of mind is called 'behaviourism' or, more properly, **logical behaviourism** (to distinguish it from a school of thought in psychology which is also called behaviourism). According to the behaviourist (we will use the shorter term here for simplicity's sake), the real function of mental language is to provide an economical way of talking about behavioural patterns. Thus, any sentence in which a mental term occurs can be paraphrased in a way that makes no reference to the mental, but instead refers to behaviour.

The best way of seeing how the paraphrasing of talk about the mental into talk about behaviour is supposed to work is to look at a specific example. Suppose that I believe that a tiger has escaped from the local zoo. How might this belief be made manifest in my behaviour? One can think of all sorts of possible behavioural consequences: I bolt the door and barricade the windows; I ring my neighbours to warn them; I do not take the dog for a walk in the park, as I usually do at that time of day.

One objection to this analysis is that it is obviously wrong to say that the sentence 'I believe that a tiger has escaped from the zoo' can be paraphrased by a sentence that describes this behaviour. Two such sentences would be far from equivalent in meaning. Apart from anything else, different people behave in different ways in the same circumstances. Moreover, although in one set of particular circumstances I will behave in the way described, I might, with the same belief, behave very differently in different circumstances. If I did not have a phone in my house, I would be unlikely to go to a telephone box to ring my neighbours; and if I thought the tiger was already in my living room I certainly would not barricade myself in with it.

Behaviourists believe they can meet this objection in the following way. Although there is no direct equivalence between my belief and my actual behaviour – since this behaviour also depends on circumstances – we can specify the behavioural *propensities* that make up any particular belief. In other words, a statement about my belief can be paraphrased not by a statement of my *actual* behaviour, but by a statement of how I *would* behave in various different circumstances, such as those suggested above.

This is quite a tricky idea, and it is worth devoting a little more time to it. The notion of a propensity is best illustrated by another example, such as solubility. When we say that sugar is soluble, we are not saying anything about what has happened or will happen to any particular piece of sugar. A sugar lump is soluble even if it has never been near a glass of water or a cup of tea, and even if it is preserved in this undissolved state for all eternity. All we mean when we say that the sugar lump is soluble is that it will dissolve *if* it is placed in water. Solubility is a propensity to dissolve in water.

Similarly, suggest the behaviourists, to say that someone has a certain belief is just a very tidy way of saying that somebody has certain behavioural propensities – that they will behave in certain ways *if* they are in certain circumstances. We can paraphrase a sentence that attributes a belief to someone with a (much longer) sentence that simply specifies all these behavioural propensities. Take the sentence 'Petra believes that a tiger has escaped from the zoo', for instance. The kind of paraphrase we are describing might begin:

> *If there is a phone in the house, then Petra will telephone the neighbours; if the tiger is not actually in the house, then Petra will barricade herself in; if . . . (etc.)*

And so it would go on, the paraphrase being made up of conditional statements, each one specifying a situation and the way Petra would behave in that situation, and having the basic structure:

> *If it is the case that . . . then Petra will – – –*

This is a general formula that could be used to paraphrase many different statements that use mental language. All we have to do is fill in appropriate conditions where the dots are, and appropriate behaviour where the dashes are. For example, the paraphrase of 'Petra feels very hot' might begin:

> *If it is the case that* Petra is wearing a coat, *then Petra will* take it off . . .

Philosophers tend to use letters instead of dots and dashes, which some people find very intimidating. But the letters do exactly the same job as the dots and dashes. We will use the letters *A, B, C* . . . to do exactly the same job that the dots are doing above, and the letters *X, Y, Z* . . . to do the job the dashes are doing. Lastly, so that we can apply our paraphrase to anyone and not just to Petra, we will use the letter P to fill the space where the name of the person will go. In this way we can use letters to present a general formula for a behaviourist paraphrase of a statement that some person believes that such and such is the case, or wants it to be so, or is sad, or happy or whatever:

> *If it is the case that* A, *then P will* X; *if it is the case that* B, *then P will* Y; *if it is the case that* C, *then P will* Z; *if . . . etc.*

In order to get a behaviourist paraphrase of a statement using mental language that details instead the person's behavioural propensities, all we have to do is to fill in the blanks (that is, the letters): a person's name where 'P' is, appropriate conditions where *A, B, C* . . . are, and appropriate behaviour where *X, Y, Z* . . . are.

We can use the idea of a propensity or disposition (the terms are interchangeable here) to give a better statement of the behaviourist position – which is that the real function of mental language is to provide an economical way of talking about the ways in which people will behave *if* they are in certain circumstances. According to the behaviourist, any sentence in which a mental term occurs can be paraphrased in a way that makes no reference to the mental but instead refers to behavioural propensities. And the point of doing this is to help us to avoid asking spurious questions such as 'What is a mind?'

A moment's thought should make apparent just how ambitious the behaviourist programme is. What the behaviourists need to show is that, by paraphrasing talk about the mental with talk about behavioural propensities, we can completely remove mental terms from our language without any loss of expressive power. If the behaviourists are able to say without using mental terms anything we want to say using them, this will demonstrate that questions such as 'What is the mind?' are pseudo-questions. But they must be able to *completely* eliminate any need for mental terminology: if any residue of mental terms remains unparaphrased, then we are entitled to ask 'So what job are these words doing? Are they not perhaps referring to minds and to mental phenomena?' And if, by paraphrasing, some of the expressive power of mental language is lost, the behaviourists have failed to show adequately what the real job of mental language is. Perhaps what we have lost is that ability to refer to minds and mental phenomena that the behaviourist claims we do not have in the first place. But if behaviourism cannot achieve the *complete removal* of mental language *without loss of expressive power*, then behaviourism has failed.

Problems for behaviourism

The prospects for behaviourism look pretty bleak even for a specific example such as the one above, let alone the complete analysis of all mental language. For instance, it is just not true that if I believe the tiger has escaped, then I will phone my neighbours provided there is a phone in the house. There may be other complicating conditions. I won't phone them if I know they are on holiday, or having tea with me. And as soon as we start to qualify the conditions for any particular piece of behaviour in this way, we will find that they get longer, and longer and longer – perhaps infinite in length. But behaviourism, which must ensure that the paraphrase completely captures the meaning of the original, needs to list all these numerous qualifications in the paraphrases it offers. The behaviourist analysis is therefore impractical.

Let us look again at the general formula for a behaviourist paraphrase of a statement that attributes a mental state – say a belief – to some person P. According to the behaviourist, to say that P believes that such and such is the case (or wants it to be so, or is sad, etc.) is just a short way of saying that:

> *If it is the case that* A, *then P will* X; *if it is the case that* B, *then P will* Y; *if it is the case that* C, *then P will* Z; *if* . . .

The objection to behaviourism that we have just seen suggests a difficulty we face when filling in the *A, B, C* . . . part of this formula. How good an objection is this? First, we must agree that the sample paraphrase we offered fails to specify the precise conditions in which P would perform the actions mentioned. Further qualifications are needed. As we begin to consider more and more outlandish possible counter-examples (say, I will not phone my neighbours if I have a fear of making outgoing telephone calls, or am tied up in the wardrobe, or have been possessed by aliens), so we find ourselves filling in the *A, B* and *C* of the above formula with longer and longer descriptions of circumstances. Perhaps, as the objection suggests, we would even need an infinitely long description in each case, to cover an infinite number of qualifications.

We also have to think about the problems we will face specifying the various possible actions of P – filling in *X, Y, Z* . . . – in a paraphrase. It is not enough to say that Petra will telephone the neighbours; this general description covers a number of slightly different actions, and we need to specify separately the circumstances in which these different actions would be performed. For instance, if Petra is panicking, she may dial the wrong number; or she may start to dial the wrong number but notice and start again, in which case, she may notice after one digit, or after two digits, etc.; and she may or may not hesitate before redialing, or have to check the number . . . For each of these slightly different actions, we have to specify in our paraphrase the slightly different conditions. And here too the possibilities are infinite.

Observations such as these can only increase our doubts about the feasibility of the behaviourist analysis. If there really are an infinite number of actions, each of which needs to have conditions for its performance specified by a description of infinite length, then the paraphrase of a simple sentence like 'P believes that a tiger has escaped from the zoo' will be not just infinitely long, but infinitely longer than an infinitely long sentence. One begins to appreciate the economy of expression that mental language offers! More importantly, one begins to see that a behaviourist couldn't even write out the paraphrase of a single sentence, let alone analyse away mental language altogether.

Is behaviourism possible in principle?

But how much does this actually matter to the behaviourist? After all, behaviourists never suggested that we should stop using mental language; they just want to show the job that mental language is really doing, so that we can see how spurious certain questions in the philosophy of mind are. Their view is that they do not need to carry out their analysis in practice – it need not even be possible to carry it out in practice. It is enough that it be possible *in principle.*

There is obviously a close similarity between something being possible in principle and its being conceptually possible: some would even say they mean the same thing. And just as with the notion of conceptual possibility, problems arise when we actually try to say what is possible in principle. Is it possible in principle, for instance, to count to infinity? When the behaviourist analysis is defended as being possible in principle if not in practice, what this seems to mean is that, although we could never actually give a full paraphrase even for the simplest sentence, we can see what sort of thing it is that we would have to do in order to arrive at such a paraphrase. Similarly, we know what sort of thing we would have to do in order to count to infinity, even though we could never actually get there. But is this enough to prove the behaviourist's point? It is not clear.

> *Suppose we concede to the behaviourists that their paraphrases only have to be possible 'in principle'. There is another, simpler objection to what they are saying. Their behavioural analysis of mental terms may work (in principle, at least) for a mental state like belief, which has a fairly straightforward connection with behaviour. But how are they going to analyse other mental states that appear, by definition, to exclude overt behaviour – such things as doing mental arithmetic, running through a tune in your head, imagining an Alpine scene, or even dreaming?*

These certainly look like problem cases for the behaviourist theory. In his major work, *The Concept of Mind*, Ryle argues that a solution is to be found in the notion of 'refraining'. He argues, for instance, that counting to ten in your head is just a matter of *refraining* from counting to ten out loud. This may seem a rather strange idea. In its defence, though, it does seem to be true that children learn how to think themselves by first thinking aloud and then learning how to do the same thing without talking. But matters get much stranger when Ryle turns to, say, imagination, which he analyses, roughly, as refraining from pretending to see!

Of course, even if Ryle's particular analyses do not work, that does not prove that behaviourism is wrong; for it would still be possible that another, more ingenious behaviourist might come up with a better analysis. To refute behaviourism once and for all we need to refine the above objection and show that it identifies an *insurmountable* problem here, a problem that no philosopher, however ingenious, could overcome.

Imagine that someone is reciting Shakespeare silently to themselves. The behaviourist might suggest that, however silent and still the person may be, they still have a number of behavioural propensities: for instance, if you ask them what they are doing they will say 'I'm running through my lines.' With this we must agree; and remembering that the behaviourist links mental states to behavioural *propensities* rather than to actual behaviour, we may begin to think that such cases do not pose as much of a problem as we thought. Perhaps running through lines in your head is just a matter of having propensities too, and all that is needed is a sufficiently ingenious analysis.

The behaviourist view also fits in well with the fact that, as long as the person is sitting there silently we have no way of knowing what is 'going on in their head' (a very unbehaviourist phrase). Similarly, we have no idea whether a substance is soluble or not until we actually try putting some of it in water. We need to provoke behaviour to ascertain what behavioural propensities are there. But there is one person for whom this is not true – namely, the person doing the mental recitation. They know what is going on in their head without any reference to their own behaviour, because for them that mental activity that manifests itself to others only in its behavioural consequences has a *qualitative* aspect. It *feels* like something to run through Shakespeare in your head, and this is what behaviourism seems to ignore.

We return here to the asymmetry that we first encountered when discussing dualism – the asymmetry between my knowledge of my own mental states and my knowledge of the mental states of others. Where dualism faced difficulties with our knowledge of *other* minds, it is our knowledge of our *own* minds that poses a problem for behaviourism. According to the behaviourist, to say that someone is in pain is just to say how they will behave in certain circumstances; therefore, the only way to find out whether someone is in pain is to examine their behaviour. But this is not true when I am talking about myself and my own pain. When I say 'My friend is in pain', I may conceivably mean that my friend has certain behavioural dispositions. But when I say 'I am in pain', I am not talking about my behaviour, actual or dispositional. At least, I am not talking *only* about that. I am talking also about a feeling, a raw experience that only a tiny minority of all the entities in the world are capable of having. This simple fact, that pain is experienced, needs to be taken into account by any adequate philosophy of mind.

Can behaviourists explain our actions?

There is a further very serious objection to behaviourism. So far we have only considered simple sentences that attribute a mental state to some person, such as 'P believes a tiger has escaped from the zoo.' But we use mental language in many more ways than this. And one of the most important uses we make of it is in the *explanation* of behaviour: for instance, we might say 'He locked the door *because he believed that* a tiger had escaped from the zoo.' This use of mental language is one that the behaviourist analysis seems unable to capture.

To understand the force of this objection, we have to go back to the general formula that the behaviourist employs to analyse mental language. We saw that to say someone is in such and such a mental state is to say something about how they will behave if things are thus and so. To say that P believes that a tiger had escaped from the zoo is to say, among other things, that P will lock the door if certain other conditions obtain. But look what happens when we try to paraphrase an explanatory sentence: 'P locked the door because she believed a tiger had escaped from the zoo' becomes 'P locked the door because she will lock the door if certain conditions obtain.' But this can hardly stand as an explanation of P's action. It just says that P locked the door because (among other behavioural propensities) that is what she will do in certain circumstances. This is like answering the question 'Why does sugar dissolve?' by saying 'Because that is what it does when placed in water.' The point is, when we ask for an event (or an action) to be explained, we want to know not just that it always happens in certain circumstances, but *why* it happens in those circumstances.

This is a very serious problem for the behaviourist. The explanation of action is one of the most important things that we do with mental language, so behaviourism's failure to analyse it represents a signal failure to paraphrase without loss of meaning. Nor is the difficulty one that could be overcome by ingenuity. Any behaviourist analysis is going to turn good explanatory sentences of the form 'P did such and such because they were in such and such a mental state' into sentences of the form 'P did such and such because, in certain circumstances, they would do such and such.'

The difficulty arises from the behaviourist's insistence that there are no such things as mental states at all. If there are no mental states, it is not very surprising that they cannot be invoked as explanations of behaviour. We shall see later, when we consider an approach to philosophy of mind called functionalism, that by relaxing this restriction we can retain a lot of behaviourism's good points while avoiding many of the objections. The insistence that there are no mental states at all also lies behind the requirement that the behaviourist analysis remove mental language completely, and thus lies behind the last objection to behaviourism that we shall consider here.

The relationship between mental states

Behaviourism has a problem with the way mental states relate to each other. Very often, when we try to paraphrase a claim about a mental state by detailing the circumstances in which certain actions will be performed – that is, when we fill in the *A, B* and *C* of our original formula – we have to include among those circumstances the fact that the agent has certain other mental states. Consider, for instance, the claim that in certain circumstances a person who believes that a tiger has escaped from the local zoo will bolt the door. These circumstances include the person's not wanting to be eaten; for if, by some chance, the person should suffer from a peculiar desire to be eaten by a tiger, then they would not bolt the door but throw it wide open instead. The paraphrase must state, therefore, that the person will bolt the door if, amongst other things, they do not desire to be eaten. But in that case, the analysis has clearly failed to remove mental language. The term 'believe' has been eliminated; but the term 'desire' has been introduced.

One possible response to this is to accept that the paraphrase will contain references to other mental states, but to try to remove these references by further paraphrasings. In the initial paraphrase we remove the reference to the belief, but introduce references to other mental states, such as the desire not to be eaten; we then paraphrase our paraphrase in order to remove these references also, and continue paraphrasing in this way until all the mental language has disappeared.

But this process is doomed to failure. What happens when we try to paraphrase 'P desires not to be eaten'? Among the behavioural propensities that go with such a desire is the propensity to bolt doors if, amongst other things, one believes that a tiger has escaped from the local zoo. So this belief has to be mentioned in the paraphrase aimed at eliminating any talk of desire. But this is the belief we started off with! The expression 'P believes that a tiger has escaped from the local zoo' has thus reappeared in the analysis. Obviously, if we try to analyse it away again, our paraphrase will contain a reference to P's desire not to be eaten, and so *ad infinitum*. No matter how many times we paraphrase in order to get rid of mental language, we cannot even remove the reference to some mental states.

The significance of behaviourism

Given the rather strange nature of the claims made by behaviourism, and the compelling nature of some of the arguments against it, you may wonder why we have bothered to dwell upon its failure at such length. There are a number of reasons for this, not least the fact that, for all its shortcomings, behaviourism does seem to be very right in asserting a connection between mental states and behaviour.

If we start from our own conscious experience, then we are bound to treat introspection – looking into our own minds – as the primary means of gaining knowledge about mental states. If we start, instead, from the way that we encounter other people's mental lives, then we are bound to treat behaviour as our main point of access, and the claim that talk about mental states is in fact talk about behaviour begins to look quite sensible. This is the asymmetry that we noted above, and it is a problem that has dogged modern philosophy of mind. The advent of behaviourism in the early part of the twentieth century put the problem on the map by asserting the importance of the mind–behaviour relationship against the mind–introspection relationship that had dominated philosophy of mind in preceding centuries. Behaviourism thus has some historical significance.

Behaviourism also represents one of the clearest – and earliest – examples of an approach to philosophy that dominated the subject in the English-speaking world for much of the middle of the twentieth century, and whose influence is still very strong. Central to that approach is the idea that philosophical problems can be solved by *analysis* – and the sort of philosophy practised in most universities in English-speaking countries is still called 'analytic philosophy'. We have not the space here to examine exactly what analysis is, but from the example of behaviourism you may be able to see that it is essentially a matter of tidying up, or making more precise, the language that we use, and establishing exactly what sorts of jobs different bits of that language are doing. Hence the common claim that analytic philosophers have forgone the customary territory of philosophy – consideration of the deep truths of the world – to concern themselves instead with questions of language; though whether that is a matter for praise or for blame is another matter.

Unfortunately, we cannot say that behaviourism succeeded in showing, as it set out to, that questions such as 'What is the mind?' are pseudo-questions that should never have been asked. The failure of behaviourism means these questions are as significant as ever, and still require answers.

Mind–brain identity

> If the mind is (contrary to behaviourist claims) something, but is not (contrary to dualist claims) a non-physical thing, isn't the obvious solution that the mind is a physical thing? The mind must be identical to the body or, more likely, to some part of the body such as the brain and central nervous system. If so, then mental states, events and processes must be identical to physical states (such as a nerve cell being excited), events (such as a nerve cell discharging) and processes (such as the sequential excitation and discharge of a series of nerve cells).

This view is commonly called the **identity theory** of mind. Philosophers normally explain what they mean by *identity* by appealing to examples. For instance, the terms 'water' and 'H_2O' are two different names for the same stuff: water is identical to H_2O. Similarly, the identity theorist would assert, 'mind' and 'brain' are just two different names for the same (physical) thing. And what the identity theorist says about mind, she also says about various mental phenomena such as your visual experience of this page. That visual experience, says the identity theorist, is identical to electrical activity in a specific region of your visual cortex, and 'visual experience of the page' is just another name for this electrical activity.

> Spelled out in this way, the theory seems obviously false. If I say that I am having such and such a visual experience, I am not saying anything about what is going on in my brain. Unless I know a lot about neurology, I don't even know what is going in my brain. So how can the two be identical?

Exactly the same situation holds, however, regarding the identity of water and H_2O. Just because water and H_2O are in fact identical does not mean that any individual using one or the other term has to know this. I can ask for a glass of water without knowing a thing about its chemical composition; and someone might study a chemistry textbook and learn lots of things about H_2O without ever realizing that H_2O is in fact the stuff that comes out of taps. Similarly, you can talk about your visual experience of the page without having the slightest inkling that you are in fact talking about electrical activity in your brain.

It is worth distinguishing what the identity theorist is doing here from what the behaviourist is trying to do. Behaviourists want to find a way of actually replacing mental language because they hold that the things to which words like 'mind' apparently refer do not in fact exist. Identity theorists are not in the least worried about replacing mental terms because, as far as they are concerned, mental terms do refer to things, just as they appear to. All the identity theorists are concerned to do is to say what those things are. In the case of the mind, says the theory, the thing referred to is the thing that in other circumstances we call the brain. But this in no way suggests that we ever should, or ever could, replace the term 'mind' by the term 'brain'.

Identity theory allows, therefore, that we do not usually know which physical processes our conscious experiences are in fact identical to. But once we establish such an identity through empirical research we are bound to accept that, if any person is having a certain experience, then a specific kind of electrical activity must be occurring in their brain too – and vice versa (if a specific kind of electrical activity is occurring in their brain then they must be having a certain experience). This must be so, since these physical and mental descriptions are describing the same event. Similarly, once we have established the identity of H_2O and water, we must accept that if we are drinking water then we are drinking H_2O. But it is here that identity theory starts to run into problems.

Problems for the identity theory

Suppose I have established the identity of, say, the experience of pain and electrical activity in a certain region of the brain – call it the pain-region. Suppose also that I have a scanning device that tells me whether or not there is electrical activity in the pain-region of anyone's brain. Now consider the following situations:

1. Someone is sitting comfortably in an armchair, watching television and drinking a cup of tea. When I ask them if they are in pain they look surprised and tell me that of course they are not. My scanner, however, shows massive electrical activity in their pain-region.
2. Someone has been badly injured. They are groaning in agony and protesting loudly how much pain they are in. The scanner, however, shows no electrical activity in their pain-region.
3. You have been badly injured and are in agony. Someone tells you that there is no electrical activity in your pain-region.

4. We encounter a race of aliens who behave in many ways as we do. If they are injured they cry out and whimper much as we do. An anatomical investigation, however, reveals that the aliens have a completely different brain structure, which relies not on electrical discharge but on the movement of very small pieces of bone china of assorted shapes. Pain in the alien is identical with a particular pattern of bone china forming anywhere in the alien's brain. There is no pain-region.

According to the identity we have established between electrical activity in the pain-region and pain, we would have to say that the person in the first example is in pain, while the one in the second is not. In the third example, you would have to accept that you yourself, despite everything, were not in pain. And in the fourth example we would have to deny that the aliens were capable of feeling pain at all since, behaviour notwithstanding, they lack the appropriate physiology. None of these conclusions seems acceptable. In each case, the scenario is readily conceivable, but the conclusion the identity theory forces on us appears misguided.

What has gone wrong? In our enquiries so far we have identified two ways of establishing what mental state a person is in. When the person is myself, I know my mental state by introspecting; when the person is anyone else, I judge on the basis of their behaviour (including their reports of their own mental states). The tension or asymmetry between these two means of gaining knowledge is problematic, but it is a real tension that derives from the actual ways in which we make judgements of what mental states people are in. Now, however, we have set both in opposition to a new, and apparently spurious, third way of working out what mental state someone is in: the scanner. What the examples above prove is that the scanner is totally irrelevant to our determination of what mental state someone is in. In the first two instances we continue to make our judgements on the basis of behaviour, irrespective of what the scanner may say. In the fourth example, the fact that there is nothing to scan is irrelevant to the question of whether the aliens are in pain. And, in the third case, it would be patently absurd to place the scanner reading above our own assessment of our mental state.

Types and tokens

This is not the end of identity theory, however. It is only the end of a particular version of that theory. In introducing the scanner, we supposed that we had established an identity between experiences of pain *in general* and electrical activity in pain-regions *in general*. That is, we supposed an identity between a *type* of mental state and a *type* of physical state. But any type has a number of different instances or, as philosophers tend to say, *tokens*. All the knives in your cutlery drawer, for instance, are tokens of a particular type – namely 'knives' – while all the forks are tokens of a different type. Now, when we assert that there is an identity between two *types*, as we do when we claim that pain (in general) is electrical activity in pain-regions (in general), we assert that every token of the first type is also a token of the second type, and vice versa. We therefore commit ourselves to saying that we have a token of the first type every time we find a token of the second type, which is why we treat the scanner as if it were a pain-detector. It was this that got us into difficulties.

The best thing for the identity theorist to do, therefore, is to deny that there is an identity between types of mental state and types of physical state. Instead, she should make the much more general claim that all mental states (irrespective of type) are in fact brain states (irrespective of type). A pain state, for instance, being a mental state, is also a brain state; but from the fact that it is a particular type of mental state (pain), it does not follow that it is any particular type of brain state.

So long as the identity theorist does not trap herself in a rash identification of types of mental state with types of brain state, she can happily accept that one pain experience (such as my experience of pain when I stick this pin in my arm now) is identical with a brain state of one type, while another pain experience (such as my experience of pain when I stick a pin in my arm half an hour later) is identical with a brain state of another type. She can also accept that an alien pain experience may be identical with some totally different type of alien brain state. Given this modification, the scanner ceases to be a way of finding out what type of mental state someone is in, though it remains a way of finding out the state of their brain.

An identity theorist who asserts that types of mental state are identical with types of brain state is called a **type identity theorist**. One who does not make this claim is called a **token identity theorist**. Both think that, when we are talking about a mental state, we are also talking about a brain state, because they both claim that mental states are identical to brain states. But the type identity theorist, unlike the token identity theorist, also thinks that types of mental state are identical to types of brain state: for example, seeing a blue triangle is always identical to a specific kind of electrical activity. Only the type identity theorist faces the sorts of objection we introduced in the scanner scenarios.

Functionalism: using the computer model

Token identity theory may avoid the kind of objection just discussed; but it does so only by remaining silent on a very important question. If one pain experience is a brain state of one type, and another pain experience is a brain state of another type, what do they have in common? What makes them all tokens of the type 'pain'?

This raises the general question: what make any particular mental state the type of mental state it is? Perhaps we can answer this question if we look back to the principal insight of behaviourism: the link between mind and behaviour. Maybe what makes a mental state one sort of state rather than another is the way that it interacts with other states to produce certain behaviour – in other words, its *functional role*.

What exactly do we mean by the phrase 'functional role' here? An analogy may help. Computer printers can be in one of two states, called 'on line' and 'off line'. What makes a state an on line or off line state is not the type of physical state involved, but the function played by that state in the overall workings of the printer. For instance, the printer is in an on line state if it will, among other things, begin printing when it receives an instruction from the computer and go off line when the 'on line / off line' button is pressed. It is in an off line state if it will reject such instructions and go on line when the same button is pressed. The combination of specific input (command from computer and pressing of button) with the current state of the printer (either on line or off line) results in specific output (such as printing 'behaviour') and a new state of the printer (which may or may not be the same as the state it was previously in). It is the specific way that a particular state of the printer fits into this interaction of input, current state, output and new state – its functional role – that makes it an on line or an off line state.

This analogy is intended to suggest that a mental state – such as a belief that a tiger has escaped from the zoo – is the sort of mental state it is in virtue of its functional role. Thus, my mental state is of a particular type if it results from certain sorts of input (such as hearing a news flash on the radio) and interacts with other states (such as a desire not to be eaten) to bring about further states (such as fear) and various patterns of behaviour (such as door bolting behaviour).

This view, that a mental state is the type of mental state that it is in virtue of its functional role, is called **functionalism**. We can see how functionalism preserves the main insight of behaviourism – the link between mental states and behaviour – while shedding the troublesome claim that mental states do not in fact exist. As a result, the functionalist avoids some of the principal objections to behaviourism. For instance, functionalism has no problem with the explanation of actions by appeal to mental states because, unlike behaviourism, functionalism can accept that mental language is about what it appears to be about – namely, mental states.

To accept that mental states exist, however, and to provide some sort of account of what makes any particular state a token of one type rather than another, is not to say what a mental state actually is. Functional roles could be fulfilled just as well by the states of a non-physical mind of the sort that dualism suggests as by states of a brain or body. In practice, however, functionalists tend not to be dualists but **physicalists** – that is, they believe that human beings are just their physical bodies and nothing more. (For further discussion of physicalism, see the chapter on Metaphysics). But functionalists do not have to be physicalists. This is a point well worth noting; for one of the things that often confuses people in the philosophy of mind is that they fail to see that the different theories which we have considered – dualism, behaviourism, token identity theory, type identity theory and now functionalism – are not all necessarily trying to answer the same question. Dualism and token identity theory are alternative answers to the questions 'What is the mind?' and 'What are mental states?', both of which are rejected as meaningless by behaviourism. Type identity theory supplements token identity theory with an answer to a further question, 'What makes a particular mental state the type of mental state that it is?' – a question to which functionalism offers a rival answer.

The best option for the physicalist might seem to be the combination of functionalism with token identity theory. This would mean holding that a mental state is identical to a brain state – say, nerve cells firing in a particular region of the brain – but is the type of mental state that it is in virtue of the functional role played by that physical state. In this way we can avoid the objections to type identity theory. If you look back at the problematic examples which we have considered, you will see that they pose no problems for the functionalist. This is because it does not matter to the functionalist what type of physical state the mental state is identical to, as long as that physical state fulfils the right functional role – which, in each of the examples, it does.

In practice, however, there are sound reasons for combining functionalism with a rather more sophisticated view than token identity theory. The reason for this is that it may be impossible to single out a specific physical state with which any particular mental state is identical. We can see why this is so if we choose a more elaborate example than we did before and consider, not a computer printer, but the computer itself. My computer is, as I write, running a word processing package, and at any one moment we can identify numerous functional states of this program. For instance, if I press the button marked 'F4' then, provided the program is in an appropriate state when I do so, the result is an 'indent' state, in which subsequent text is indented until I press another button. If I press the buttons 'Ctrl' and 'F2' together, the program goes into a highly complex state in which pressing further buttons may initiate spell checking or word counting processes.

I have talked here of the program as the thing that is in these various functional states; but, of course, no one would be tempted to think that there is anything on my desk other than a computer – a complex arrangement of metals, semi-metals and plastic in which electrical currents and potentials are flowing and changing at very high speed. We are not tempted to be dualists when it comes to programs and computers. So, if there is nothing other than the computer, the functional states must be physical states of that computer. What then is the physical computer state to which the 'indent' state is identical? Perhaps we can pick out a particular circuit in the computer that is in a charged state whenever the program is in this 'indent' state, and in an uncharged state when it is not. The state of this circuit looks like a likely candidate for the 'indent' state.

But now suppose that I finish word-processing and start playing a computer game. The very same circuit fulfils a totally different function in the new program – perhaps it goes into a charged state whenever my spaceship's energy shields are up. Thus the 'indent' state is not identical to the charged state of the circuit, but to the charged state of the circuit *given that* the word processor package is running –

that is, given that the rest of the computer is in a certain state. This suggests that we cannot identify the 'indent' state with the charged state of a single circuit, but only with the physical state of the computer as a whole (including the charged state of that one circuit). And, similarly, it may be that we cannot identify a mental state with the state of any part of the brain but only with the state of the brain as a whole. In fact, given that the brain is only part of the body, we may have to identify each mental state with the state of the body as a whole.

But perhaps this will not do either. For suppose that, as well as being in the 'indent' state, I am also in the 'bold print' state. By the same arguments, the 'bold print' state would also be identical with the physical state of the computer as a whole. But if both functional states are identical to the same physical state, they must also be identical to one another. In fact, by this argument, all the functional states of the program at any one time would be just one state. But that is clearly absurd. The 'indent' state has a completely different functional role to the 'bold print' state, which is why we talk about there being two states here rather than one. The implication of this reasoning is that the functional states of the computer cannot be identical to the physical state of the computer as a whole either.

So what are functional states? One suggestion is that, as long as we confine ourselves to thinking about a computer as nothing more than a lump of metal and plastic in which various electrical events are taking place, it does not make sense to talk about functional states at all. Normally, however, we approach a computer with certain goals and projects of our own; we interpret its behaviour in ways that are determined by our particular interests; and we attribute functional states on the strength of our assessment of what it is that the computer is doing. Viewed with disinterest, the computer does not have functional states; but viewed in the light of our particular interests in the tasks it can help us perform, it does. Yet it is unclear whether this approach can successfully be fleshed out. And even if it could be, it is doubtful whether we could extend it to cover mental states. For while I may interpret the behaviour of others and attribute mental states to them on the basis of my interpretation, surely I arrive at my assessment of my own mental states not by such an interpretation but by direct access to those states. My being in pain does not depend upon my having a functional state of a certain sort attributed to me by someone, not even by myself. Being in pain is being in pain.

Back to the mysteriousness of consciousness

We seem to have returned to the place we started from: the everyday yet peculiar phenomenon of consciousness. It is literally an *everyday* phenomenon, since it is an inescapable part, as well as a necessary condition, of the experience of every one of us at every waking moment. In fact, we could just as well say it *is* our experience. And it is *peculiar* in that it stubbornly resists an attempt at explanation or elucidation. One branch of philosophy of mind that focuses on the nature of consciousness as human beings experience it, and that tries to describe precisely what happens when someone is conscious of something, is **phenomenology**. The phenomenological approach typically starts out by describing the way things actually appear to us, rather than discussing the role of brain processes in causing consciousness, or whether mind is identical with brain.

Although we cannot here discuss phenomenology at any length, one particularly interesting and important idea that has emerged from this approach is worth noting: the thesis that consciousness is always *intentional*. The term 'intentional' as used here does not have its familiar meaning of purposive, or deliberate. Rather, it refers to the fact that consciousness is always directed towards something. Just as we cannot be seeing without seeing something, nor hearing without hearing some sound, so we cannot be conscious without there being something we are conscious of. It may be a light, a smell, a memory, a pain, a mathematical theorem or any number of things; but consciousness must always have its object. This is the **thesis of intentionality**.

One way in which this thesis is important is in helping us to understand that consciousness is not a *thing*. It is closer to an activity or an attitude. This is why I cannot just introspect and see it there, in the mind's eye. When I make something the object of my consciousness, that thing 'fills' my consciousness, so to speak; the thing takes over my consciousness. Yet my consciousness does not *become* the thing towards which it is directed. No matter how completely my mind is focused on the scene I am viewing, the music I am hearing or the idea I am contemplating, there is an irreducible difference between *being* a thing and *being conscious of* that thing. This observation underlies a famously paradoxical description of consciousness by Jean-Paul Sartre: 'consciousness', he says, 'is what I is not, and is not what it is'.

Another way the thesis of intentionality is important is in suggesting that the best way to think about consciousness may be to concentrate our attention on the things we are conscious *of*: that page, this light, that sound. If this is correct – and it certainly seems plausible – then we must acknowledge that consciousness cannot be understood apart from its objects – the things it is directed towards. Understood as a mode of intentionality, consciousness is the way we take things to be. But just as there are many kinds of object, so there are different kinds of intending. Your awareness of the whiteness of a page, the words on that page and what they mean, the pictures on the wall, the sounds you hear, your memory of a face, all require different kinds of intentional act. Some of them are quite complex. If you have a painting of a person on your wall you are not only taking it to be a two-dimensional object with colours on one side, but also a representation of someone. You grasp it, as all these things, in a sophisticated intentional act that you perform without reflecting on just how complex it is.

The complex nature of the intentional act is further revealed if we reflect on our experience of a single object. Suppose yourself to be standing in front of a house. What do you see? The house? Well, not exactly. If you standing by the front door what you can see is the front-facing part of the house. Look up: now you see the upper floor windows, the tips of the chimney tops, and aerials or a satellite dish. The lower part of the house is now partially out of your vision. Lower your gaze and walk round the house. As you do this you see obliquely the corner, the side wall, then the back, new aspects of the building appearing as others fall away. Examining the house is a complex combination of presences and absences: you recall past perspectives and anticipate new ones as you make your circuit of the building. But the house is not just the sum of these 'appearings'. We experience the aspects as aspects of the total intentional object, the house. They only make sense *because* we intend them as aspects of the house.

When we undertake this kind of patient description of what it is like to actually have a conscious experience of something, we soon come to realize that the mind does not receive bits of pure data, raw impressions that it then has the task of combining and construing as a world. We saw in the Theory of knowledge chapter that this way of viewing sense-experience tends to lock the impressions 'inside' the head, which opens the door to scepticism: for who is to say that the inner impressions correspond to what is 'out there' in the real world? The attraction of the intentional approach to mind and world is that it underlines the essentially 'public' nature of the mind. The mind is not storing up the data from 'out there', because it is 'out there' itself, in its experience of the world as intentional phenomena.

Phenomenology does not eliminate the fundamental mysteriousness of mental life or consciousness, any more than do the various other attempts to grasp the nature of the mind that we have considered in this chapter. But though we still have no final answers to the basic puzzles that motivate philosophy of mind, in spite of all this philosophical activity, we should not conclude that nothing has been achieved. Philosophy is often accused of going round and round in circles: and the failure of philosophers to solve the problem of the relation between the mind and body after thousands of years of trying is often cited as an example of such pointless gyration. But this complaint is misguided in two ways. First, it ignores the fact that this sort of philosophical investigation has produced – and continues to produce – significant scientific insights and advances. Second, the complaint misunderstands the nature of philosophy. The problems may not have been solved; but our understanding of their character, depth and complexity has been enhanced. Consequently, our way of thinking about the mind has changed constantly, and continues to change today. Rethinking the questions we ask is often just as valuable as finding answers.

4 Philosophy of science

The remarkable phenomenon of scientific progress

It is obvious that the world has changed greatly over the past couple of centuries, more rapidly and more dramatically than during any comparable period in human history. Exactly why this has happened is an interesting, important and controversial issue. But hardly anyone would deny that one of the main factors responsible for these changes has been the tremendous progress made in the theoretical and applied sciences. We live in a world of skyscrapers, cars, planes, televisions, telephones, computers, artificial lights, electrical applications of all kinds, plastics and other synthetic materials, antibiotics, X-rays, photographs . . . The list of the things made possible by modern science could be extended indefinitely; these things surround us, and we have become totally dependent on them.

But while the impact of science and its remarkable rate of progress may help to explain the way our world has changed, this progress itself calls for an explanation. It is, after all, quite an astonishing phenomenon. Our scientific understanding of the world has advanced further in the past few centuries than it did in the whole of human history prior to this period. And the rate of progress in the sciences is also striking when compared to other areas of human endeavour. We need not deny that there can be and has been progress in fields such as literary criticism, philosophy, history or sociology. But the kind of progress and the rate of progress made in the natural sciences still seems to be of a different order. So how is it to be explained?

> *Is the success of science really such a mystery? Compare, say, psychology with astrology, or modern medicine with medieval medicine, or modern astronomy with ancient astronomy. The difference is obvious: modern science rests on true assumptions, and what went before rested on false assumptions. So long as you believe that the stars govern your character, or that sickness is due to the presence of bad blood, or that the sun moves around the earth, you won't make much progress. But when you start to work with correct assumptions your researches set off on the right track, and progress is more or less inevitable.*

This response is certainly plausible on the face of it. But from a philosophical point of view it is problematic. After all, why do we believe that the assumptions on which modern science rests are true? Our main reason for thinking this is that research based on them tends to be more successful than research based on other assumptions. For instance, astronomers who start out by accepting a heliocentric view of our solar system are able to make more accurate predictions than geocentric astronomers could manage. And their description of how celestial bodies behave coheres better with other parts of science, such as the theory of gravity. But it now looks as if we are saying something like this:

> *The success of science is due to its truth; and we know it is true because of its success.*

The problem with this is that the thing that needs to be explained – the success of science – figures in the explanation, which is a bit like defining a word by constructing a definition that contains the very word we are trying to define. So to say that science has been successful because its assumptions are true is one of those explanations that looks good at first but turns out, on examination, to be somewhat hollow. Yet there is more to be said on this issue, and we will return to it again below.

What other explanations of the remarkable advances made by modern science might one offer? Broadly speaking, there are two kinds of explanation:

- Those based on factors *external* to science: for example, the level of funding that has gone into science, connections between science and the military, connections between science and commercial interests, the intelligence of individual scientists, or the effectiveness of professional scientific organizations in disseminating information and promoting cooperation.
- Those based on factors *internal* to science: for example, the methodology that scientists typically employ, or the theoretical assumptions that they generally take for granted.

These two kinds of explanation are not exclusive; both could contribute to our understanding of scientific progress. Nevertheless, philosophers of science have generally focused on the second kind – the internal factors. Their underlying belief is that there is something about the way science works, the way it conducts itself, that is primarily responsible for its extraordinary success in modern times. One of their main goals, therefore, has been to analyse scientific *method* – that is, the ways in which scientists arrive at and justify their conclusions. Moreover, if it is indeed the methodology of science that is mainly responsible for its success, then an account of scientific methodology will also provide the basis for distinguishing between science and non-science. In other words, our account should help us answer more general questions like: What is science? What makes an activity scientific, as opposed to unscientific or pseudo-scientific?

What makes science scientific?

Here is one plausible view that is likely to occur to many people when they consider this question:

A scientific approach to a problem can be distinguished from an unscientific approach by the fact that its claims have to be supported by evidence. Compare, for instance, the creationist view of how human beings came to exist with the Darwinian view. Creationists say that the story told in Genesis is literally true. They don't go out and collect evidence for their theory; they just accept what is written in the Bible. And their acceptance of the Bible is not based on further evidence or on reason; as they themselves say, it rests on faith. The theory of evolution, by contrast, is based on countless observations, by Darwin and thousands of other scientists, of fossil records, resemblances and differences between species, mutations, extinctions and so on. And even though it explains these phenomena much better than any rival account put forward to date, if new evidence came to light that pointed to a different explanation, scientists would trade in the old theory for the new.

Clearly, there is something right about this claim. The familiar story about Galileo's experiment with falling objects illustrates the point very well. In the late middle ages, the views of the ancient Greek philosopher Aristotle were held in the highest esteem, not just on philosophical questions but also on matters of scientific fact. So great was the authority of Aristotle – the medievals often referred to him simply as 'the Philosopher' – that it was considered sufficient in some circles just to cite his opinion as a way of establishing the truth of a claim. Now, Aristotle had asserted that heavier objects fall to the ground more quickly than lighter objects. This view had gone pretty much uncontested for almost two thousand years. According to the legend, Galileo proved it to be false by dropping objects of different weight from the top of the leaning tower of Pisa. The story may be apocryphal, but it has survived because it captures so vividly the contrast between the old and new ways of approaching scientific questions.

Modern scientific knowledge is thus based on experience or, more specifically, on careful experimentation and observation. That much is uncontroversial, and perhaps helps to distinguish science from at least some unscientific practices. But we need to go much more deeply into *how* science rests on experience if we are to understand the nature of science and scientific methodology.

For example, scientists are clearly interested in making *predictions*. Indeed, when we talk about the 'success' of modern science, we perhaps mainly have in mind its ability to make reliable predictions. This ability is not equal in all fields: the predictions of meteorologists, for instance, are often inaccurate. But in many areas the accuracy and precision of scientific predictions is truly astonishing. Astronomers can predict to the second when future solar eclipses will occur; engineers can predict exactly how much stress a structure can withstand before it breaks; and chemists can describe with great precision the consequences of mixing a given combination of chemicals. It is the reliability of its predictions that has made science so powerful. Clearly, though, all these predictions rest on various assumptions.

Take a simple example. If I leave an iron nail in a cup of water for a week, it will rust. The chemist can tell us why: water reacts with iron to form iron oxide, the brown deposit we call rust. How do we know what will happen to the nail? The natural answer is to say that we know from past experience that iron rusts when it is exposed to water for a certain time. In effect, we are putting forward this claim about iron as a general truth; and we are also claiming that this general truth will be borne out in the case before us. But that raises the question: How can we justify moving from our limited experience of past cases to asserting bold generalizations and predictions about the future, both of which clearly go beyond mere reports of what we have experienced? This is the *problem of induction*.

Galileo Galilei (1564–1642)

Galileo is one of the most important figures in the history of science. He is perhaps most famous for having been the first to make astronomical observations with a telescope. This enabled him to discover that Jupiter has moons and that our own moon has mountains and craters – discoveries that in subtle ways supported the controversial heliocentric view of the solar system proposed a century earlier by Copernicus. As is well known, after publishing his astronomical findings Galileo was forced to recant by the Catholic church, which believed the Copernican view to be at odds with scripture.

But Galileo's most profound contribution to science was his development of a new kind of physics that challenged, and soon replaced, the older Aristotelian physics. Aristotelian physics described the *qualities* of things as they appear to the senses; it explained the behaviour of things by positing essential natures (for instance, a stone was said to fall to the ground because its natural state is to be at rest); and it viewed the earthly realm as essentially different from the heavenly realm. Galileo based his physics on general principles that are abstracted from experience – for instance, the principle of inertia, which he was the first to formulate. He mathematized physics, giving mathematically precise formulations of mechanical laws such as those governing projectiles, pendulums and free falling objects. And he broke down the distinction between the earthly and heavenly realms, positing his principles as genuinely universal laws that operate uniformly throughout the universe.

think critically! Deductive and inductive reasoning

Deduction is a reasoning process in which a certain conclusion follows *logically* from a set of premises. For example:

> *Premise 1*: All water contains oxygen.
> *Premise 2*: The liquid in this jar is water.
> *Conclusion*: Therefore, the liquid in this jar contains oxygen.

A deductive argument is **valid** if the conclusion really does follow from the premises, as it does in the example just given. Notice that whether the premises are actually true is irrelevant to the question of validity, so the following argument is also perfectly valid:

> All politicians are goats.
> No goats like cheesecake.
> Therefore, no politicians like cheesecake.

It is valid because *it is impossible for all the premises to be true and the conclusion false*. But, of course, the conclusion is false. Given that the argument is logically valid, that tells us that at least one of the premises must be false. Although it is valid, the argument is still not **sound**. For a deductive argument to be sound, it must meet two conditions:

1. It must be valid
2. All the premises must be true.

Induction is also a reasoning process, but one in which the conclusion does not follow *logically* from the premises. Instead, the premises support the conclusion in a looser way. Here is an inductive argument:

> *Premise 1*: Iron nails rust in water.
> *Premise 2*: Iron washers rust in water.
> *Premise 3*: Iron knives rust in water.
> *Conclusion*: Therefore, all iron objects rust in water.

Here it is possible for all the premises to be true and for the conclusion to be false. However, the premises still *support* the conclusion in the sense that if they are true then it is *probable* that the conclusion is true. And the probability of the conclusion being true could be increased by the addition of further premises.

Strictly speaking, all inductive arguments are deductively invalid. This is because the conclusion does not simply unpack what is already contained within the premises. It goes beyond them, making claims about future events, perhaps; or about all members of a certain class (such as the class of all iron objects), most of which have not been observed. But inductive arguments can be *stronger* or *weaker*. An inductive argument is *weak* if, in spite of the fact that the premises are true, *the conclusion could very easily be false*. Here is an example of a weak inductive argument:

> World War I started in Sarajevo.
> Therefore, odd numbered world wars start in Sarajevo.

An inductive argument is *strong* if the truth of the premises is such that *the conclusion is overwhelmingly likely*. Statements describing what we call laws of nature are supported by strong inductive arguments.

The problem of induction

The basic problem of induction is this: What justifies our moving from a finite number of particular observations to conclusions that cover cases we have not observed? The two most common forms of this sort of inference are:

(1) *Moving from the past to the future*:

In the past, July has always been warmer than March.
Therefore, next year July will be warmer than March.

(2) *Moving from the particular to the general*:

Jim bleeds when cut; so does Jamal; so does John; so does Jill; so does Juanita . . .
All human beings bleed when cut.

Obviously, both of these forms of inductive reasoning are absolutely basic to everyday life. Why do I believe that a drink of water won't poison me, or that dark clouds overhead portend rain, or that jumping off a tall building will kill me? In each case, I base my belief on experience — either my own experience, or other people's experience that I have heard about. It also seems obvious that induction is basic to science. Take any law of nature, such as 'Water boils at 100 degrees Celsius at a specified pressure'. We believe this because samples of water have been observed to boil at that temperature under those conditions on numerous occasions and have never been observed to boil at any other temperature.

But pointing out that inductive thinking is basic to both science and everyday life does not *justify* it as a rational procedure. The issue is not: Could we live normal lives or do science without thinking inductively? The issue is: When we reason inductively, are we being *rational*?

To sharpen and deepen our understanding of this problem, let us focus on a simple example. I am about to drink a cup of coffee. If someone asked me why I believe this drink will give me pleasure rather than kill me, I would answer that I have drunk thousands of cups of coffee over the past twenty years, most of which have given me pleasure and none of which has killed me. Of course, it is just possible that the drink before me contains poison, in which case my belief that it is safe to drink is false. But the fact that it *might* be false does not prove it to be irrational; it just means that it is not absolutely certain. It would be irrational to pour the coffee down the sink or to hire a food taster just because there is a remote (we hope) possibility that someone may have poisoned my drink.

Why am I so confident that drinking the coffee won't kill me? The obvious answer is that the circumstances in which it would prove fatal to drink it are very unlikely to occur: for instance, an enemy slipping cyanide into my cup; a terrorist polluting the water supply with a deadly poison this morning; my body having recently developed a rare medical condition that makes coffee dangerous to it. Unless such circumstances obtain, I assume that drinking coffee this morning will have the same consequences as it has had on every other occasion that I've drunk coffee. Thus, my confidence in the harmlessness of the drink before me seems to rest on two assumptions:

1. No unusual circumstances are present this morning;
2. In the absence of unusual circumstances, drinking coffee this morning will have the same consequences as it has had on all previous occasions.

Both beliefs are based on past experience. Belief (1), as we have already noted, is not completely certain. But what about (2)? Is this belief more certain? At first sight it would seem so. If either belief turned out to be false I would be surprised – or, more precisely, those who survived me would be surprised. But the kind of surprise experienced would be different in the two cases. If (1) turned out to be false, people would experience the kind of surprise that usually accompanies events that we don't expect but that we recognize may possibly happen. If (2) turned out to be false, however, their surprise would be of an altogether higher order. In fact, most people would not accept even the possibility that (2) could be false. If, at the coroner's inquest, a doctor was to report that death was caused by drinking coffee that, on this occasion and for no particular reason, happened to prove fatal, their testimony would be automatically rejected by the coroner, the jury, the police and everyone else. Why?

Assumption (2) actually rests on a deeper, more general assumption: namely, that nature operates in a uniform manner. In other words, we assume that the same causes will always produce the same effects. If drinking coffee refreshes me on Tuesday and kills me on Wednesday, there *must* be some significant difference in the two sets of circumstances to account for the different outcomes: for example, poison in the coffee, or a change in my physical condition. Another way of saying that nature operates uniformly or consistently is to say that its workings are *law governed*. Some of the generalizations we form on the basis of experience express what we take to be laws of nature: for example, light travels at 299,792 kilometres per second through a vacuum. Such generalizations express truths that we believe are genuinely universal; they hold throughout the universe and allow no exceptions. To say that nature operates in a uniform manner is equivalent to saying that everything that happens takes place in accordance with universal laws of nature.

We can now identify not one but *three* problems thrown up by the way we posit laws of nature:

1. *The basic problem of induction.* What justifies the move from a limited number of observations to a generalization or prediction that covers as yet unobserved cases?
2. *The problem of 'projection'.* Why are some inductive generalizations viewed as mere generalizations to which there may be exceptions, while others are treated as expressing exceptionless universal laws?
3. What justifies our belief that nature as a whole operates uniformly?

Let us address the first problem directly and leave the others until later.

The first person to voice doubts about the rationality of inductive reasoning was the eighteenth-century Scottish philosopher David Hume (see the box). The reason for his doubts can be stated simply: *induction is not deduction.* In a valid deductive argument – or at least in one that is fairly simple – we can just 'see' how the conclusion follows from the premises. (If I like any kind of music, and if reggae is a kind of music, then it *obviously* follows that I like reggae.) But in an inductive argument this is never so. No matter how many pieces of copper we have tested to see if they conduct electricity, it does not follow *logically* that the next piece of copper we test will conduct electricity.

Can we evade this problem, at least sometimes, by using deduction wherever possible? Suppose I want to infer that the piece of untested copper before me will conduct electricity. Instead of making an inductive inference from tests performed on other samples of copper, why not simply construct a deductive argument along the following lines?

All copper conducts electricity.
This is a piece of copper.
Therefore, this conducts electricity.

The argument is certainly valid. Moreover, this is undoubtedly the kind of reasoning that is frequently used in science and everyday life. But it should be obvious why this move does not solve the problem. The premise 'All copper conducts electricity' is a generalization. We believe it to be true on the basis of numerous observations made in the past. In other words, this premise is itself the product of an inductive inference, so the problem of induction simply arises again with respect to this premise. What entitles us to move from *many* particular observations of copper conducting electricity to the generalization that *all* copper conducts electricity?

David Hume (1711–1776)

David Hume is widely regarded as the greatest of all British philosophers and one of the most important thinkers of the modern era. Born in Scotland, he was educated at Edinburgh university and while still a student decided to pursue a career as a man of letters. His *Treatise on Human Nature*, published when he was 26, was not well received in spite of its obvious originality. Hume continued to write, however, and eventually became famous — and also infamous — not just for his contributions to philosophy but also for his monumental history of England and other 'popular' writings on politics, economics and matters of taste. But his lasting reputation is based on his highly original contributions to metaphysics, epistemology, ethics and the philosophy of religion.

Hume was notorious in his day for his sceptical attitude towards religion. This attitude was based on a more far-reaching scepticism that takes in most of our beliefs about the world. Hume argues that whenever we make claims about matters of fact that lie beyond our own actual experience (such as future events, or past events that we have not ourselves witnessed), we rely on our knowledge of causal relations. Such knowledge rests entirely on experience. I could not know that water will turn to ice when cooled just by examining water itself. This is something I have learned from past observations. But there is no *rational* justification for my belief that the next time I cool water down to zero degrees it will turn to ice rather than, say, catch fire. This possibility is not ruled out by reason; nor is it ruled out by experience, since experience only tells us what has *already occurred*, not what *will occur*.

So why do we assume that the future will resemble the past in a regular and predictable way? Hume's answer is that after we have seen two things 'constantly conjoined' (that is, one always being accompanied by the other), our mind forms the habit of expecting the first thing to be followed by the second. He concludes that 'all inferences from experience are effects of custom, not of reasoning'.

The clear implication of this, which Hume cheerfully accepts, is that most of our knowledge has a non-rational foundation. Certain assumptions and kinds of inference are basic to our way of thinking; we cannot think otherwise. But they are based on instinct or habit, not on reason. Hume goes on to argue that neither reason nor experience reveals to us the truth about the things that traditional metaphysics discusses — things such as God, the soul or the material substances that supposedly cause our sense-perceptions.

Clearly, we can't use deduction to justify induction. But can't induction be used to justify itself? Stated very generally, the problem is: How can we prove that past experiences are a good guide to future experiences? Well, we've all used inductive reasoning in the past; we've done so on countless occasions and with great success. Thus, since in the past our previous experiences have been a good guide to the future, we may reasonably infer that in the future they will continue to be a good guide.

This is a nice try. But it cannot be accepted as a rational justification of induction. One objection that might be made to it is that in fact inductive reasoning often fails. Occasionally, people do confidently drink their morning coffee only to find that it contains poison! More seriously, many generalizations that have been formed on the basis of experience turn out to be false: for example, the claim that humans are the only animals that use tools was universally believed until it was falsified by Jane Goodall's observations of chimpanzees.

There is, though, a deeper logical problem with this attempt to use induction to justify induction. The argument is, in fact, a perfect example of the fallacy known as 'begging the question' (see the box in the Theory of knowledge chapter). The argument might be laid out as follows:

Premise 1: Induction proved reliable on occasion 1.
Premise 2: Induction proved reliable on occasion 2.
Premise 3: Induction proved reliable on occasion 3 . . . (etc.)
Conclusion: Therefore, induction is reliable.

The conclusion of the argument is that induction is reliable. But this conclusion is arrived at by means of an inductive inference from the premises. Therefore, *Anyone offering this argument already assumes that inductive inferences are reliable.* If they did not assume this, the premises would not lend any support to the conclusion. The argument thus assumes what it is supposed to prove − namely, that past experience is a good guide to future experience. This assumption is not built into any of the premises; it is built into the logical structure of the argument.

If induction cannot be justified either deductively or inductively, then does it follow that it cannot be justified at all? Many philosophers, following Hume, have indeed drawn this conclusion. But others have thought that we should not be so ready to declare inductive reasoning non-rational. Some have tried to justify it in terms of probability. They argue that while induction can never yield conclusions that are certain, it can yield conclusions that are *probable*. When we make a generalization, for instance, the previously observed cases are the evidential support. If the generalization is based on only a small number of cases, then we will usually recognize that it could quite possibly be mistaken. But as we witness more cases that confirm our generalization and never encounter any counter-instances that disconfirm it, we affirm the generalization with increasing confidence. To be sure, we can never claim that our conclusion is absolutely certain; but in many cases its truth seems to be extremely probable.

This probabilistic defence does capture one important aspect of induction: in many cases, the confidence with which we assert a generalization or a prediction depends on how many confirming instances have been previously observed. For example, the generalization that you cannot get a decent cup of coffee on a plane flight is made more probable with each negative experience you have of in-flight coffee. Nevertheless, this probabilistic defence of induction is unsatisfactory in at least two ways. One problem is that in many cases our confidence in an inductively derived conclusion is completely unaffected by further confirming instances. For example, the proposition that all human beings are mortal is not made one jot more probable by another day's obituary notices. The same goes for generalizations that express laws of nature. In the case of many generalizations, there is a point reached − and sometimes it is reached quite quickly on the basis of very few confirming instances − where nothing further could increase our confidence in the truth of the proposition. It stands on the threshold of certainty, so to speak, and the only reason we do not view it as completely certain is that it is not a logical truth (that is, a statement whose denial would lead to a contradiction).

There is a second and more fundamental objection to the probabilistic defence of induction: it seems to miss the point. The basic problem, remember, is whether inferring conclusions about the unobserved on the basis of the observed can be rationally justified. The probabilistic argument says that it is justified because the more cases we observe, the greater is the likelihood that any unobserved cases will be similar. But the question still remains: *Why* do further confirming instances make the inferred generalization or prediction more probable? The main point urged by critics of induction such as Hume is precisely that this belief − the belief that there is some sort of connection between observed and unobserved cases − has no rational basis. Thus this argument, like the attempt to justify induction by appeal to induction, *begs the question*: it assumes what it is supposed to prove. In fact, at bottom it is really only a different version of that other argument.

The problem of 'projection'

According to Hume, there is no rational basis for supposing that correlations we have observed in the past − for example, the correlation of a flame with heat − will continue in the future. The next flame we encounter could conceivably cool us instead of warming us. Nevertheless, we do expect such correlations to continue; indeed, we regard them in some sense as *necessary*. A flame is *necessarily* hot; put it under an ice cube and the ice is bound to melt.

On Hume's view, there is not really any necessary connection between two things or between two events. This idea of a connection is merely a 'fiction' that we foist on nature. What happens, he says, is that when we experience two things invariably correlated, our mind forms the habit of expecting them to appear together in the future. Thus, when I next see a flame under some ice, I expect the ice to melt. Repeated observations of this or similar processes have made this expectation very strong – so strong, in fact, that we find it hard to take seriously the possibility that putting a flame under some ice would not be followed by the ice melting. If we perceive the first event we will necessarily expect the second event. But this necessity is a *psychological* necessity; it is not something we actually *perceive* to be linking the two events. However, we project it onto the events being observed and conclude that in nature itself a cause is necessarily connected to its effect. We think that although it is *logically* possible for the ice not to be melted by the flame, it will nonetheless necessarily melt – the necessity in question being natural rather than logical.

> *That's all very well, but isn't Hume overlooking an important point? Repeated observations of a correlation between two things or events do not always lead us to expect that they will be correlated in the future. Until you get to the last page, every sentence you read in a book is followed by another sentence; but you don't expect that this will be true of every further sentence you encounter. Every president of the United States has been a white male; but we don't think that in this case there is any necessary connection between the office and these qualities.*

This is clearly correct. It was on the basis of this observation that the American philosopher Nelson Goodman reformulated the problem of induction in a way that puts certain aspects of it into sharper relief. The heart of the matter, according to Goodman, is the difference between two kinds of hypothesis. Why do we regard some hypotheses – such as that all water freezes at zero degrees Celsius – as legitimate inductive generalizations, but regard other hypotheses – such as that all US presidents are white males – as illegitimate, even though they both seem to be supported equally well by experience? Using his term 'projection' to cover both predictions and generalizations (both are hypotheses that 'project' what we have already observed onto what we have not observed), the problem can be stated thus: What is the difference between legitimate and illegitimate projections? This is Goodman's reformulation of the problem of induction.

> *Why not distinguish between them in this way: Legitimate projections express laws of nature; illegitimate projections do not?*

In a sense, this seems to be right. But it does not really solve the problem; it only pushes it back a step. For the question is: Why do we regard some projections as expressing or resting on laws of nature but view others as projecting merely accidental regularities? To illustrate the problem Goodman constructed an ingenious thought experiment that has since become famous in philosophical circles. It is known as the 'grue paradox'.

To make his point, Goodman invented a new term, the predicate 'grue'. It can be defined in this way:

A thing is 'grue' if it is either

1. examined before 1 January 2000 and found to be green, or
2. examined after 31 December 1999 and found to be blue.

Prior to the year 2000, thousands of emeralds have been examined; every one has been found to be green. This regularity in our experience thus supports the projection:

All emeralds are green.

But it also, and to exactly the same extent, supports the projection:

All emeralds are grue.

Now, suppose it is 1 January 2000. An emerald sits in a sealed box. It was deposited in the box mechanically, and its colour has not yet been determined by any sort of examination. The box is about to be opened so that the stone can be examined. But before it is opened, you are asked to predict the colour of the stone. If you are at all concerned with making a correct prediction, you will presumably predict that the emerald in the box will prove to be green. Asked to explain your prediction, you will presumably say that it is an induction from the fact that all emeralds examined hitherto have been green. But it is equally true that all emeralds examined hitherto have been grue. So an exactly similar piece of inductive reasoning would support the prediction that the emerald in the box is grue. But if the emerald in the box is grue, then — because it is now after 31 December 1999 — it will not be green but blue!

We have here a paradox. The argument shows that from a purely logical point of view it is just as reasonable to predict that the emerald in the box is blue as it is to predict that it is green. But this contradicts our deep seated belief that the emerald is far more likely to be green than blue. Indeed, if there was a decent prize at stake, any philosopher or logician who seriously thought it was a toss-up between green and blue would be looked on as crazy.

You might think that one thing wrong with the argument is that it rests on a bizarre, artificial concept, invented by a philosopher. But the strangeness or artificiality of the concept 'grue' — a quality that has given a new meaning to the term 'gruesome' among philosophers — does not affect the basic point being made. The two predictions bear exactly the same relation to the evidence that supports them; they are in fact supported by exactly the same evidence, and must therefore be, in some sense, equally rational.

Needless to say, not every contemporary philosopher accepts Goodman's argument. But most would acknowledge that it does succeed into bringing into focus a very deep problem in the philosophy of science: Why are some predicates more projectible than others? Compare these two statements:

All water contains oxygen,

All the tanks beside the beds in this hospital contain oxygen.

Both are universal statements based on a limited amount of evidence. But we only regard the first as law-like. We might well predict that the next sample of water and the next bedside tank we encounter both contain oxygen. But if we were wrong about the bedside tank we would only be moderately surprised. If we were wrong about the sample of water we would be totally bewildered.

Many philosophers of science, particularly those associated with the school known as logical positivism, have sought to discover some feature that is *intrinsic* to certain concepts but not to others that would justify our making law-like projections in some cases but not in others. According to Goodman, however, there is no such feature. The difference between 'green' and 'grue', or between 'water' and 'bedside tanks in this hospital', does not lie in their logical character. The difference is simply that we are more used to projecting some predicates than others. Goodman describes those we are more accustomed to projecting as being better 'entrenched'. And this is the basis on which we regard some projections as more rational, and more certain, than others.

A discussion of this 'solution' to the paradox would take us too far afield. But it is interesting to note how reminiscent it is of Hume's own 'solution' to the problem of induction. According to Hume, the basis on which we make our inductions is what he calls 'custom' or 'habit'; this is what leads us to project our past experiences into the future. According to Goodman, the reason we do this more confidently in some cases than in others has to do with how *used* we are to making certain kinds of projection — in other words, it has to do with custom or habit. A critic would say of both Hume and Goodman that they have merely described what we do and have not shown how inductive thinking is *rational.* Hume would undoubtedly acknowledge this, adding that his whole point is that our knowledge of the world, in so far as it is based on induction, has a non-rational foundation. Goodman, however, would argue that the critic, like Hume, has too abstract a concept of rationality. There is more to being rational than thinking deductively. Indeed, we should recognize that allowing one's beliefs and reasoning processes to be informed by 'custom' is, *and should be*, also part of our notion of what it is to be rational.

Induction: who needs it?

One of this century's leading philosophers of science, Karl Popper, put forward a quite different solution to the problem of induction. Popper fully accepts Hume's point that inductive arguments are, strictly speaking, invalid; but he does not draw Hume's sceptical conclusion that science has a non-rational foundation. This conclusion does not follow, he argues, because science does not in fact proceed inductively.

It is a plausible view that scientists first make observations and then, on the basis of those observations, form generalizations; but it is a view that Popper totally rejects, derisively labelling it the 'bucket theory of knowledge'. According to him, this is not what scientists actually do; nor is it what they should do, since it is not a method that would generate valuable results. After all, scientists are clearly more interested in making some observations rather than others. Their research is directed, and their experiments and observations serve definite purposes. When they spend billions constructing a particle accelerator, the goal is obviously not just to add a few more choice titbits of information about the behaviour of subatomic particles to our current body of knowledge. The main purpose is, rather, *to test theories*. This is the basic idea behind Popper's account of how science works.

Popper describes his own view as the 'searchlight' theory of knowledge. The point of this label is to emphasize the way in which scientific research is always focused on a certain area and is conducted with definite expectations and objectives in mind. The method he describes is known more formally as the **hypothetico-deductive method**. It involves the following steps:

1. Put forward a hypothesis (*H*).
2. Deduce a consequence (*C*) of this hypothesis.
3. Through experiment and observation, see whether *C* occurs.
4. If *C* does not occur then *H* must be false, so a new hypothesis is needed.
5. If *C* does occur then *H* is corroborated to some extent. To further corroborate it, one should deduce further consequences and repeat step 3.

The key idea here is that science proceeds (and progresses) through a series of conjectures and attempted refutations; scientists construct hypotheses and then try to falsify them.

A couple of examples from the history of science serve to illustrate the way the method works in practice. At the end of the nineteenth century, the dominant theoretical model with which physicists worked posited an invisible substance, the ether, that permeated the universe and provided a medium through which light waves could travel. This was the *hypothesis* that needed to be tested. A deduced *consequence* of this hypothesis was that the velocity of light from a source towards which the earth is moving will be different from the velocity of light from a source at right angles to the earth's motion through space. The famous Michelson-Morley *experiment* of 1887 tested for this, and found that there was no difference. The conclusion eventually drawn from this was that the hypothesis in question was false and a new hypothesis was needed. (Enter Einstein.)

In the case of the ether, the hypothesis was falsified. For an example of a hypothesis being corroborated, consider the researches of the great French scientist Lavoisier (1743–1794) into the nature of combustion. His *hypothesis* was that when substances burn they take in something from the air. From this principle he deduced the *consequence* that if a substance is burned and no part of it escapes during the burning, it should weigh more afterwards than it did before. He *tested* for this by burning some mercury under suitable conditions and weighing the calx (the remaining ash). As predicted, the calx was heavier than the original mercury, a finding that *corroborated* Lavoisier's initial hypothesis.

> *Don't scientific experiments do more than simply 'corroborate' hypotheses? Don't they, at least sometimes, conclusively prove a theory to be true? After all, scientists base their current research on theories, principles and facts that are accepted by everyone – for instance, Boyle's law, or the theory of evolution, or the fact that the earth orbits the sun and that light travels at 299,792 kilometres per second.*

According to Popper, these beliefs are exceptionally well corroborated; but it would be incorrect to say that their truth has been fully confirmed. His argument is simple and is based on elementary logical principles. If I say that the truth of a hypothesis (*H*) implies a given consequence (*C*), my statement has the form:

If *H* then *C*.

This is a conditional statement. Now, according to an elementary logical principle known as *modus tollens*, given the truth of this conditional statement, we may infer that if *C* is false then *H* is false. Thus, it is possible to *falsify* a hypothesis conclusively, as Galileo did when he refuted Aristotle's ideas about falling bodies. On the other hand, if we assume the conditional statement is true and then argue that since *C* is true then *H* must be true, we commit a fallacy – specifically, the fallacy of 'affirming the consequent' (see the box). The problem is that the consequence one has predicted could occur even though the hypothesis is false. In Lavoisier's experiment with mercury, it is possible that the calx became heavier not because the burning mercury combined with something in the air but for some other reason: for example, it could have combined with part of some solid substance such as the tray on which it was placed.

Scientists are, of course, fully aware of this. That is why a good deal of their work involves eliminating alternative hypotheses that would also explain the phenomenon under investigation. For example, to eliminate the possibility that the mercury combined with the tray on which it was placed, we could weigh the tray before and after the experiment. This too follows a Popperian procedure. The hypothesis to be tested is that the burning mercury combines with its tray. The consequence deduced from this hypothesis is that the tray will weigh less after the experiment than before. If the weight of the tray turns out not to have changed, then the hypothesis is falsified. And the falsification of that hypothesis indirectly corroborates further the hypothesis that the mercury combines with something in the air.

It is not sufficient, however, simply to say that scientists strive to construct hypotheses that can withstand attempts to falsify them. After all, anyone can do that! Consider this hypothesis:

The speed of light is above 10 kilometres per hour.

It is hard to imagine this being refuted. But even before scientists had determined the speed of light, no one would have advanced this hypothesis as one worth testing. The hypothesis that light travels through a vacuum at 299,792 kilometres per second is much more likely to be wrong, since it is more specific. Being more specific, it is, in principle, much easier to falsify. But if it withstands attempts to falsify it, it represents a far more valuable and interesting achievement. The difference between the two hypotheses is analogous to the difference between predicting the result of a football game and predicting the exact score. Predicting the result is easier because your prediction contains less information; it is therefore compatible with more outcomes than is the other prediction. Predicting the score

think critically!   Valid and invalid inferences

Some patterns of argument are so common that they have been given names by logicians, whose business it is to classify, analyse and evaluate argument forms. Two of the most common valid forms of argument are *modus ponens* and *modus tollens*. In representing the form of an argument we use letters like *P* and *Q* to stand for complete sentences that can be either true or false.

Name	Form	Example
Modus ponens	If *P* then *Q*	If 4 > 3 then 4 > 2
	P	4 > 3
	Therefore *Q*	Therefore 4 > 2
Modus tollens	If *P* then *Q*	If Einstein was Chinese then he was Asian.
	Not *Q*	Einstein was not Asian.
	Therefore not *P*	Therefore Einstein was not Chinese.

Two fallacies (invalid patterns of argument) are also, unfortunately, so common that they have been given names.

Name	Form	Example
Affirming the consequent	If *P* then *Q*	If Churchill was French then he was European.
	Q	Churchill was European.
	Therefore *P*	Therefore Churchill was French.
Denying the antecedent	If *P* then *Q*	If Churchill was French then he was European.
	Not *P*	Churchill was not French.
	Therefore not *Q*	Therefore Churchill was not European.

is riskier; you stand more chance of being wrong; but for that very reason, if you are right, the feat is more impressive. In Popper's terms, the more detailed, riskier predictions have more 'empirical content', and are therefore more valuable. The goal of science is thus not simply to construct hypotheses that withstand falsification tests; it is to generate hypotheses that can do this even though they have as much empirical content as possible.

Popper also uses the idea of **falsifiability** to demarcate science from non-science. The claims advanced in other spheres such as religion ('God loves you') or astrology ('When Mars appears in Taurus, Librans are more likely to fall in love') are usually unfalsifiable, where they are not actually falsified; nothing is allowed to count as evidence against such claims. This is what reveals them to be essentially unscientific. Modern science really took off when it more or less self-consciously began using the hypothetico-deductive method. In doing so, it turned away from speculative claims that cannot be subjected to any kind of empirical test. Voltaire's satirical novel *Candide* is one of the best-known attacks on that kind of speculation. When Pangloss holds on to his hypothesis that 'everything is for the best in this best of all possible worlds', regardless of how much suffering he experiences and observes, it becomes evident that he will allow no experience to falsify it. The unavoidable conclusion one draws from this is that the hypothesis is vacuous. It has no empirical content, because no experience could possibly prove it false.

Popper wields his falsifiability principle in a similar way to attack other supposedly anti-metaphysical pretenders to scientific credibility, such as Marxism and psychoanalysis. The problem with statements like 'Every dream is a wish fulfilment' or 'All ideological disputes are the expression of a class conflict', he argues, is that they are propounded in such a way as to exclude even the possibility of falsification. Any falsifying evidence will always be dismissed or reinterpreted so as to leave the main hypothesis intact. But the truly scientific attitude is not to 'ride shotgun' alongside one's favourite hypotheses; it is, rather, to expose them as much as possible to the possibility of falsification. In this way one can be sure that only the strongest survive. This open-minded, critical attitude is the hallmark of genuine science.

Problems with Popper's account of scientific method

Popper's account of scientific method is appealing in many ways. It provides an answer to Hume's sceptical challenge: the invalidity of inductive reasoning does not undermine the rationality of science, since scientific theories are not arrived at by induction. It captures important aspects of how scientists actually work. And it provides a criterion for distinguishing the scientific from the unscientific and the pseudo-scientific. Nevertheless, there are problems with the Popperian view.

Take Popper's answer to the problem of induction. His insistence that scientists do not simply collect data in an arbitrary manner and then produce generalizations on the basis of this data is clearly correct; but it is equally true that scientists do not simply come up with hypotheses at random. Given any phenomenon that needs to be explained, there are always an infinite number of hypotheses that one could offer. For instance, one could try to explain the fact that a piece of mercury becomes heavier when burned in any number of ways:

- When heated to a certain temperature the mercury reacts with oxygen in the surrounding air.
- Certain elements in the surrounding air are attracted to the mercury because it is hot.
- Molecules from nearby objects are attracted to the mercury, as moths are to a light, because it glows.
- The 'soul' of the mercury dies when the mercury is burnt, and dead souls weigh more than living souls.

It is obvious that such explanations could be multiplied indefinitely. But it is equally obvious that the great majority of them would never even occur to a scientist, and if they did occur they would be rejected immediately. This shows that just as scientists are selective in what data they collect and what experiments they perform, so there must also be some *principles of selection* governing what hypotheses they are likely or willing to entertain. Moreover, although it is difficult to state precisely what these principles are, it seems plausible to suppose that induction plays a key role in determining which hypotheses are postulated. The sight of an apple falling to the ground may or may not have triggered a train of thought in Newton's mind that led to his theory of universal gravitation; but the falling apple could have had no significance if it had been an isolated incident. Newton, like everyone else, already believed that bodies heavier than air fall to the ground if unsupported. And he had arrived at this belief by forming a generalization based on countless observations. To be sure, the theory of gravity itself cannot be viewed as just another such generalization; it took a Newton to formulate it. But induction seems to play an important role in providing a basis for the more imaginative kind of hypothesizing.

A second objection to the Popperian view is that his concept of falsification is too simple. According to Popper, scientists test a hypothesis by deducing consequences that it entails and then conducting experiments to compare these predictions with reality. If the prediction is wrong, the hypothesis is thereby falsified. But one can only validly infer the falsity of the hypothesis so long as one holds other assumptions in place. Suppose, for instance, that you were testing the hypothesis that an electrical current sent through a wire coiled around an iron bar will turn the bar into a magnet. The predicted consequence of this hypothesis is that when the current is flowing the bar will attract iron filings. But now suppose that when the experiment is conducted the predicted result does not occur. Must you immediately conclude that the hypothesis is false? Of course not. The negative result could be explained in any number of ways: perhaps the current was not turned on; perhaps the current was not powerful enough; perhaps there is a break in the circuit somewhere; perhaps the bar is not made of iron; perhaps the filings are not made of iron; perhaps some other force is acting on the filings and keeping them from moving. The general point here is that, strictly speaking, it is not possible either to verify or to falsify individual hypotheses in isolation. When scientists interpret an experimental finding as signifying that a certain hypothesis must be false, they can only do so because they are holding in place a complex body of assumptions that rule out such possibilities as faulty technique, corrupted data, impure specimens or the falsity of other theoretical beliefs on which their predictions are also based.

A third problem with Popper's view of science concerns the way he uses falsifiability as a criterion for distinguishing the scientific from the unscientific. According to at least some theorists, if we take this seriously we would have to exclude from the pantheon of science some of its most illustrious, useful and widely accepted principles. Consider, for example, this Darwinian principle: The species that survive in the course of evolution are those that are best adapted to their environment. On Popper's view, if this hypothesis is to enjoy scientific credibility it must be falsifiable. But how might one set about falsifying it? To do so would involve searching for evidence of a species surviving in spite of its being environmentally disadvantaged. But the fact that it has survived could be taken as prima facie evidence that a species is well adapted — which is how it will be construed by anyone already committed to the Darwinian principle. The point here is not that the principle in question is entirely unproblematic; the point is simply that Popper's falsifiability principle may be too rigid and too crude. There are hypotheses it would brand as unscientific that are an integral part of our system of scientific knowledge.

What about truth?

All this talk about scientific method — induction, deduction, verification, corroboration, falsification and so on — is very interesting, but aren't we ignoring the most important notion of all in science: namely, truth? After all, isn't truth supposed to be the ultimate goal of science? So how, exactly, does the concept of truth fit into the picture?

The nature of the relation between scientific method and truth is a large and difficult issue. One natural account of how they are related would be this: Use the right method and you will arrive at the truth; use the wrong method and you will probably fall into error. On this view, sound methodological principles are like the lights on an airport runway, guiding us to our destination. This was certainly the view of the great pioneers of modern scientific method — Bacon, Galileo, Descartes and others — and with certain qualifications it is probably still the view of the majority today.

In philosophy, though, things are rarely so simple. An obvious question that arises for this traditional view is: How do we know when we have actually arrived at the truth? When a plane touches down on the runway we feel a bump that tells us we have landed. Is there any proof that we have reached the truth, other than the fact that we have been following an approved method? This is a tough question, even for more recent theories of science. Take Popper's account, for instance. Popper is a firm believer in the existence of objective truth. He also believes that when we use the method of conjectures and refutations that he recommends, we steer towards this truth. But as we have already seen, according to Popper the hypotheses that scientists put forward cannot be conclusively verified. They can either be falsified or, if they resist all attempts to falsify them, they can be corroborated indirectly. But it follows from this that we cannot ever know for certain that we hold the truth. All we can be sure of is that if we conduct our enquiries in the right way our theories will come *ever closer* to the truth.

> *But if we can't know when we are there, how can we know we are* nearly *there? If we can't know for certain that our theories are true, how can we be sure that they are* close *to the truth?*

This is a reasonable question. To many, it shows the traditional conception of objective truth (a conception Popper more or less endorses) to be deeply problematic. For this reason, some philosophers of science have put forward a very different view of scientific truth and, with it, a radically different account of scientific progress.

In the chapters on Metaphysics and Theory of knowledge we touched on some of the issues involved in the debate between realists and non-realists. In particular, we looked at Kant's idea that the mind 'shapes' the world it seeks to know, and at the implications of Berkeley's insistence that we cannot know what cannot be experienced. These ideas, if accepted, are likely to make us suspicious of any talk about a reality existing independently of us and hence also of a realist conception of truth.

Remember that the word 'realism' is a technical philosophical term. It has nothing to do with practicality or hard-headedness. Rather, it is a label for the view that our assertions are true or false according to how well they correspond to the way reality is, independent of our relation to it. This is the traditional (one might say the 'orthodox') view of truth. There are several different kinds of realism. In the Theory of knowledge chapter we discussed one kind — 'representative realism' — in some detail. Representative realism holds that our sense-impressions represent to us an independently existing reality. This is compatible with 'scientific realism' (which is the kind of realism that is of particular interest to the philosopher of science). The two kinds of realism may even overlap. But they are not quite the same.

Scientific realism is the doctrine that science provides us with a true picture of an independently existing reality. The scientific realist sees science as something like a map. A map can represent a territory with greater or lesser degrees of accuracy. But if it is accurate, then corresponding to the place on the map where three roads are shown to meet half a mile south of a church there will be a place 'on the ground' where three actual roads converge half a mile south of an actual church. Thus, according to the scientific realists, the key concepts of good scientific theories – such as electron, gene, black hole – refer to real things that actually exist; and scientific theories accurately describe the relations that obtain between these things. In this way, say the realists, science 'carves nature at the joints'.

The main alternative to realism, in philosophy of science as elsewhere, is non-realism. As with realism, there are different forms of non-realism, but they all cluster around one central idea: the idea that the truth of our assertions about the world is *not* independent of our relation to the world. More specifically, *whether* our claims are true or false is bound up with how we *determine* whether they are true or false.

Now, this definition of non-realism is rather too general to be illuminating. And it strikes many who encounter it for the first time as a rather implausible view. After all, assertions such as 'The moon is smaller than the earth' are surely true regardless of how one happens to ascertain their truth. Nevertheless, many of the leading philosophers of science are non-realists of one sort or another. To better understand why, let us examine briefly some of the key ideas put forward by another major contemporary philosopher of science, Thomas Kuhn.

Kuhn's account of how science advances

Kuhn, like everyone else, is struck by the remarkable progress that has been made by the natural sciences over the past few centuries. On the conventional view, which scientific realists typically endorse, this progress consists in the gradual accretion of information about nature that enables scientists to provide an ever more accurate and ever more extensive representation of the way the world is. But Kuhn challenges this view. Central to his challenge are two distinctions that he makes: one between pre-scientific activity and science proper, the other between 'normal science' and 'revolutionary science'.

Both these distinctions hinge on Kuhn's notion of a **paradigm**. A paradigm, roughly speaking, is an exemplary model of successful science: for example, Ptolemy's geocentric astronomy, Newton's physics, the electromagnetic theory of light, or Darwin's theory of evolution. Such paradigms dominate a field for a time. While they are dominant, they provide scientists in that field with a theoretical framework, a set of assumptions, an orientation toward particular sorts of problems, and rules for how these problems should be approached and proposed solutions appraised.

'Pre-science' is the term Kuhn uses to describe the situation that one finds in a theoretical field before a single paradigm has been widely accepted. In this situation, researchers may disagree over what phenomena need to be studied or explained, what methods they should use, and which observations are relevant. Nor will there be a single set of theoretical premises that they can take for granted as a foundation from which to work. This was the case, for instance, in bacteriology before the work of Louis Pasteur, or in psychology before the twentieth century. These handicaps prevent the various activities of those researching in a particular field from constituting a science. According to Kuhn, the transition from pre-science to science typically occurs when one school of thought triumphs over its rivals and thereby establishes a paradigm. From then on, there is general agreement about which phenomena are worth studying, which problems need to be addressed, what methods should be employed, and how findings should be presented. Instead of continually worrying about the theoretical foundations of their discipline, scientists can take a body of theory and data as given and start to engage in more specialized research. In this way, the discipline as a whole becomes pro-fessionalized.

Within science proper, Kuhn distinguishes two kinds of activity. What he calls **normal science** is the tightly disciplined activity in which most scientists are engaged most of the time. It consists, for the most part, in working out the limits and implications of the dominant paradigm in a given field. A good contemporary example of normal science is the human genome project – the attempt to locate and classify all the different genes in a human being and to analyse exhaustively the structure of human DNA.

Contrasted with normal science is what Kuhn terms **revolutionary science**. This involves responding to problems thrown up by normal science, problems that lead to a theoretical crisis within a given field. Revolutionary science seeks to resolve a crisis by constructing a new paradigm to replace the one that has generated the crisis. The history of science, according to Kuhn, consists of periodic revolutions, or paradigm shifts, separated by rather longer periods of 'normal' scientific activity. Examples of paradigm shifts are the transition from Newtonian to Einsteinian physics, the displacement of Aristotle's account of motion by Galilean mechanics, and the revival of atomic theory by Dalton. In each case, once established, the new paradigm makes possible and helps to direct scientific research in the relevant field. Thus, once Dalton had convinced his fellow chemists that the atoms of each element had a particular weight that distinguished them from other elements (a revolutionary idea), scientists could then set about the 'normal scientific' task of discovering the exact atomic weight of each element.

Disputes within normal science – for example, over the exact distance of some star from the earth, or the chemical composition of a DNA molecule – are conducted under the rubric of a particular paradigm. For this reason they can usually be resolved according to criteria accepted by all parties to the dispute. But conflicts *between* paradigms cannot be settled in this way. In part this is because such conflicts often involve fundamental questions about the values underlying scientific research – questions about which problems are most worth solving and about the direction that a particular discipline should take. According to Kuhn, though, a more fundamental reason is that the conflicting paradigms are *incommensurable*: they rest on incompatible assumptions, and define many of their key terms differently; consequently, there is no common ground that can serve as a basis for resolving the conflict between them in a neutral manner.

What changes in a paradigm shift?

It is at this point that Kuhn's account of how science progresses connects up with the debate between realists and non-realists. In his best-known work, *The Structure of Scientific Revolutions*, Kuhn compares the adoption of a new scientific paradigm to the kind of change that is involved in a *Gestalt* switch, as when a person goes from seeing a drawing as representing a duck to seeing it as a picture of a rabbit. And he claims, plausibly, that experiments performed by psychologists into this kind of phenomenon have put it beyond doubt that what we perceive is conditioned by the interpretative presuppositions and mechanisms that underlie and are involved in the act of perception. *Gestalt* switches thus illustrate the general thesis that the things we know – the objects of cognition – are shaped or affected by what we bring to the act of knowing them. Moreover, Kuhn believes this is so at all levels of human knowledge.

The same general principle operates in cases of rudimentary sense-perception, where the objects in question are such things as the drawing of the duck rabbit, and in the sophisticated observational research undertaken by scientists. This is why Kuhn claims that scientists before and after a paradigm shift may be said to be contemplating 'different worlds'. But there is one important difference between the *Gestalt* switches investigated by psychology and paradigm shifts in the sciences: only the former can be identified and discussed by reference to an external standard. I can recognize that when I switch from seeing some lines on a page as a drawing of a duck to seeing them as representing a rabbit I experience a *Gestalt* switch (and not, say, a perceptual change occasioned by the substitution of one drawing for another), because I can refer to the lines on the page that remain the same throughout. But in the case of paradigm shifts in the sciences there is nothing that functions as an external standard in this way. Consequently, one can never prove directly that a paradigm shift changes the character of the world itself, which is the object of scientific cognition. But in Kuhn's view, this non-realist way of viewing the change makes better sense of the way scientists respond to revolutionary changes in their field.

> *Surely, it would be simpler and more reasonable to say that paradigm shifts in science merely involve changes in the way scientists interpret their data. It seems extravagant and implausible to say that a change in scientific thinking actually alters the nature of the reality that scientists are investigating.*

To the realist, non-realism will always seem implausible. This is because in our everyday thinking we are all realists. Realism thus has common sense on its side. But, as we have already observed, before dismissing an idea in the name of common sense we should reflect on the fact that some of the most successful scientific theories — for example, the heliocentric view of the solar system, Newton's theory of gravity and Einstein's theory of relativity — all contradicted common sense to some extent. Moreover, non-realists like Kuhn have positive reasons for rejecting the realist view of paradigm shifts, most of them having to do with the way theory and observation are related in science. Two points made by Kuhn on this matter are particularly interesting.

First, he argues that the realist view — which takes different theories to be only different interpretations of reality — relies on a notion of data as something that is simply 'given' to the observer. But whatever one takes as the 'given' of scientific observation, this notion remains highly problematic. If the basic data are taken to be the relatively complex things that are subject to investigation — elements, electromagnetic forces, organisms, pendulums and so on — then, Kuhn argues, what one actually observes is inevitably conditioned by the dominant paradigm. For example, someone comparing the face of a man and the face of a monkey in pre-Darwinian times would probably be more struck by the differences than by the similarities. After Darwin, the similarities become more obvious. Or again, an Aristotelian physicist observing a stone swinging on the end of a rope would see a stone trying to reach its natural state of rest on the ground but prevented from doing so by the rope; but someone working under the paradigms established by Galileo and Newton would see a pendulum acting according to the laws of gravity and energy transference. The point in both cases is that what the two observers experience — the immediate content of their experiences — is not the same.

Second, while it may be true that normal science is, to a large extent, concerned with the interpretation of data, this activity is only possible because — and as long as — the data in question are 'stable'. This agreement on the nature of the data is in turn made possible by the fact that members of the scientific community in question share a paradigm. For example, biologists and chemists finally agreed that living organisms did not spontaneously germinate only after Pasteur's experiments established a new paradigm that posited micro-organisms that were too small to be seen. Prior to this, some regarded spontaneous germination as a proven fact, others as an impossibility. According to Kuhn, whenever a paradigm becomes problematic, the data are also liable to become unstable and can no longer be regarded as simply 'given'.

The upshot of these and similar arguments is that scientists can have no access to reality as it might be in itself, independent of their experience of it. Therefore they cannot know to what extent, if any, their descriptions of nature correspond to 'independent' reality. In fact, the concept of reality 'in itself' (things as they 'really are') is useless from a philosophical point of view. From a philosophical vantage point, we may as well say that there is no such reality, and therefore that none of our descriptive statements can be true of it – that is, they cannot be unconditionally true. But the descriptions of nature offered by scientists can be true or false of nature *as it is experienced by them* – that is, relative to the context provided by the dominant paradigm within which the scientists are currently working.

Unsurprisingly, this view of scientific truth is highly controversial, not least because it seems to imply some form of relativism. Since different paradigms distinguish different periods in the history of a scientific discipline, Kuhn's theory appears to make it possible for the same statement to be both true and false relative to different historical contexts. For example, the statement 'There is no action at a distance' is true in so far as it describes the way things are, or were, as experienced by a pre-Newtonian scientist. But it is false in so far as it contradicts a true statement about the world as experienced by a scientist working with a Newtonian paradigm. Different paradigms also distinguish the various disciplines from each other. In a similar way, therefore, two apparently conflicting statements can both be true relative to their different disciplinary contexts.

Scientific progress revisited

Where does all this leave the idea of scientific progress – which was, after all, the phenomenon that we set out to try to explain?

> *Progress in science presumably means getting closer to the truth. So if there is progress in science, this means that later theories must, in some sense, be closer to the truth: they must correspond to independent reality more closely than do earlier theories. If we dispense with this traditional, realist notion of truth, won't we have to dispense with the notion of progress as well?*

This problem has been raised by many of Kuhn's critics. The general problem – whether the concept of progress in science only makes sense given a realist view of scientific truth – could occupy us for many pages. All we can do here is sketch Kuhn's response and let the reader judge whether it is adequate.

Kuhn concedes that his view of science is incompatible with the Popperian concept of scientific progress, according to which science progresses in so far as it constructs theoretical accounts of nature that approximate more and more closely to the way things really are. But since (as even Popper concedes) we have no access to a completely objective reality, Kuhn views this notion of progress as empty. And since the scientific theories that succeed one another do not develop our conception of nature in a uniform direction – Einstein's physics, for instance, is closer in some respects to Aristotle's physics than to Newton's – it is also a notion of progress that is historically implausible. In its place, Kuhn proposes an *evolutionary* concept of progress.

Normal science, he claims, is essentially a puzzle-solving activity. Its practitioners work on specific, well-defined problems that have definite solutions.

It therefore tends to accord a high value to puzzle-solving ability. And it tends to generate and select those theories that improve on previous or competing theories in particular respects — most importantly, their greater puzzle-solving power or potential, and their possession of associated qualities such as simplicity, predictive accuracy, practical fruitfulness, and compatibility with theories developed in other disciplines. Using these criteria, Kuhn argues, it should be possible to determine which is the more recent of any two theories in a given field. Science can thus be said to progress in the sense that it produces theories that better satisfy its own criteria of success.

Obviously, this account of scientific progress does not close the debate. On the contrary, it opens up a whole range of new questions:

- Are the criteria just mentioned the only ones by which scientists evaluate theories?
- Can they be ranked in order of importance?
- What is their status? Is there one set of criteria (and one particular ordering) valid for all scientists at all times? Or do the criteria vary from one period to another or between disciplines?
- If they do vary, can one set of criteria be shown to be better than another, and if so, how?

Kuhn's views on science have been tremendously influential, and not just within the philosophy of science. In other fields of enquiry, especially in social sciences like psychology and economics, scholars have taken very seriously the idea that progress within a field requires the establishment of a paradigm. For only where there is agreement over fundamentals — which problems are important, what methodology should be used, which assumptions can be relied upon, what constitutes success, and so on — can a discipline achieve the kind of integrity, unity of purpose and continual forward momentum that the natural sciences exhibit so impressively. Paradoxically, however, Kuhn's views have also been interpreted by many in a thoroughly relativistic way as undermining the whole idea of objective progress in science or any other field.

We began by noting the remarkable rate of progress in the natural sciences over the past few centuries and by asking for an explanation of this phenomenon. Our enquiries have led us to consider, among other things, the nature and rationality of inductive reasoning, the hypothetico-deductive method, the verification, falsification and corroboration of hypotheses, the debate between realism and non-realism, and the concept of scientific truth. In the end, we found that even the concept of scientific progress is not as clear cut as we supposed. How one understands the notion of progress turns out to be bound up with one's view on various other matters — truth, realism, the status of methodological principles, and so on. We can confidently predict that the natural sciences will continue to make progress. But we can also predict, with almost equal confidence, that a fascinating debate will continue into exactly how, why and in what sense this is so.

5 Ethics

In this chapter we will be concerned with questions about right and wrong, the good and the bad; this is the practical aspect of ethics. We will also consider the nature of our beliefs about such matters; this is the theoretical aspect. Ethical theory approaches its subject matter in the same way that other disciplines do: its aim is to achieve clarification, insight and, if possible, truth regarding the questions it asks. Its questions include:

- What do moral concepts like 'good' and 'right' mean'?
- Are our moral judgements objectively true or false, or do they express subjective preferences?
- Can specific moral rules such as 'Don't lie' or 'Help those in need' be rationally justified?
- What motives do we have for living morally?

On the practical side, ethics is the business of conducting one's life in the right way, as well as trying to ensure that society operates according to acceptable moral principles. This involves making concrete choices and performing specific actions. Here we face questions such as:

- Should I give something to this charity and, if so, how much?
- Should lie to help someone I love?
- How should I balance the pursuit of my own goals with making a contribution to my community?
- Should our society allow euthanasia and, if so, when and under what conditions?

However, while we can make a general distinction between the theoretical and the practical in ethics, we cannot keep them entirely separate. Reflecting on morality may be part of a process in which we work out what to do; moreover, the decision to reflect is itself an action, a way of conducting our lives. This interrelatedness of the theoretical and the practical will become very evident in the following pages. We will start by looking at some of the things that people often say about morality, uncovering some of the assumptions that underlie these opinions, then go on to examine some of the main ethical theories. Throughout our enquiry the terms 'ethics' and 'morality' are treated as synonymous.

Can we make moral judgements?

Let us begin by considering a view we have probably all heard expressed at one time or another.

> *Don't be judgemental. Moral judgements are oppressive. Morality is a private matter, and as no one is in a position to know what is right for others, so no one has the right to condemn their behaviour. Moral opinions differ, as do lifestyles; we should recognize this and be tolerant. We should live and let live.*

How convincing is this view? Here are a few possible objections to some of these claims.

'Moral opinions differ'

The first thing to question here is whether in fact there is a great deal of disagreement about ethics. One is struck rather by the enormous amount of *agreement* about which people or actions are good and which are bad. After all, there doesn't seem to be much controversy about the respective moral status of Gandhi and Hitler, or about which is better, committing a murder or saving a life. Furthermore, even if such disagreement was the norm, would it follow that no view could be correct? Surely not. There is fierce disagreement about global warming, genetically modified crops and the theory of evolution, but this does not prove that no one is right and no one is wrong about these matters. The same point applies to ethics. Disagreement may be a sign of nothing beyond the fact that people disagree.

'Live and let live'

Anyone who believes this is not avoiding morality; they are committing themselves to an ethical position – albeit a vague one. Advocating universal tolerance, or respect for diversity, is itself a moral stance. Similarly, the demand that we should not be 'judgemental' implies a preference for one kind of behaviour over another; it implies that people who are judgemental are in the wrong while those who avoid judging others are in the right. Thus it is impossible to espouse this point of view without at the same time implicitly betraying it.

'Morality is a private matter'

It is unclear how this could ever be true. Morality, almost by definition, concerns how we treat each other. Moreover, we identify what someone's morality is (1) by what they say, and (2) by what they do. By what they say, people *tell* us what they value – which things matter to them and which things do not. By what they do, people *show* us what they value. In cases where a person's words conflict with their actions most people would regard the actions as the surer guide. But neither is private. It is therefore difficult to imagine what a 'private morality' would look like in practice.

  If someone with a 'private morality' saw a defenceless person being attacked in the street, would it be 'right' for her to intervene if she disapproved? Intervention would obviously involve others, and so would not be a private act. She might do nothing more than voice her disapproval: 'Hey, leave him alone!' But this would still not be a purely private act. Even if she walked on by, silently thinking 'That is wrong', she would still be passing a judgement on another person who is 'out there' in the public world. Perhaps those who say that morality is a private matter just mean that each of us should pass judgement only on our own actions and come up with prescriptions for ourselves alone ('I must not attack defenceless persons'). But why impose these restrictions? Where do they come from? Why do they only apply to me? Surely they apply to me because they would apply to anyone else in the same situation as me. But if this point is conceded it again becomes hard to see how morality could be essentially private.

The view that morality is a private matter perhaps rests on the idea that morality is like taste in some way. Almost everyone accepts that taste is a personal thing. If I like cheese and you do not there is no point in my telling you that you are wrong and that you *ought* to like cheese. And just as there is no sense in arguing about taste, the argument goes, there is no sense in arguing about morality. Background assumptions like this one – often unspoken but nevertheless influencing our opinions – are called presuppositions. A large part of philosophy is about uncovering presuppositions, bringing them into the light in order to examine them to see what they are worth. If the above objections to the 'morality is private' view have any force – and I think they do – this should make us suspicious of the underlying presuppositions concerning the nature of moral judgements. They may not be like judgements of taste at all.

Consider another commonly expressed opinion, similar to the previous one in some ways, but not necessarily open to the same objections

Do (and think) what you like as long as you don't hurt anyone else.

This principle appeals to many of us. It expresses an outlook that is tolerant and liberal, and probably rooted in the belief that individuals should have the freedom to decide their own destiny, that no one has the right to decide it for them. But it is clearly still an ethical standpoint, whether we agree with it or not. A person holding a view like this would almost certainly go on to make further moral judgements; for instance, they would presumably think it is normally wrong to coerce people to do things against their will, and they may be quite willing actively to protect someone from coercion by a third party.

So although we may be able to 'travel light' in terms of settled views about how people should act, it is not easy to shed moral principles altogether. Nothing we have looked at really represents an escape from ethics. If we are involved with other people we are involved practically with moral matters: we make judgements and choose courses of action. Some people do not like what this seems to imply, hence the objection to being 'judgemental' – a word that carries the connotation of standing over other people in a censorious, authoritarian manner. But even a rejection of authoritarianism connects with a moral standpoint, a point of view containing principles that guide our judgements and our actions. And this standpoint necessarily implies a commitment to certain values.

Emotivism

Here is one possible answer to the question of what morality is based on:

> *Moral talk is just the expression of personal feeling. If I say that something is right or wrong I'm just giving vent to my feelings. If I tell you that it's wrong to force someone to do something against their will I'm only doing so because I feel bad about it and want you to feel the same way as well. Choosing the 'right' principles just doesn't come into it, since feelings can't be either right or wrong.*

This view is called **emotivism.** Its central claim is that when we use moral language we are usually just expressing our emotions. For example, I feel disgust at the sight of a strong person bullying someone weaker and I express my aversion through words like 'unjust', 'unfair' or 'wicked'. I may offer arguments as to why you should also condemn the bullying; but no matter how I dress things up in fancy language about good and evil, all I am really doing is trying to get you to feel as I do.

On this view moral judgements are neither true nor false. The statement 'Slavery is unjust' may have the same grammatical form as a statement like 'Grass is green', but this should not mislead us. 'Grass is green' describes the way things are in the world; 'Slavery is unjust' does not. Deep down, it is analogous to utterances like 'Hooray for Rangers!' or 'Liposuction – yuk!' For this reason, critics of emotivism have referred to it derisively as the 'Boo-hurrah!' theory of morality. If emotivism is correct, it seems that what really matters about our moral utterances is not their truth or falsity but how effective they are at triggering feelings similar to our own in our audience. My moral talk is aimed at causing a certain feeling in you by hitting the right emotional buttons; I find your emotional-ethical PIN number and get the required response. On this view, even the most eloquent condemnation of an act of violence is really just an expression of my 'heartfelt' feelings.

It is probably worth acknowledging at the outset that a claim like this cannot be strictly proved or disproved. Ethics is not like mathematics, where we generally expect theorems to be accompanied by rigorous proofs. The emotivist offers an account of what goes on when we make moral judgements. The question we have to ask is not whether emotivism can be proved true or false but whether it gives an adequate picture of moral discourse and moral life.

The emotivist reduces moral talk to expressions of the speaker's feelings, and thus denies that morality has anything to do with truth. The effect of this is to flatten out different claims about right and wrong so that there is nothing to choose between them — torturer and victim may certainly feel differently about their situation, but neither is morally better or worse than the other. We cannot even say

> ### think critically!   Emotive language
>
> Words have the power to suggest much more than their strict dictionary definitions. Associations stick to them obstinately, like fluff to Velcro, evoking feelings and images in the listener or reader. These associations can be charged with positive or negative feeling. Compare 'freedom fighter', 'guerrilla' and 'terrorist'. Any of the three might be used to describe the same sort of person, but with steeply descending degrees of approval. Words with an especially strong emotional charge are called *emotive*; they are beloved by poets, but also by advertisers and politicians. A speech loaded with the right emotive language can carry great persuasive force through the way it makes the recipient feel rather than think. It is thus vital that we keep our critical faculties awake — that we do not assume something has been proved simply because our feelings have been aroused.

that certain feelings are morally better than others. That I have the feelings I have is just a brute fact about me, possibly explainable as the result of various causes acting on me in the course of my life – genetics, conditioning, education, propaganda etc. – so it is pointless to try rationally to criticize or applaud this.

Emotivists thus tend to see ethics in terms of *causes*. They view our moral judgements as expressing our emotions, which are themselves just the effects of various causes. The problem is that emotivism is so much at odds with our experience of what is involved in participating in moral life that it is hard to take it completely seriously. Against it one can argue that at least some of our moral judgements are not just the effect of non-rational causes as they are based on *reasons*. In fact, most of the time when we praise or blame people for their actions we think we can support our judgements in a rational manner. Thus, we have reasons for condemning an act as unfair or for declaring it to be honourable, reasons that are open to discussion and possible disagreement on rational grounds. Emotivism, in effect, tells us that we are deceiving ourselves about this.

The crucial question to answer is whether ethical judgements connect with events and things in the world or just signal our various emotional states. In practice, we usually make a distinction between people who are just expressing (or appearing to express) feelings in emotive language and those who are making a judgement about something that we can assess for ourselves. Indeed, we are often very critical of speakers who try to persuade by means of mere oratory rather than argumentation. Thus, if you think that you make ethical judgements because some things in the world matter to you more than other things, and that it is important to get these judgements right, you are unlikely to be impressed by an emotivist account of what you are doing.

Another problem with emotivism is that does not make clear how feelings relate to moral language. If feeling is all that morality amounts to, we might wonder whether there are particular emotions that we should call 'moral' and, if so, how we would recognize them. Are there just two relevant feelings: approval and disapproval? Or do different moral terms (such as 'unfair', 'virtuous', 'honourable', 'evil') each relate to different feelings (such as resentment, approbation, admiration, hatred)? The alternative seems to be an undifferentiated wash of feelings that, in a way that is unclear to us, metamorphose into 'moral talk'.

One way of thinking about emotion is as something that unites us, that we can share through word, gesture or image. Language certainly plays a big role here: love, grief, joy and so on get communicated. It is a welcome part of our lives. But it may not be what we want when it comes to ethics. Emotions can be contagious, and we can be highly receptive to them in the appropriate circumstances; but this can leave us open to manipulation by emotionally persuasive language and other rhetorical tricks. (Anyone who wants a particularly graphic and sinister example should see a film of one of the huge Nazi party rallies of the 1930s.)

But emotions, as well as uniting us, can also isolate us. If someone feels strongly about something and tries to convince us that we too should feel the same way, we may not want to go along with her. The force with which someone expresses an argument is no real recommendation as to its value. Assuming that the person hasn't simply swept us off our feet with her eloquence and that we are able to keep some kind of independent critical attitude, we will surely feel that we need a good reason to throw in our lot with her. That is the point: good reasons are what proper arguments – as distinct from subliminal advertising, seductive images and emotionally charged ranting – are all about. It is in the world of advertising that the line between the two is most obviously blurred. Everything from cars to political parties can be marketed through images of sex, power and so on – images that seek to associate the product with feelings promoted by the adverts, but that don't really answer the question 'What is this thing that they are trying to sell me *actually like*?'

In the end, the question is not just about whether emotivism is true but also about the possibility that it might *become* true. Emotivists talk in terms of unmasking what we are doing in order to show what is 'really' going on. If we take them at their word and treat all talk of right and wrong as mere emoting, we might end up by creating an emotivist world. In a world in which moral language is essentially manipulative, we might come to see only narrow self-interest in any kind of appeal for help as we calculate what might be in our interests. I have my feelings about what is desirable and you have yours; I will only ally myself to you if you compel me through brainwashing or brute force, or if it serves my interests. Power, self-interest and manipulation become the final realities.

Situation ethics

Can we find a more satisfactory account of moral judgement and its relation to action? Perhaps. We might accept that 'doing the right thing' involves making a judgement at a particular time and place, but reject the idea that this must involve the imposition of standards or rules on the huge variety of events and people that we meet.

> *Every situation is different. You have to respond to each new situation afresh, trying to do what seems to be the right thing according to the new set of circumstances you find yourself in. Life never repeats itself, so why impose an unchanging set of rules on it?*

This is the approach preferred by what is called **situation ethics.** It seems to avoid the dead hand of imposed formulas or conventional codes of behaviour. It also rejects the idea that acting morally is essentially the application of a rule. In this respect it looks plausible, since much of the time that is not what we seem to be doing. We try to 'judge each case on its merits'. But in other respects the view expressed here is questionable. If you think that ethics is about more than just feeling, then presumably you will have reasons for choosing to do one thing rather than another in a given situation. In this, ethical judgements and choices are not so far away from the other kinds of decisions we make. Of course, many of our actions are performed fairly automatically; but in cases where we have to make non-trivial choices we will presumably not act in a purely arbitrary way. Our actions reveal what is important to us in these cases. Even if we seem to be acting completely differently in a new situation to the way we acted before (say, lying in one case, then telling the truth in the next) we will almost always have a reason for acting differently that is discoverable on reflection.

If 'situation ethics' is still supposed to be ethics in any recognizable sense, the person claiming to practise it can be asked what it is about the new situation that calls for a new response. We are all used to the idea that although it is wrong to lie, there may be some circumstances in which lying may be acceptable (to spare someone's feelings, for example) but that does not mean we have given up acting on any principle whatsoever. It just means that the principles and values that underlie our actions get applied in ways that seem appropriate to the new situation. So we will at least be aiming at an underlying consistency in our responses to new situations, even though we are not always consciously applying a rule.

Consider how we respond to concrete moral dilemmas where we are faced with a choice of two evils — for example, we must decide whether to tell the truth to someone and cause them pain or instead to lie and spare them this suffering. It seems that we have a set of basic assumptions that inform what we do on a day-to-day basis: for example, that it is generally wrong to lie, that it is wrong to cause people unnecessary pain, that suffering is generally a bad thing, and so on. The fact that we may not make these explicit to ourselves does not mean they are not there. Moreover, these assumptions can often be articulated in the form of general principles. This is an important point, because it means that the business of ethics has something about it that is *rational.* We can reflect on the reasons for our actions. We may even be able to criticize, modify and improve our moral opinions and attitudes, a possibility that the emotivist and situationist both seem to exclude.

However, a basic problem (or set of problems) that any critical reflection on our moral values and principles has to confront concerns their origin. Where do they come from? Why do I have these values rather than some others? Do the views I hold merely reflect the particular culture and historical period to which I belong? If so, how can we justify saying that one moral code is more correct than another, when so much apparently comes down to the accident of where and when one was born? This is the problem of ethical relativism.

Ethical relativism

Hardly anyone would dispute that our beliefs, including our moral values, to some extent reflect the society to which we belong. But for ethical relativists, this idea is only a starting point. Relativists do not simply call attention to the fact that different cultures often espouse different moral codes. They also deny that any one culture can be said to be right or superior in its values, beliefs or practices compared to any other. (The contrary view holds that there are standards of right and wrong that apply across cultures and periods in history. This view goes by a variety of labels, the most common being 'ethical objectivism', 'ethical absolutism' and 'ethical universalism'.) There are different varieties of **ethical relativism**, of varying degrees of subtlety and sophistication. A very popular version of it continues the argument in the following way.

> *'Right' and 'wrong' can only mean right and wrong in a particular culture. It is totally misguided to use the standards of one culture (invariably one's own) to pass a moral judgement on an action performed within the context of a different culture. As no one can be said to be right or wrong in a dispute like this, it's better simply to say 'You're right from your side and I'm right from mine'. Respect the diversity of cultures. No one is right, so live and let live.*

This is a view that many people today find both plausible and appealing. It is plausible just because of the diversity of codes and practice found among different societies. In some cultures, for instance, sex outside marriage is absolutely taboo; in others it is permissible within prescribed limits. For long periods of time, even in supposedly 'enlightened' places, slavery was accepted; nowadays we view it as morally loathsome. A similar diversity of opinion could be found on many other moral issues: abortion, infanticide, euthanasia, capital punishment, corporal punishment, eating meat, usury, homosexuality, polygamy, to name just a few. How plausible is it to suppose that, in spite of this diversity, there is a single moral code that is binding on all people, no matter which culture they belong to?

Ethical relativism is also appealing, at least in part, because it expresses a rejection of arrogant ethnocentrism. For example, the Europeans of the recent past often acted as if their way of doing and seeing things was the only correct way.

Other cultures were viewed as 'primitive' or 'godless' – or at any rate inferior. If they did things differently, that just meant they were wrong; they had little to teach the more 'advanced' societies and much to learn from them. This kind of confidence in the superiority of one culture's beliefs and practices is now much less common. There is a greater humility about these matters, at least in some quarters. But we should remind ourselves that there is a big difference between a willingness to accept that no one group *may be* right and the claim that no one *can be* right. We should also be aware of the radical nature of the claims of the thoroughgoing relativist, who holds that outside of the practices of a particular cultural group, ethical judgement has no application. This view implies that you cannot judge the practices of any culture because there is no overarching ethical code above or between cultures that provides you with the necessary criteria – a position that generates some serious problems. Let us first look at the ideal of tolerance that many relativists seem to be arguing for.

Ethical relativists advocate that we should adopt a tolerant attitude when we encounter different cultures who have differing, even contradictory, approaches to ethics. Let us respect them all, they say. We have already noted a couple of problems with this 'live and let live' attitude. First of all, it is not actually entailed by the existence of ethical diversity; just because there is more than one view about what is morally right it does not follow that all views on the subject must be equally correct. Diversity does not by itself entail relativity. Second, even if one accepts that no one moral code is correct, what follows from this? Immorality? Indifference to morality? Indifference to all moralities but our own? Self-conscious ethnocentrism? It is not at all clear what the central relativist thesis entails. Third, if we maintain that we should respect all moral codes equally and not judge cultures by moral standards that the people in that culture do not accept, then we cannot consistently preach universal tolerance, or respect for cultural diversity, or celebration of difference, or what have you. These ideas express particular ethical values, espoused in some cultures but not in others. The ethical relativist cannot float above the different cultures, telling societies how they should treat one another while at the same time denying there are any transcultural moral values.

Take a look at the following list. Imagine the implications of holding a thoroughgoing relativist or absolutist position on all of them.

1. Aztec ritual slaughter of prisoners by ripping hearts out of live bodies.
2. Nineteenth-century imperialism.
3. Equality between women and men.
4. Nazi policies towards the Jews.
5. Suttee, the Hindu custom of putting the widow on the funeral pyre with her dead husband, practised in some parts of India until fairly recently.
6. The suppression of suttee by the British.
7. Free speech.

8. The conquest and settlement of America by Europeans.
9. The conquest and settlement of Britain by the English.

The purpose of the list is to try to make us confront the full implications of the relativist position. We must be clear that we may not sneak in our values by the back door. Take the case of number 5. It won't do to say that you are happy to be a relativist about this if the woman consents to being incinerated with her dead husband, but not if she is coerced. Why should her wishes count? If you think they must, then you appear to be applying number 3 – the principle that men and women are equal – in an absolutist way. Now consider number 6. Were the British right to suppress suttee? Perhaps you think that they should not have been in India in the first place, in which case it looks as if you are viewing number 2 in a non-relativist way. But since they were there, would it have been right for them to adopt a policy of 'live and let die' to suttee, even if the widows asked them not to?

We should also remind ourselves that a modern society is rarely homogeneous and may well have deep divisions within it regarding questions about right and wrong. Think of the controversy over abortion in the USA, for instance, or the debate about divorce in Ireland. Within any large society there are usually numerous subcultures, often characterized by different moral outlooks – religious fundamentalists, technocrats, environmentalists, academic specialists, specific ethnic groups, and so on. And hardly any societies are sealed off in their own little worlds; they trade, fight, form alliances and influence each other most of the time. It is thus misleading to picture each culture (or subculture) as having an entirely separate set of beliefs and going its own sweet way. Sometimes it is hard to know where one culture ends and another begins. All these considerations make it difficult to say to the members of any society, including one's own: 'Your moral code applies only to you; you may not apply it to other societies'.

In addition to all the foregoing difficulties, relativism runs up against a further objection. If words like 'good' or 'bad' as I use them simply mean whatever my culture says is good or bad, then when I object to something generally held to be morally acceptable in my culture I must be wrong, for the only guide to what is good and bad or right and wrong is the moral outlook that prevails within my culture. But this would rule out the possibility of society making moral progress and would make all attempts at moral reform pointless. If what is right is determined by what most people currently think is right, then the idea of trying to make our society better makes no sense. For that matter, the idea of our society becoming morally worse would make no sense either.

But hardly anyone would accept these conclusions. Anyone, relativists included, who has ever voted in an election, signed a petition, written to their political representatives or taken part in a demonstration has indicated that they believe there can be changes for the better and changes for the worse. And some of our most important moral heroes are people who seemed at first to be heretics because they did not share commonly held views on what is right: people like Jesus,

Socrates, Gandhi, the abolitionists and the suffragettes. What would ethical relativists of the kind we have been considering make of the movement to abolish slavery, or the more recent civil rights and feminist movements? An inability to make sense of the notion of moral progress is surely a serious drawback to any ethical theory.

In spite of objections like these, we may feel that ethical relativism embodies an insight, however confused, that cannot be so easily disposed of by a demonstration of the incoherencies and consequences of some of its more vulgar versions. Part of its attraction may lie in the sheer incredulity that people feel when confronted by absolutism. It seems unlikely, to put it mildly, that a moral code with its objective criteria of right and wrong could exist somehow 'out there', applicable to all cultures and periods. Many of us would balk at the idea that moral norms are objective in this sense – part of the furniture of the universe, as it were, and independently 'there' whatever we happen to think about the matter. And if we cannot accept this view of morality we may feel the attraction of relativism.

There seem to be two distinct but interrelated issues that call for further consideration.

- The problem of the origin and basis of moral codes.
- The problem of applying moral norms across cultures and periods.
  Let us examine these in more detail.

Where do moral codes come from?

Ethical relativism is in part a reaction to the many different conclusions people seem to have reached about morality. If we look back in history we see beliefs about right and wrong that look as if they are rooted in a way of life formed by historical forces, environment, war, accident etc. These ways of life seem to determine what will count as 'good' for the people that live them. So the people in a given culture will approve or disapprove of eating pork or eating people for reasons that have to do with their shared experience, not the intrinsic 'rightness' or 'wrongness' of these practices. Of course, they may believe that they have adopted the one right way of doing things, but this need not convince an outsider. And if that outsider is aware of a plurality of cultures, each with its own codes, she may come to believe that one's moral values depend on one's way of life, rather than the other way round. 'Eating people is wrong' is the ethic of my culture because we don't eat people here, and not vice versa.

This perspective has some plausibility. Yet we could object that moral codes are not as different from each other as the relativist supposes. What cultures share is more significant than what divides them. On this view, the 'Western' businessman, the Ancient Greek and the Aztec priest have, at bottom, the same underlying concerns and needs – they are all human, so they share the human condition. The same sorts of things are important to all of them: for instance, securing the means of life; establishing and enjoying meaningful relationships; raising children; expressing themselves through work and play. And perhaps included in this list of universal concerns is the desire to understand and communicate to others the fundamentals of morality. Thus the variations, or many of them at least, are on the surface and only serve to mask an underlying universality to ethics. However, a relativist might respond in the following way:

> *There are very great actual differences between cultures, and these cannot be explained away as surface phenomena. And even if all humans are faced by certain very basic questions posed by a common biology and shared earth, they keep coming up with very different answers. They share the earth, but inhabit different worlds. You cannot strip away culture in order to get at a more basic humanness that would be of any use in trying to establish a common moral code; what you uncovered would be just too basic. All the interesting issues regarding moral values occur at the level of culture, which is where the big differences are, and where no single 'right' answer can be found.*

Those who take this view, if they are consistent, will have to apply it to their own moral beliefs, regarding them as every bit as culture dependent as any others. From this perspective, absolutist claims seem untenable, even arrogant, and relativism still appears to be the more plausible position.

To whom do moral norms apply?

The issue seems clear enough. If the only basis for morality is history and culture, it is hard to see how any one moral code could be 'better' than another. While the practices and beliefs of a culture may inspire admiration or aversion in an outsider, they cannot be subject to a rational appraisal. I may be appalled that culture X practises polygamy, infanticide or female circumcision, but that is just because I happen to be from culture Y. Perhaps those who belong to culture X would be equally revolted by some of the things we do (such as imprisoning people for taking drugs or allowing extramarital sex), or by some of the things we accept (like factory farming). And if I had been raised in culture X my views would be very different from what they are. There are no criteria that could be applied to different cultures in order to see how they measure up to some absolute standard of right and wrong.

The more thoughtful relativist, asked to account for what we think of as moral progress, will accept that change does occur in a culture, but will point out that heretics/reformers usually make their case against the way their society does things by appealing to ideas that are already present in that society. The reformer says something like: 'We say we believe in this, but why don't we practise it?' or 'We ought to extend this belief to cover this other area too.' Think again of campaigns to abolish slavery and to establish equal rights for men and women. They had a measure of success precisely because people could connect what the reformers were saying to the core beliefs already held in that culture (in this case, beliefs about equal treatment that originated in the view that all human beings are God's children). Indeed, if such a connection could not have been made it is hard to see how the question of reform could have come up in the first place.

Of course, all of these considerations only apply within a culture; other cultures with other core beliefs may not make these connections at all. Moreover, ethical relativists still have to reject any objectivist or absolutist concept of moral progress, since there is no independent standard that one could use to show that the new situation is objectively morally better. All they can say is that practices that seemed acceptable within a given culture at a certain time come to appear unacceptable at a later date (and vice versa).

As long as relativists avoid making non-relativist claims that their theory does not allow, they can perhaps avoid obvious inconsistency and even put forward a plausible case. Yet there remain some considerations that may lead us to challenge the relativist account of what morality amounts to without automatically embracing the counter-intuitive absolutist position that moral truth somehow hangs in the air, quite apart from what anyone thinks or how anyone lives. Let us look again at the story we have just given about how someone might come to embrace relativism.

An observer looks at the plurality of moral codes and concludes that as morality is subject to great variation between cultures, there can be no possibility of choosing between them objectively. But why not? True, people and cultures differ; but must this mean that no choices can be made between them, or that no culture can judge any other? It is actually very hard to witness some practices and not make moral judgements about them — consider apartheid as practised in South Africa until recently.

The relativist looks like someone who has suffered a debilitating loss of confidence in the truth of her ethical standpoint, perhaps coming to view it as mere prejudice, the effect of a conditioning that has started to wear off; certainly, she has become acutely aware of how difficult it is to offer a non-relative justification of one's views. This takes us to the heart of the matter. The relativist's loss of confidence in her 'local' moral values is understandable, but that does not necessarily mean it is justified. One response to it that might help to restore some of that lost confidence would be to make a similar point to one discussed when we looked at emotivism. We saw there that an alternative to the 'morality as feeling' approach might be to direct our attention not to the supposed hidden causes of moral judgements but, rather, to their *objects*. This means focusing not on the feeling 'behind' a judgement (rage, disgust, delight . . .) but on the things that the judgements are about (torture, racism, kindness . . .). It means asking whether our judgements are justified, and trying to form judgements that make sense, that have good reasons behind them, that reflect our principles, and so on.

If we try this approach on the relativist, we are arguing, in effect, that recognizing that we see things from a particular cultural standpoint need not cripple our capacity to make moral judgements. This involves a certain appeal to reason, to the idea that we can rise above the things that have helped to shape our perspective and form our own rational judgement. According to this view, the person who says 'torture is wrong' can back up her claim with reasons. The case she makes may be more or less convincing, but it is not just arbitrary or an expression of purely personal taste. And although it is bound to be affected by her upbringing and cultural traditions, these are also open to examination.

This is an important claim. We are capable of bringing even our cultural background before the court of critical scrutiny, of reflecting back on what has influenced us in a kind of stocktaking exercise that may lead us to reject 'the way we have always done things here'. Perhaps we can never be absolutely sure that our views are right; indeed, we may take the view that the goal of correct moral judgement is an ideal that can never be finally attained, but can usefully be aimed at. Our judgements will thus have to be provisional in the sense that they are always open to criticism. Implicit in all this is the notion of a dialogue with others governed by shared norms and a willingness to engage in that dialogue is what we may call the rational attitude.

This is all very well, our observer tempted by relativism might retort, but you have not really answered the question: What counts as a good reason? The answer to that question may not be the same in different cultures. For example, in some places, the fact that a practice accords with tradition is considered a good reason for continuing it; in other places it may be sufficient that one is following the prescriptions laid down by a sacred text or by an authority figure. Decisions can be made on the basis of dreams, the interpretation of dreams by a seer, personal revelation, moral intuition or majority opinion. Can we dismiss all such ways of arriving at or justifying a moral decision as 'irrational'? Furthermore, isn't there something a bit unreal about the idea of a pure 'appeal to reason'? Ethical disputes are not settled by the methods used in debating societies; people will differ — sometimes sharply, even violently — over what counts as persuasive, because different things matter to them. That is usually what we mean when we say that people have different values.

This is a good point, and one that critics of relativism should accept. They should thus avoid conceiving of ethical disputes too abstractly and be willing to flesh out their idea that such disputes take place against the background of a shared world and a common humanity living in it. The argument might go something like this:

> Values don't just float around, unconnected to how we think the world is. We believe that certain actions are acceptable or not in a world that shows up for us in a certain way. Our values are intimately

connected to the way we understand the world and to the things we think are significant about it. But this significance is not a matter of whim: I don't just 'happen to disagree' with the Nazis. If I were to meet a sincere Nazi, my rejection of his or her values is part and parcel of my view that beliefs about the superiority of the Aryan race, the innate wickedness of the Jews, the all-seeingness of Adolph Hitler etc., are factually incorrect as well as morally detestable. Values are not an afterthought, still less an optional extra. What we think of as good and what we think of as true-about-the-world are inextricably interwoven. Questioning someone's ethics means questioning their beliefs about the world.

How convincing you find this argument will depend, at least in part, on how much you think that conflicting values can be resolved by reason, by an appeal to a shared world. To go back to the question of what counts as a good reason, perhaps some cultures come up with different answers simply because different things are important to them. Perhaps the way they understand the world differs so radically as to make the sort of argument in the last paragraph impossible. How can you get a dialogue started if both parties cannot even agree on how to describe an action or a situation, or on what would count as evidence, or on whether dialogue is possible? Perhaps different people sometimes understand the world in such fundamentally different ways that some ethical codes just can't be compared to others at all: they just reflect those very different understandings. If this is true, then a degree of mutual incomprehension may be inevitable and insurmountable.

Yet if we don't live in a shared world we do share the same crowded planet and, as we have already noted, we do not have the option of making no judgements at all. Even if ethics are invented by humans, and even if specific moral codes reflect the culture and the conditions that create them, that does not make morality something we can dispense with. Nor will the difficult problem of how to live together and make sense of different value systems go away. No one acts as if nothing is better than anything else: the choice seems to be between dialogue and conflict.

Facts and values

What makes relativism so plausible, and what makes the questions it raises so difficult to deal with, is really something very simple: value judgements can't be proved true or false. I can prove that grass is green or that the earth is round. But it's quite impossible to prove that racism is bad or that murder is wrong.

There does seem to be something peculiar about value judgements. Unlike most other judgements we make, they do not appear to be based on anything. Put simply, on the one side we have the world of facts – the things our five senses tune into, that scientists can investigate, that we can be right or wrong about: for example, it is raining; there is a tree in the garden; Paris is the capital of France. On the other side we have the realm of values – what we are talking about or invoking when we say that things are good, bad, right, wrong, beautiful, ugly and so on. The difficulty lies in relating one to the other, in grasping the connection – if there is one – between *describing* how the world is and *prescribing* what people ought to think or do. Where (if anywhere) do values fit into the furniture of the universe? And how can factual claims provide logical support for value judgements? These problems all cluster around what is often referred to as the **fact–value gap**.

All the problems we have examined so far can be seen to turn on the central issue of the status of our value judgements. Emotivism and relativism are both attempts to explain how our values fit into the world, the former basing them on our feelings and the latter on our culture. Both are examples of **reductionism**. Reductionists define one thing in terms of some other, more basic phenomenon. They claim that the thing being defined (V) is 'nothing but' this other, more basic thing (F). Emotivism, for instance, says that moral utterances are 'really' just an expression of our feelings. Reductionists boil values down to certain facts and in the process the values usually evaporate away: the fact (F) is what the value (V) 'really' amounts to. So this would be one solution to the problem posed by the fact–value gap: collapse the values back into the facts.

An alternative to reducing values to facts is to see whether the facts can somehow *imply* certain values. Maybe there are 'moral facts', in the sense that a complete description of the world would include a description of the moral qualities of people, actions and situations. If so, then the way the world is obliges us to adopt certain values and perform certain actions. This sort of view is called **ethical naturalism**. An obvious problem with it is that people's values differ, sometimes very markedly, even in cases where there is no dispute about the facts.

Consider the controversy over assisted suicide. The facts are rarely in dispute. Suppose that John Doe is 67; he has been diagnosed as having liver cancer by three specialists; each of them predicts he will probably die within six months; he says that the pain and nausea he is experiencing prevent him from enjoying life any more; he has stated orally and in writing that he would like a doctor to give him a lethal injection in order to put him out of his misery; there is no reason to suppose he is anything other than fully rational and perfectly sincere. Some people believe that in these circumstances the right thing to do is to respect the person's wishes. Others think that assisted suicide is fundamentally immoral. Of course, the dispute could conceivably be factual. The opponents of assisted suicide might base their opposition on the assumption that if it is allowed in any circumstances, this will have the long-term effect of devaluing human life in our culture. In that case, the whole controversy could come down to the question of whether or not this assumption is factually correct. In some cases, though, the dispute is clearly not

think
critically!

The 'is—ought' problem

Consider this argument (A):

> Stealing is illegal.
> According to the law, pirating software is a form of stealing.
> Therefore pirating software is illegal.

The argument is clearly valid — the conclusion follows from the premises. But notice, the premises and the conclusion are all statements of a similar type; they are all *factual* claims simply stating that something *is* the case. Now consider another argument (B):

> Stealing is illegal.
> According to the law, pirating software is a form of stealing.
> Therefore one ought not to pirate software.

This argument is invalid. I can, without contradicting myself, admit that the premises are true yet still reject the conclusion. I may, for instance, believe that civil disobedience is justified in this case.

The root of the invalidity in (B) is the logical difference between 'is' and 'ought'. The premises are both 'is' statements; the conclusion is an 'ought' statement. In general, the conclusion of a valid deductive argument cannot introduce new claims that are not implicit in the premises. But the introduction of an 'ought' into the conclusion of argument (B) does just this, which is what makes the argument invalid. To make the inference valid we need to introduce an 'ought' claim into the premises. For instance (C):

> Stealing is illegal.
> According to the law, pirating software is a form of stealing.
> One ought not to do what is illegal
> Therefore, one ought not to pirate software.

This is valid (with the conclusion of (A) — pirating software is illegal — as an unstated intermediary step). But the problem now for anyone wishing to prove the truth of the conclusion in this way is to prove the truth of the premise 'One ought not to do what is illegal'.

A similar point applies to all attempts to derive evaluative or normative conclusions from purely descriptive premises. For example, the fact that a man has killed dozens of innocent people for his own sadistic pleasure does not *logically* entail the conclusion that he is morally bad. To derive this conclusion validly one must add a further premise: 'Someone who kills innocent people for their own pleasure is morally bad'. The evaluative conclusion may now be derived, but only because the premises of the argument now contain a value judgement.

about the facts but about basic values. Some people think assisted suicide is just fundamentally unethical; others think it is fundamentally unethical to let people suffer unnecessarily against their will. When the dispute is of this sort, digging up extra facts will not help to resolve it.

The problem of the fact–value gap has also been described as the problem of deriving an 'ought' from an 'is' (see box on previous page). I am faced by a situation that can be described in purely factual terms. Can I discover what I should do just by looking at the facts? Some philosophers have argued that it is indeed possible to derive an 'ought' from an 'is'. The American philosopher John Searle is the author of a well-known attempt to do this. Searle concentrates on the example of promising. In his view, if I utter words such as 'I promise to . . .', then I take on the obligation of doing what I promised. It is now my duty to fulfil my promise to you, so I ought to do whatever I promised to do. From the 'brute fact' that I spoke some words it follows that I ought to do something.

Is this case, has an 'ought' been validly derived from an 'is'? A problem with Searle's argument is that when I made the promise I was actually entering into the social practice of promising, whose main rule is that one ought to keep one's promises. Entering into this practice is like agreeing to play a game. So by entering I have agreed to play by the rules, which means that I have accepted an 'ought' at the very start. There is a lot more than just brute facts (the sounds of my words) involved when I utter words like 'I promise to . . .' For this reason, Searle's argument is unpersuasive. It does not really derive an 'ought' from an 'is'; instead, it derives an 'ought' from a description of a situation that already implicitly contains a normative dimension.

All attempts to derive an 'ought' from an 'is' face the same challenge: to describe a situation in which the facts somehow logically dictate what a person is obliged to do. But every attempt to do this runs up against the same problem – it always makes sense to ask why one should not act otherwise. For example, if you tell me that I should not drop litter, I can ask why not. If you say that litter spoils the appearance of the street, I can ask why I should care about that. If you say that it detracts from other people's enjoyment, I can ask why that should matter to me. Ultimately, you may be led to say something like 'You should care about other people because that is part of being a good person' or 'You should care about the environment because we all have a basic duty to do so.' But I can still respond with questions like 'Why should I try to be a good person?' or 'Why should I do my duty?' (In the end, the question at issue here is perhaps the most fundamental question in ethics: Why be moral? We shall return to this issue later.)

It is hard to see how ethical naturalists can meet this kind of 'open question' argument. They want to say that at some point the facts 'speak for themselves'; it is just obvious, they claim, that some things are good or that some actions ought to be performed. But the critic of ethical naturalism denies that the facts ever speak for themselves. It is we who decide which facts shall count decisively with us. Thus our judgements about ethics (and about politics and art) can never be about brute facts alone. They contain value judgements, and these can never be wholly reduced to, nor validly derived from, descriptions that are purely factual.

Prescribing

If ethical naturalism is not able to bridge the fact–value gap, then the status of our ethical judgements is still questionable. We still have to take seriously the possibility that they have no objective validity and are more like expressions of personal preference or taste than rationally grounded, informed judgements. Let us therefore approach these questions from the 'other side' of the fact–value gap, and see whether it is possible to recognize anything distinctive about ethical language. To do this, we need to see how it fits into a more general picture of how we use words.

If I say 'This is good' I seem to be describing something. And in many cases I can support my judgement with reasons. For example, if I say that my CD player is good, and you ask me for my reasons, I can give them: it produces clear sound, is easy to operate, looks stylish, and so on. In other words, it is a good instance of a certain kind of thing: it does those things that CD players are supposed to do well and thus satisfies certain criteria sufficiently for me to describe it as a good CD player.

Perhaps if I describe something as 'good' in the moral sense we can offer a similar analysis. Suppose I see a friend sacrifice his own pleasure in order to spend time comforting someone in need, and I describe his action as morally good. Asked why, I point out that his action was selfless, that it showed a sympathetic understanding of another's needs, and so on. For some ethical naturalists, nothing more needs to be said: these facts 'speak for themselves'. But this does not seem right. For one thing, regarding 'This is good' as a sort of shorthand for 'This has qualities x, y and z' runs up against the problem of the open-question argument. It is always reasonable to ask: 'But are qualities x, y and z *really* good?' If 'good' meant nothing more than 'has qualities x, y and z', this question would make no sense. Secondly, if I say an act is 'good' in the ethical sense, I am surely doing more than saying it has certain characteristics: I am also *commending* it. The question is: What am I doing when I express commendation?

Commending is related to choosing. It implies an attitude on the part of the speaker. It would be decidedly odd for someone to say 'That is morally good' and then add 'but I am absolutely indifferent to it'. Moral language is wrapped up in what we care about, reject, admire, despise, wish to become, and so on. When we commend an act as 'good', we are implicitly selecting that act as good for us to do – and good for others to do as well. So we can be said to be *prescribing* that act, and this involves not so much a description as an *imperative* or command. If I say that keeping promises is right, I am effectively telling you to keep your promises.

It may well be true that when we say something is 'good' or 'right' we are implicitly telling people how to act. But that just says something

*about the nature of moral language. It doesn't actually tell us anything
about what we ought to do. This is the central question of ethics, but
so far none of the theories considered — situation ethics, emotivism,
relativism and naturalism — have been able to address this issue
satisfactorily. How does recognizing that moral language is
prescriptive help?*

When we say that moral judgements are prescriptive, we are not saying anything
about their content. Their content can vary enormously: 'Keep your promises!'
'Avenge any harm done to you!' 'Do not resist evil!' These commands obviously
express very different moral outlooks, but they all have at least one thing in
common: they are all prescriptions. This fact concerns not their content but their
form. However, if all moral judgements have a common form, this fact may itself
have moral significance. Whether it does — whether or not the 'form' of moral
claims has implications as to what their content should be — is a difficult question.
But many ethical theorists have argued that this is indeed the case. One of the first
thinkers to advance something like this position was Immanuel Kant (1724–1804;
see the box in the Metaphysics chapter). His account of how we determine what we
ought to do remains one of the most stimulating and influential ethical theories
ever developed. Although we cannot here examine Kant's entire theory, we can
look at certain key ideas within it that may help us gain further insight into the
issues we have been discussing.

The Kantian approach: universalizability

We have seen that our use of moral language is very often not merely descriptive
but also prescriptive. When we use moral terms we are often, explicitly or
implicitly, issuing commands. Kant recognized this but made an important
distinction between two kinds of command. Some are what he calls **hypothetical
imperatives**: these tell someone what they must do in order to achieve some end.
For example, I can tell you how to get somewhere ('Catch the number 57 bus'), or
I may tell you which CD player to buy ('Get this make — it's great value for
money!'). Imperatives like this all say something like: 'If you want x, do y'; 'If you
want to go to the art gallery, catch the number 57 bus'; 'If you want a good
bargain, buy this piece of equipment.'

Now, it might be possible to understand moral imperatives as being of this form.
It is perfectly possible to say 'Keep your promises, because if you don't no one will
trust you and you won't like that', or 'Help people in need because then they will
be more likely to help you in the future.' But a moral command can also be
understood in a different way, as what Kant calls a **categorical imperative**. This
kind of command has the form: 'Do *x*!' It does not tell you to do something for the
sake of something else or in order to achieve some goal. Instead, it tells you that

you have an absolute and unconditional duty to act in a certain way (or to avoid acting in a certain way). It tells you to be honest not so that you will be respected or successful in business but simply because you *ought* to be honest. This is an approach that sees value judgements not as calculations based on facts, but as starting points of supreme importance for us.

Having made the distinction between hypothetical and categorical imperatives, Kant proceeds to argue that all moral imperatives ultimately boil down to one central command of morality, which he calls *the* categorical imperative. This is the fundamental moral principle from which, he claims, all more specific moral rules can be derived. This principle has also been called the 'universalizability' principle. Let us see what it involves.

If someone is really acting ethically, we assume they are acting 'on principle'; we do not expect to find that they are making up special rules for themselves. And if they pass judgement on others we do not expect them to be doing so on the basis of rules that do not also apply to themselves.

While it is obviously true that we are all different, and have to deal with different situations, most people do demand equal consideration. Take the example of housework. Most of us now think that women should not be left to do the bulk of the household chores just because they are women. This is a claim about fairness, a demand that the same considerations apply to different people, other things being equal. Of course, one can object that other things are never equal. Circumstances differ, and a person trying to act according to some principle certainly has to take account of real differences of circumstance. For example, the principle that each member of a household should make a fair contribution to the upkeep of the home will have to be applied in a way that takes into account the age of the person, their capabilities, their responsibilities outside the home, and so on. But even so, the circumstances are never so different that no principles apply. This is recognized in the legal system; the circumstances of two cases are never identical, but if they were held to differ completely the courts would never be able to apply any laws.

The categorical imperative

The idea that our principles be universalizable follows fairly naturally from these considerations. A genuinely moral principle must be capable of being applied consistently. Specific imperatives may only apply to me or to you in a particular situation: 'Open the door!' 'Throw that ball!' But a genuinely moral imperative *applies to anyone in a similar situation*; it must therefore always be based on a universal principle. 'Keep your promises' has to apply to *all of us*, including myself. Kant expressed this as the requirement that *you should always act so that the principle behind your action could be willed as a universal law.* He calls this *the* categorical imperative, the fundamental principle of morality. What does it mean?

Suppose that I am thinking of breaking a promise because it is no longer convenient for me to keep it. I said I would pay you back the money I owed you before the end of the week, but I wanted to take advantage of a one-day sale in a shoe shop, so I spent the money on a new pair of trainers. What is the principle I am acting on here? Presumably it is something like: 'I will break my promises when keeping them would deprive me of something I want.'

Now, can I sincerely wish that everyone acted on this principle? It seems not. If it became a universal principle, a maxim that everyone followed, the whole institution of promising would break down. Nobody could trust anyone to keep promises, so nobody would ever bother to make a promise. (Notice that breaking promises, like lying or stealing, is parasitic on its opposite; it can only occur as an exception to the rule.) Thus I cannot will the principle consistently. When I break my promise I am, in effect, wanting everyone else to follow one principle ('Keep your promises') while allowing myself to follow another principle. In making an exception of myself I am being inconsistent. I am thus acting on a principle that cannot be universalized, and this indicates that I am acting unethically.

The categorical imperative expresses an enormous respect for human beings as rational agents, creatures endowed with the capacity to act on principle. Indeed, for Kant it is the principle underlying one's action that is the distinguishing mark of moral action, not the particular goal one aims at. Kant emphasizes this respect for agents in another version of the categorical imperative: *Always treat people as an end in themselves, never merely as a means to an end.* This means that we should not use other people as a way of getting what we want. They, like ourselves, are rational agents, and the same duties and demands apply to them as much as to us. Interestingly, Kant claims that the two versions of the categorical imperative – the 'universalizability principle' and the 'ends principle' – really say the same thing. This claim is certainly intriguing, but it is far from obvious, and generations of scholars have puzzled over the reasons behind it.

Problems with Kantian ethics

The idea of the categorical imperative seems to chime with traditionally accepted notions of right behaviour in many parts of the world. The so-called 'Golden Rule' of the Christian tradition says 'Do unto others as you would have others do unto you.' The same rule appears in the Analects of Confucius, and variations on it can be found in the scriptures of Judaism, Islam, Hinduism, Buddhism and Taoism. However, in its religious form the rule seems to involve both an imaginative effort to enlarge our sympathies (putting oneself in another's place), and a demand for equal treatment. Kant's categorical imperative, on the other hand, seems only to embody the latter requirement, being based on our capacity to reason. This may be a strength. If we relied entirely on our imaginations and sympathies, ethics might be even more patchily applied than at present. But the Kantian approach, with its very heavy emphasis on always acting rationally, may lead us to underestimate the importance of sympathy (feeling for another), empathy (feeling with another), compassion (suffering with another) and a whole range of other feelings that many regard as in some sense vital to morality. Emotivism views morality as based entirely on emotion; with Kant, we are in danger of going to the other extreme and allowing emotion to play no part at all in our moral lives.

> *All this talk about acting on principle is all very well; but aren't we neglecting one very obvious and important thing — namely, the* consequences *of what we do? Surely, consequences must count for something. In fact, why not say that the right action is the one that produces the best consequences?*

This observation raises another very serious problem for the Kantian approach to ethics, which defines morality in terms of one's duties and obligations. Kant holds that what decides whether or not an action is morally correct is its 'form': does it accord with or contradict some general principle? This approach to ethics is called **deontological**. It has many strengths, as we have seen; for instance, it captures the idea that moral principles must apply universally and impartially. But it also has a number of weaknesses, and perhaps the most serious weakness is the way it tends to discount the importance of consequences when evaluating actions.

The lack of consideration for consequences can be seen as an aspect of a more general problem. Kant's notion of the categorical imperative is rather formal and empty. We are told the *form* of our duty: namely, to act in accordance with the categorical imperative. But we need a clearer idea of the *content* of morality, of what our duty actually is. The principle of universalizability is a framework that only tells us what shape a moral judgement must take; it offers us little help in coming to a decision about what the content should be. What should we regard as a duty? When there is a conflict of duties, which should we choose? Suppose, for instance, that the only way I can protect an innocent person from harm is by telling a lie. Which imperative should I obey: the command not to tell lies, or the command to protect the innocent?

The abstract nature of the categorical imperative seems to leave us with imperatives that command us without making it clear exactly why we ought to obey them. Cut off from all considerations of the actual society we live in (the facts), we lose the sense of what morality is for. We want some indication of the ends to be willed, and what it is reasonable to will. This implies a more concrete idea of the Good that we are supposed to actualize in our society. Kant leaves us duties that we perform because they must be performed, like mountain climbers scaling a mountain 'because it's there'. We want more information about the way ethics relates to the lives that we actually live. In particular, we want to know what the *point* of morality is. Is moral action intrinsically valuable, with no point to it beyond itself? Or does the point of moral action lie beyond itself, perhaps in the probable consequences of the action? One ethical theory that believes it has a plausible answer to these questions, an answer that also recognizes the importance of consequences in a way that Kant's theory does not, is utilitarianism.

Utilitarianism: maximizing happiness

Utilitarianism is a form of ethical naturalism. Ethical naturalists, as we saw earlier, believe that we should ground our ethics in the ordinary ('natural') features of the world. Utilitarians are naturalists because they want to look at the facts of our lives in order to determine what is the right thing to do. Utilitarianism is also a form of **consequentialism**, which means it holds that the moral worth of an action is determined by its consequences. In its simplest form, utilitarianism says that if you have a choice between two courses of action, you should follow the one you think is most likely to bring about the greater good overall. This formula is still rather vague, of course; we need to know what constitutes the best consequences or the 'greater good'. Utilitarians have a straightforward answer to this question: they say that what is ultimately good is pleasure or happiness. These things are ultimate goods in the sense that we value them for their own sake, not merely as means to something else. It makes sense to ask someone why they want money, or why they want to learn the piano, or why they want to climb mountains. But it does not make much sense to ask a person why they want to experience pleasure, or why they want to be happy. What can they say in response, other than that being happy is better than being miserable?

Utilitarianism gets its name from the word 'utility', which in this context *means* pleasure or happiness. The terms 'pleasure' and 'happiness' do not mean exactly the same thing, of course. We think of pleasures as relatively short-lived experiences, and we tend to associate pleasurable feelings with specific activities such as listening to music, eating food or climbing a mountain. Happiness, on the other hand, is normally conceived to be a general state of being that characterizes longer portions of a person's life. We can imagine a person experiencing quite a lot of pleasure without being happy: for example, someone who was constantly getting high on drugs might meet this description. But we also think that there is usually a fairly strong connection between the two. A life with little pleasure and much pain cannot be considered a happy life. To live happily is to experience many pleasures – preferably somewhat varied pleasures – and not too much misery. For the sake of brevity we shall normally speak only of happiness here, with the understanding that this term includes within it the idea of pleasure.

The central tenet of utilitarianism is usually called the **principle of utility**. It states that actions are right in so far as they promote happiness, and wrong in so far as they promote unhappiness. The happiness in question is not just that of the agent – the person performing the act – but of everyone affected by the action. Indeed, utilitarianism has always been a radically egalitarian theory, insisting that every person's happiness counts equally. In this respect, at least, it shares with the Kantian view a concern for impartiality. The basic moral imperative advanced by utilitarianism is thus that we should try to promote 'the greatest happiness of the greatest number'.

There are some definite attractions to the utilitarian outlook:

1. It has common sense on its side. Everyone recognizes the value of happiness, and the idea that morality is fundamentally about trying to increase happiness and reduce misery is comprehensible, plausible and appealing. It appeals to our natural belief that morality should have something to do with making the world a better (that is, happier) place.
2. It advocates an attitude that is fair and unselfish.
3. It offers a coherent criterion – a rule or standard – for settling moral disputes, 'the greatest happiness principle' (GHP). This would be a common currency among the diverse and complex problems prevalent in modern societies. The GHP is something we can all agree on, whatever else divides us, since presumably we all want there to be more happiness. This is not to say that the GHP offers an immediate answer to all our particular ethical questions, but it does offer a way of getting at those problems through an agreed criterion.
4. It is a 'minimum commitment' philosophy. In adopting it, we are not required to believe more than the GHP. It does not seek to be a Grand Theory of Everything, nor does it rest on controversial metaphysical or religious claims. It is well suited to the modern world in being worldly and secular. At the same time, no one is asked to relinquish whatever other religious or metaphysical beliefs they may already hold.
5. It involves calculations and assessments understandable to all. We calculate costs and benefits much of the time in our daily life, from when we go shopping to when we choose careers. So it comes quite naturally to us to think of evaluating actions by assessing their likely consequences. Thus the GHP is attractively unmysterious. Happiness is what matters and we all know why. There is no fixation on performing an action just for the sake of tradition, or just because it is held to be one's duty.

Problems with utilitarianism

Utilitarianism has a number of things going for it. Nevertheless, its advocates have to face some very troubling questions that cast doubt on the theory's adequacy as a complete account of how we ought to think about morality. Let us consider a few of these.

Can pleasure or happiness be measured?

One set of problems utilitarians have to deal with concern how happiness is to be measured. Even if a single person can compare and assess the different levels of happiness she enjoys at different times in her own life (and this is not obviously true), it is extremely hard to compare the happiness of different people. People devote themselves to all sorts of things: sport, hard work, family, art appreciation,

John Stuart Mill (1806–1873)

John Stuart Mill was born in London, the son of the well-known political theorist James Mill. He received a remarkably thorough education at home, and became, as his father had hoped, an effective spokesman for the utilitarian outlook that had been developed first by David Hume and later by James Mill's friend Jeremy Bentham.

Mill wrote on many topics, but his most widely read works today are two short books, *On Liberty* (1859) and *Utilitarianism* (1863). In the former, he defends the so-called 'harm principle', which says that the only legitimate reason for anyone, including governments, to limit a person's freedom is to prevent harm to others. In *Utilitarianism* he defends a more sophisticated version of utilitarianism than Bentham had espoused. While he agrees with Bentham that pleasure is intrinsically valuable, he argues that not all pleasures are qualitatively equal. Some, he says, are just better than others: the 'higher' pleasures of the mind are generally to be valued more than the 'lower' pleasures of the body.

Mill was very close to and eventually married the feminist Harriet Taylor. She greatly influenced his thinking, and inspired his late work *The Subjection of Woman*, in which he advocates women's suffrage.

sex, food, television, God, politics, literature, gardening and train-spotting all have their adherents, each of whom can claim that their chosen activities make them happy. But it is not clear how we can decide which produces the most happiness. They may not even be comparable.

This incommensurability of different pleasures was not a problem for Jeremy Bentham (1748–1832), one of the fathers of utilitarianism. According to Bentham, the various pleasures only differ from one another in two respects: intensity and duration. All other things being equal, longer pleasures are better than shorter ones, and more intense pleasures are better than milder ones. If this is true, then we can perhaps rank pleasures quantitatively; but we cannot say that one kind of pleasure is qualitatively better than any other. Bentham was certainly prepared to grasp this nettle; consistent with his theory, he boldly declared that if the quantity of pleasure produced is equal, pushpin (a simple game) is as good as poetry.

This way of thinking may simplify our calculations, but it is hard not to think that some activities (such as painting the Sistine chapel or making scientific discoveries) are somehow worth more than others (such as watching the shopping channel on cable TV all day), even if the quantity of pleasure is the same. This is the view of John Stuart Mill (see the box) who holds that pleasures vary in quality as well as quantity, distinguishes between what he calls 'higher' and 'lower' pleasures, and famously declares that 'it is better to be Socrates dissatisfied than a pig satisfied'. But does a scale that places art and literature above television or sport merely reflect the perspective (and the prejudices) of an intellectual who is better at reading than at football? It is no good saying that anyone who knows both will place reading above football; some people who have tried both prefer sport. Who is to say that enjoying one's physical prowess is a 'lower' pleasure?

Problems of measurement and calculation also crop up at the social level. What, exactly, is meant by 'the greatest happiness'? Is it better to have many people quite happy or a few people very happy? Should we be trying to increase population just as long as those born can be expected to be at least moderately happy, since that way we increase the total quantity of happiness? The GHP alone does not provide answers to such questions. And the questions themselves cast further doubt on the feasibility, or even the intelligibility, of measuring happiness at all.

Is happiness our only goal?

Utilitarianism typically presupposes that pleasure or happiness is the ultimate goal of all our actions. Strictly speaking, this view is not essential to utilitarianism as

> **think critically!**
>
> # Intrinsic and instrumental value
>
> To value something is to hold that the world is a better place because that thing exists. Speaking generally, there are two ways we might value something: as an *end in itself* or as a *means* to some other end. We value most things in the second way; we see them as valuable because they enable us to get to something else. For example, we value money for the things it can buy, washing machines because they give us more free time, telephone directories because they facilitate communications. We say these things have **instrumental value**.
>
> Some things, however, are valued for their own sake and not simply because they help us towards something else: for example, pleasure, happiness, friendship, love, beauty, virtue and justice have all been touted as being goods of this kind. When something is valued for its own sake it is said to possess **intrinsic value**. It is, of course, possible for something to be valued both as a means and as end. For instance, many people think of education in this way.

an ethical theory, but it lends support to the thesis that happiness alone is intrinsically valuable as the one thing that we pursue for its own sake. However, we can raise questions about this picture of human motivation. Consider the following two examples.

First, imagine the case of Joan of Arc. It seems unlikely that her campaign to rid France of the English was motivated entirely or even mainly by the search for pleasure. It is hardly credible that she was experiencing pleasure as she stood at the stake and the flames began to rise around her body. Although it is just possible that she was getting some weird kind of kick out of being burned alive, we have no evidence to support this. It seems more plausible that she – like many other people who sacrifice themselves for some ideal – was experiencing pain for the sake of something she valued more highly than pleasure. Was she happy? Possibly. She might have felt happy that she had fulfilled her mission, saved France, done God's work etc., despite the pain of the fire. But this would surely involve looking beyond her moment on the pyre: it would mean looking at her life's work as a whole. And in that case it is not clear that happiness is a determinate thing that she or anyone could aim at.

Second, imagine that science has produced an amazing new invention, the hedon machine. All you do is plug yourself in and it gives you delightful sensations: pure pleasure, artfully varied to avoid monotony. If you do plug yourself in you will enjoy yourself indefinitely. In fact, you will never want to unplug yourself. If someone successfully attracts your attention long enough to ask you if you want to come out to do other things – go walking, attend concerts, read books, and so on – you will refuse. Being plugged in is so great you want nothing else. This is guaranteed pleasure beyond the wildest dreams of the early utilitarians. Of course, if everybody plugged themselves in to a hedon machine there would be no one left to maintain the machines, supply food etc., but we need not worry about that here. Our question is: Would you want this for yourself? The majority of people would probably say no, on the grounds that a life hooked up to the hedon machine would not be a proper life for a human being. There are things in life that we aim at and value other than just pleasure. Although it is not always easy to articulate what a life spent plugged into the machine would lack, words like 'reality', 'truth' and 'authenticity' come to mind.

This example also brings out another dubious aspect of utilitarianism's assumptions about human motivation, namely, the idea that there is some thing (pleasure) that is the real thing we are aiming at in all the particular things we do (horse-riding, playing the guitar, eating, rowing, reading . . .). I do not wake up in the morning thinking: 'How can I maximize my pleasure today? I know, I'll go rowing.' Rather, I have a desire to go rowing and not, say, cycling; and if I derive pleasure from the activity this is, at least in part, because I am doing what I wanted to do. The redundancy of pleasure in this context is emphasized when we imagine the hedon machine as a real option for us. Few people find it very appealing. Even if we conceive of utility as happiness rather than pleasure, the theory is no less problematic. Happiness is often thought of in relation to the general shape of a life, applicable to people in diverse situations, doing disparate things.

If this is right then it is unhelpful to imagine happiness as a kind of product that arises from a particular action or a single event. We can, if we wish, say that everyone – Joan and the soldiers who burned her, the couch potato and the athlete, the mountain climber and the bookworm – are all 'in pursuit of happiness' but it is not clear that anything much is being said. If 'happiness' is used as a general term that covers various kinds of satisfaction that people might get from doing the things they want to do, but is not actually locatable as a distinct and determinate pay off for any particular activity, it is not much help to the utilitarian. One of the advantages of utilitarianism initially seemed to be that it promised to base morality on something calculable, thereby simplifying our moral choices. We now seem to be left with the alternative of the hard-headed assessment of pleasure (which we don't in fact always pursue), or the vague notion of happiness (which we cannot measure).

Can we – and should we – be motivated by a desire to promote the greatest happiness?

Utilitarianism tells us we should try to maximize the happiness of all those affected by our actions. But virtually no one actually lives according to this principle, which seems to call for a degree of selflessness, even a willingness to sacrifice one's own happiness, that it is unrealistic to expect from people. After all, anyone who took seriously the injunction to maximize the happiness of all those affected by one's actions would have to be some kind of ethical superman or superwoman, righting wrongs and helping others most of the time.

From the utilitarian perspective, we are arguably guilty of a moral failure every time we indulge ourselves by drinking wine or buying luxury items instead of giving our money to some worthy cause. Moreover, as a consequentialist moral theory, utilitarianism is characterized by an absence of particular duties that a particular agent might be called on to perform. It does not seem to recognize the special claims that family or friends may make on us, for instance. Strict utilitarianism seems to imply that putting the people we love ahead of strangers cannot be morally justified. Claims of loyalty must bow before the claims of 'the greatest number'.

Does utilitarianism justify unethical actions?

Probably the most serious objection that has regularly been levelled against utilitarianism is that it can be used to support actions and policies that most people would consider morally wrong. Consider a gang rape, for instance. Any reasonable person would condemn it. But if we take the strict utilitarian view seriously, we have to ask whether the rape increased or decreased the total amount of pleasure experienced by all those affected. Now, one might say that the distress experienced by the victim, including all the resulting unhappiness and loss of pleasure she suffers in the long term, outweighs the pleasure experienced by her attackers. But supposing it does not? Does that mean that the act is morally acceptable, or not so bad after all? Surely not. And even if the utilitarian calculation showed that the rape caused more misery than pleasure, *that* is not the reason it is morally wrong. If we are asked why gang rape is wrong, most of us would not even think to enter into such calculations; we would probably say it is wrong because it was contrary to the victim's wishes and therefore involved a violation of her rights.

Imagine another situation in which the police and judiciary know that if they imprison an innocent person for a terrorist bombing (they cannot catch the real perpetrators) it will have the effect of calming public fears and restoring confidence in themselves. If this is a course of action that will maximize overall happiness, it seems that they would be able to justify it on utilitarian grounds. But once again, this conclusion would be utterly contrary to what we might call moral common sense. Punishing innocent people is *unjust*. It is a violation of their *rights*. It is not something they *deserve*. But utilitarianism appears willing to ride roughshod over matters of justice, rights and desert, if doing so is likely to maximize overall happiness. As Bentham once candidly but ominously remarked, it views all talk of 'rights' as so much 'nonsense on stilts'.

A utilitarian response

In spite of these objections utilitarianism remains an appealing ethical theory for many people. True, its defenders say, if you interpret the doctrine too simplistically it will run into difficulties: the kind of calculations it proposes will seem too mechanical, its account of human motivation will appear inadequate, and it will entail conclusions that are incompatible with our ordinary sense of justice. But utilitarianism does not have to be construed in this simplistic way. For instance, it is not a necessary part of utilitarian theory that we be able to measure precisely and compare every kind of pleasure as experienced by every person. It is sufficient to be able to make general – and of course fallible – assessments of what the consequences of our actions are likely to be. On the whole and in the long term, will we be increasing the amount of happiness in the world, or will we be adding to its store of misery?

Nor need a utilitarian insist that we all become round-the-clock do-gooders. Mill gave a plausible response to this objection when he argued that the general happiness is usually best served by individuals working to secure the well-being of themselves and those around them (family, friends, colleagues and neighbours). Not that saintliness is morally wrong; indeed, the saintly types who devote themselves to others perform a valuable social function: apart from the material benefits they confer on those they aid, they present us with an ideal of selflessness that inspires the rest of us to be less self-interested and more concerned for the welfare of others.

But this does not mean that a world of self-sacrificing saints would be a happier place.

The argument that utilitarianism may justify actions we would normally consider unethical is a more serious problem. Of course, one response open to utilitarians is simply to say that our ordinary moral intuitions are wrong. If common sense tells us that the rights of a single individual should count for more than the happiness of many, then so much for common sense! After all, would the champions of individual rights stick to their guns no matter what? If terrorists with deadly chemical weapons were trying to subvert the legal system, is it obviously better to let hundreds of thousands perish rather than see an injustice done? Would that be rational?

These are fair questions. And we should certainly be open to the possibility that moral common sense may be wrong. After all, it was common sense that declared sex before marriage, homosexual relationships and miscegenation to be immoral. One of the functions of an ethical theory like utilitarianism is to provide a fresh and critical perspective on beliefs and practices we take for granted. But this point, valid though it is, does not overcome the difficulties concerning issues of justice and individual rights. These require, at the very least, a significant modification to the theory.

Act and rule utilitarianism

So far, we have been discussing a kind of utilitarianism known as **act utilitarianism**, which judges the moral worth of *particular actions* by their consequences. The problem, as we have seen, is that this theory may condone actions that we would normally consider immoral. In response to this objection some utilitarians have developed a more sophisticated version of the theory called **rule utilitarianism**. Instead of saying that we should always perform the act that promotes the most happiness overall, rule utilitarianism says that our actions should be guided by rules that, if followed by everyone, would lead to the greatest happiness overall – even though in certain cases we would not be maximizing happiness.

The accumulated wisdom of millennia have taught human beings what the general tendency of certain classes of actions is – whether they serve, in the long run, to promote our well-being or not. For example, we have learned that killing, stealing, lying and cheating tend to cause misery, while kindness, honesty and keeping promises tend to promote happiness. Our moral code should correspond to this accumulated knowledge. In this form, utilitarianism looks a lot more like what most people intuitively feel that a moral code should be. It upholds the principle that innocent people should not be knowingly imprisoned, despite any supposed short-term gain in utility, because in the long run that sort of behaviour will lower the general happiness: there would be less respect for the law and we would all feel less safe.

Rule utilitarianism is a bit like the highway code. It demands that we consider what the effect would be if certain types of action became general. Not indicating before I turn may save me a little energy on a particular occasion when I know I can get away with it, but what if everybody failed to indicate? The general result would be more accidents and hence more misery. It is important to notice here that the principle of rule utilitarianism is different from the principle of universalizability, which is a formal rule requiring me not to contradict myself. Rule utilitarianism asks us to consider the *practical consequences* of certain actions becoming general, and may also have the added benefit of saving time in making calculations. We are not asked to try to assess, in each new situation, what the best overall outcome would be; we just follow the rule that has been established on the basis of the GHP. Only if two rules clash do we need to make a particular calculation based on the GHP.

Rule utilitarianism looks like a neat solution to some of the problems faced by act utilitarianism, but it is not itself free from difficulties. One problem is especially troublesome: Given that a rule has been established, should we ever allow exceptions to it? If so, when? Recall the highway code example. We are told to follow certain rules even if breaking them would cause no harm and would probably increase overall happiness. For instance, we stop at a red light and wait there until it changes to green, even though we are in a hurry and can see that no traffic is coming. But now imagine a fire engine, racing to a burning building. Any delay may mean lost lives. Would the fire engine be justified in ignoring the red light, given that no accident would occur as a result? A 'strong utilitarian' would demand that the rule be kept, however good the reason for breaking it might seem. The rule is there to maximize welfare, and to allow exceptions undermines the principle of rule utilitarianism.

There is, of course, a certain irony here: the utilitarian, setting out to follow undogmatically only those courses of action likely to maximize happiness, is now the enforcer of a rule that will, if applied rigidly, quite possibly increase suffering. So perhaps exceptions should be allowed. This is the view of the so called 'weak utilitarian', and it seems to represent a more sensible approach. However, once we start trying to work out when we can afford to suspend the rules and when we should stick to them, we risk the collapse of the entire edifice. Now the rules only seem to have force when and if individual calculators calculate that they should. In effect, we are saying something like: Follow the rule (which has a broad utilitarian justification) except when doing so will fail to maximize happiness. But following *this* guideline requires us once again to assess each situation individually.

In short, rule utilitarianism must either be adhered to rigidly, in which case it will have to defend just the kind of blind, rigid adherence to rules from which utilitarianism is intended to free us; or it permits exceptions to the rules, in which case it collapses back into act utilitarianism.

One thing that rule utilitarianism obviously shares with Kantianism is a conception of morality as essentially a matter of establishing and then following a set of clear-cut rules. Ethical relativism, in so far as it identifies morality with a set of existing cultural norms, exhibits the same tendency. The idea that morality is all about rules is fairly widespread. One reason for this is that moral codes are closely linked to legal codes, and a legal code consists of a body of laws (which, ideally, are completely unambiguous). The law of the land in a sense provides us with a paradigm of a practical code that can guide our conduct. Another paradigm, which also reinforces the idea that morality is all about rules, is that of the Ten Commandments and the rest of the law that Moses gave to Israel. Western culture is steeped in this tradition, so it is bound to inform our thinking. However, the ancient Greeks – to whom we are also deeply indebted for some of our ideas about ethics – did not share this overriding concern (some would say obsession) for rules. In their view, ethics was not so much about justifying and obeying absolute moral rules as about cultivating a certain kind of *character*. In recent years, this approach to ethics has seen a significant revival. We will conclude our enquiry by seeing if it can offer a way around the kinds of difficulties that beset the other views we have been examining.

Why be moral?

Let us first reorientate our enquiry by returning to an absolutely fundamental question: Why be moral? This question has appeared on the horizon several times but we have not yet really addressed it. Here is one response:

> Nobody would act 'ethically' if they didn't have to. It's all an elaborate game you have to play, a price you pay for being in society. Morality is a set of rules to make you conform, a way of holding back the strong from doing what they want. Truly strong people just take what they want, unless they've been brainwashed into feeling guilty about it. There's only one rule really worth worrying about: don't get caught.

To help us think about the implications of this sort of challenge to ethics, let us see if there is a convincing argument for ethical behaviour, even in a case where no obvious benefits seem to flow from it. Suppose that you discovered a ring with the magical property of making the wearer invisible. Imagine it! You can go anywhere, do anything, protected by invisibility as long as you wear the ring. You can do what you like, see what you want to, take what appeals to you. Armed with this ring, is there any reason why you should not just follow your desires?

It is possible that you would no longer be impressed by the maxim 'Honesty is the best policy', since your invisibility would enable you to get what you want with impunity. Anyway, if you are careful you will be able to lead a double life: morally upright when visible, ruthlessly self-interested when unseen. Honesty does not seem to be the best policy for you in your new circumstances. In the unlikely event of your caring about setting a bad example, you can relax; since no one need ever know who is the true author of your nefarious deeds, you will be leading no one astray. So much for rule utilitarianism. As for the principle of universalizability, the temptation to regard it as emptily formal and thus disposable, or to interpret it in a way that suits your desires, may well be overwhelming. After all, no one else is ever likely to have a ring like this, so why bother yourself with questions about how it would be if everyone did.

If we are to defend the claim that one ought to act ethically we shall have to do more than simply invoke Kant's categorical imperative or the principle of utility. The question here is: Why should I not simply pursue my own interests, without concern for anything or anyone else? Perhaps we need to look more closely at what exactly is 'in my interests', all things considered, whether or not I have a ring of invisibility. Investigating this goes beyond the question of particular acts and rules, and considers the kinds of lives human beings might lead.

We are time bound, social creatures. We have an idea of ourselves that goes beyond the here and now. That is why it makes sense for us to recall, to learn from past mistakes, to anticipate, to plan, to hope and fear, to make resolutions, and so on. I have an idea that I am a certain sort of person, responsible for acts performed in the past, able to assess the effects of what I plan to do next. If I knock things over a lot, then people I know will think of me as clumsy; if I am often late I will be thought of as unpunctual. This ongoing sense of who I am is formed largely through my relations with others: it does not occur in isolation from the world I live in. Being human, and hence a social animal, means more than just sharing space with others. Human sociality implies language, a way of understanding what goes on in our world. That does not mean that we cannot disagree about all sorts of important things, but it does mean that we cannot disagree about *everything*. In spite of our many disagreements, there will always be a vast amount that we are not putting into question at any one time. This shared world is like a backdrop against which any disagreement will show up and without which any kind of dialogue would be literally unthinkable. Without a shared world and a shared language disagreements could not be articulated or recognized in the first place.

Finding the magic ring or winning millions in the national lottery may help me deal with some problems, but some very basic questions will still remain unanswered. The sorts of choices I make now are helping to contribute to what I will be in the future. I am a person, someone who *becomes* someone. So it is reasonable to relate ethics to the larger question of how well my life might go, given the opportunities available to me. The question is not just 'What is the morally right thing to do here and now?' but also 'What kind of person am I? What kind of person do I want to be? What kind of life do I want to live?' How I answer the first question is inseparable from how I answer these other questions, even if I never consciously make the connection. This will apply just as much to the wearer of the magic ring, even if he never takes it off. After a life lived in pursuit of his private advantage, always doing what he takes to be 'in his best interests', he will have become a certain character – perhaps the kind of person who, say, spies on people, steals from them, and generally places his personal advantage ahead of others. In other words, he has become a voyeur, a thief and a selfish deceiver, at least on a part-time basis.

This may not bother him. He might think he is beyond our petty ethics, for although he did use invisibility to deceive, calling it 'wrong' or 'bad' merely expresses a value judgement, and 'there is nothing either good or bad but thinking makes it so'. One response to this is to point to the kind of language we are using to describe him: 'voyeur', 'thief', 'selfish', 'deceiver'. Earlier we saw that some theorists wish to make a very sharp distinction between facts and values. The idea that there is a sharp distinction here may be popular, but it is nevertheless problematic. The words just mentioned are not purely descriptive or purely evaluative but can be thought of as performing both functions. 'Thief' is a factual term, at least in ordinary and legally uncomplicated contexts; either one is a thief or one is not. But it is certainly not a *neutral* term; if you use it incorrectly you could end up in court, charged with defamation. People do not like being called a thief. The same is true of many other words. Take the word 'mean', for example. If someone tells me that Mary is mean, I might ask them why they think that. They proceed to give me examples as evidence (she never buys a drink when it is her turn, never lends money but borrows it herself and begrudges repayment, is always thinking of what something will cost her, and so on). Then I go and see for myself and find she does indeed act in this way. She is mean. This is a factual description, but it is also evaluative.

The existence of adjectives like this tells us something about the nature of values in general. In naming propensities or dispositions of people, such terms indicate that we understand character in a way that blends the descriptive (what is) with the normative (what one ought to do or be like). For this reason, an account of human life that limits itself to factual descriptions, eschewing evaluations and prescriptions, is bound to be unsatisfactory. We can *try* to give a value-free account of human actions, as in 'A took money from B; he said he would give it him back in less than a month but did not do so.' However, although this tells us something about an event, it deprives us of the tools to understand its meaning. We can only approach this meaning if we grasp what the purposes and motivations are for the people involved, since this will shed light not only on the meaning of an isolated event (an unpaid loan), but on what will possibly happen in the future (no more loans, a degree of social isolation for A, A's likely reaction to this, etc.). Thus we cannot dispense with the meanings that people ascribe to character and action if we want to understand what they are doing. And these meanings are saturated in normative language.

The mistake underlying this attempt to separate out the descriptive and the evaluative lies in imagining that the only 'real' things are brute facts, objects and the relations between them. But the world is not a mass of neutral facts, on which we shine the torchlight of our value judgements: it always already appears to us as meaningful. Human beings live their lives against a backdrop of significance and value that is not unreal merely because such things are not physical objects.

Aristotle (384–322 BCE)

Aristotle ranks alongside his teacher Plato as one of the most original and influential philosophers of all time. The range of his interests was vast. His surviving works including writings on biology, astronomy, physics, metaphysics, epistemology, logic, rhetoric, ethics, political theory and poetics. These writings occupied such a central place in Western philosophy that by the end of the middle ages Aristotle's philosophy was practically synonymous with The Tradition. Despite a reaction against Aristotle at the beginning of the modern epoch (led by thinkers like Descartes and Hobbes), he has never really gone away and is currently undergoing something of a revival. Much of this renewed interest has centred on his *Nicomachean Ethics*, which develops an account of ethics in terms of the virtues.

One of the distinctive features of Aristotle's view of the world is his assumption that everything has a purpose or function. He applies this principle just as much to things in nature as to human artefacts like tables and chairs, which are very clearly designed to serve some end. In Aristotle's view, a full account of anything would include an explanation of its 'final cause' or purpose: the account itself provides what philosophers call a **teleology** (from *telos*, meaning end or purpose). This kind of teleological thinking is central to Aristotle's ethics since he assumes, from the start, that human beings have a *telos*. This purpose is to actualize one's potentialities, to achieve self-realization by cultivating those qualities that we associate with human flourishing. This one does by exercising them. A person who regularly performs acts of kindness acquires the habit of being kind; one who practises temperance becomes temperate. Practising the virtues is thus both a means to and a constitutive part of the good life for a human being.

'Courage' and 'meanness' are not things in the way a stone or a tree are things, but they do belong to a world, and this means they are not merely the projections of individuals *onto* the world.

Virtue ethics: a question of character

Philosophers who hold the sort of view just described sometimes point to the ancient notion of moral virtue. This is an approach to ethics that starts out by asking what qualities make a person a good human being. These qualities — courage, honesty, trustworthiness and the like — are called *virtues*. They are essentially dispositions to act and feel in a manner that is both part of and leads to what we think of as the good life for a human being – what might also be called human flourishing.

This approach to ethics was characteristic of the ancient Greek and Roman philosophers, notably Plato and Aristotle, but it has enjoyed a revival in recent years. An advantage of this approach is that it seems to meet the problem of what is to count as good that we encountered in our discussion of the categorical imperative. The duties that the categorical imperative urged on us seemed to hang in mid-air, without justification. I could ask: 'Why these duties? Why should I only act on universalizable principles?' An advocate of the goodness-as-virtue view has an answer: the virtues should be cultivated because they contribute to human flourishing.

When we look at the virtues as described by Aristotle we find that they are described as a propensity to think, desire, feel and act in an integrated manner; in other words, they help us to become a person for whom thought, feeling and action are in harmony. This is the kind of person who derives satisfaction from doing the right thing but does not do the right thing *in order* to maximize her pleasure or gain some other extrinsic benefit. She becomes this kind of person by cultivating certain habits of feeling and thinking, the habits that contribute to a happy life because they erase the distinction between 'I *ought* to do this' and 'I *want* to do this'. In a more modern vocabulary we might say that the Aristotelian person is happy because she is not in conflict with herself, but is instead integrated and relatively free from neuroses. This is a way of flourishing. Such a person is unlikely to imagine that a magic ring would provide a better kind of happiness through the acquisition of extrinsic benefits.

Virtue ethics, as this approach is commonly called, is another kind of ethical naturalism. It claims that our identification of certain qualities as virtues is based on a true understanding of what we are and what we should strive to be. As a variety of naturalism, it is of course open to some of the standard objections to this approach. These include:

- Doubts about the accuracy of the account of human nature on which it rests.
- Doubts about the objectivity or universality of the values that inform its conception of human flourishing. Other cultures have different notions of what it is for a human being to 'turn out well'. For example, many cultures in the past have placed an extremely high premium on physical courage and martial prowess. By comparison, we are perhaps more inclined to emphasize emotional sensitivity and intellectual acumen. Once again, we run up against the problem of relativism, this time with reference to the notion of human excellence. Who is to say which ideal (or ideals) we should prefer?
- The 'open question' argument. Even if the facts are as the virtue theorist says they are, they need not compel us to adopt one specific ideal of human excellence. We can always raise questions like: Is this ideal really good? Why should we prefer it to other possible ideals?

In the end, a virtue ethicist can only point to examples (real or ideal) of what they call human flourishing and ask us to agree with their judgement. The judgement they make is, of course, a value judgement — or perhaps more accurately, a *value laden* judgement. But that need not imply that it is at all arbitrary. We make analogous judgements about all sorts of things: houses, cars, trees and cats. We all recognize the difference between a well-constructed house, attractive in appearance, pleasant to live in and built in a convenient or picturesque location, and a cold, cramped, leaky, dilapidated slum that is infested with cockroaches and situated next to a toxic waste dump. Almost everyone will agree that a cat who enjoys the care of a loving family, ample food, a warm spot by the fire, a glossy coat, sharp teeth, keen senses, freedom to come and go as it pleases, and an active social life with other cats is 'living well' (in the feline sense) compared to a solitary, mangy, flea-ridden, half-starved stray that limps around on three legs, peering out of one eye for pieces of litter that may contain scraps of stale food. By the same token, it really is not open to us to accept any kind of life as a possible example of human flourishing, nor any kind of character as exemplifying human excellence. If someone recognizes what moral behaviour is and still rejects it, perhaps opting for the magic ring and all the 'advantages' it brings, there do not seem to be any extra things one can say to recommend goodness over evil, apart from using the sort of terms we discussed earlier. When I describe a person as 'truthful', 'trustworthy', 'kind hearted' and so on, anyone hearing this description is expected to recognize immediately the connection between virtue and flourishing. The kind of character and the way of living described are, one might say, self-recommending.

But it is always possible that my listener may not see things this way. For example, he may find the ideals he is asked to applaud disgustingly conventional and turn away from them in favour of more extreme and one-sided ideals, such as those represented by ruthless but successful criminals. If the Aristotelian view is correct, such a person displays a kind of culpable ignorance in pursuing the 'wrong' goals. The thief is not just doing his own thing: he is doing the wrong thing in every sense of the word. And if the Greeks are right in seeing moral virtue as a necessary condition of human flourishing, the person who fails to see this will eventually suffer the consequences of his error. His unfortunate fate was described enigmatically by Plato: he will become more and more like himself.

Virtue ethics claims to bring the theoretical and the practical together. Its strongest argument is that unethical behaviour is also unreasonable, because it does not lead to a flourishing life. It holds that our values and our ideas about how people should behave can have objective validity because they are based on truths about human beings. So perhaps the finder of the invisibility ring will throw it away and cultivate the virtues instead. Perhaps!

We began the chapter by claiming that ethics is both theoretical and practical, concerned with knowing and doing, thinking and choosing. Many of the theories we have considered seem to be flawed, in that they each tend to focus on some important aspects of ethical life while ignoring others. Each is thus unsatisfactory in so far as it presents a distorted picture not only of ethics but of human action and thought. *Emotivism* recognizes that moral judgements express feeling, but it neglects the role of rational reflection in our moral lives. *Situation ethics* calls attention to the importance of the context in which we have to make our moral choices, but it exaggerates the uniqueness of these contexts and thus fails to see that situational similarities allow us to formulate general precepts. *Relativism* makes us aware of the importance of understanding moral norms in relation to the culture within which they function, but it is unable to justify taking a critical perspective on any particular set of cultural norms and practices.

Kantian ethics reinstates reason, but at the expense of feeling, and it fails to see that morality needs to be linked to people's legitimate desire for happiness. The *utilitarian* reduces ethics to nothing other more than a set of prudential rules aimed at maximizing happiness, but in so doing oversimplifies its account of human motivation and refuses to take seriously moral concerns such as justice and individual rights. *Virtue ethics* is perhaps the most balanced theory, but it tends to take for granted assumptions about human nature and the objective validity of normative judgements; it also runs the risk, like relativism, of failing to recognize the critical function that moral principles can play in relation to one's own ethical tradition.

Perhaps what emerges most clearly from all of this is the *complexity* of moral life. All the theories illuminate some important aspects of morality, but none offers an adequate account of the whole. This is because the whole is too big and irregular and complex to be captured by a single theory. There have been quite a few ethicists who have hoped that morality could be simplified – notably Kantians and utilitarians, both of whom seek to deduce all moral precepts from one or two fundamental principles that are binding on everyone. But this dream of reducing moral reasoning to a few simple inferences or calculations is an illusion. This does not, of course, mean that morality itself is in some sense illusory. It just means that no theory can ever replace the need for each of us to exercise what Aristotle calls 'practical wisdom', as we are called upon to deal with the ethical problems that arise in the course of a normal human life.

6 Political philosophy

There are few more important problems than that of how society should be organized. It is an issue that generates tough questions – who should rule, the relation of power to authority, the nature and purpose of law, and many more. Problems like these have been the matter of political philosophy since ancient times, and they remain important today. Our starting point, however, is a topic of particular importance to modern political philosophy: the concept of *freedom*. Its centrality to recent political philosophy reflects the enormous prestige it has enjoyed in the modern world, where it has become perhaps the supreme political and social value. In examining the concept of freedom we will be led to many of the principal and traditional questions mentioned above. Given its importance, it is surprising to find that there has been a good deal of disagreement about what exactly we mean by 'freedom' and 'the free society'.

First, a working definition:

> *Freedom is doing what you want to do, without being stopped by anyone else.*

This is the common sense idea of freedom. A person is free when she can make her own choices without restraint or compulsion. Freedom of movement is a classic example of this, being precisely the thing that prisoners are denied. What is prized in freedom seems to be the minimum of barriers blocking the individual from doing what she wants, with the ideal of complete freedom being liberty to do whatever one wants to do, with no barriers at all. But as 'whatever you want to do' might include *anything*, including actions like murder, rape or extortion, this is not a realistic basis for a society composed of people as they are now. The strongest would tend to exercise *their* freedom at the expense of the rest. So we need a limit on freedom. And it seems intuitively clear what this should be:

> *You should be free to do what you want, provided you do not cause harm to others.*

This principle is commonly known as the **harm principle**. The notion of freedom underlying it has been called **negative freedom**. It is 'negative' because it is freedom *from* constraint. No one is compelling the individual to pursue or avoid a particular kind of life or set of ideals, because this is something she will determine for herself. One way to think of it is to imagine each life as a blank piece of paper, left open for the individual to fill in as she chooses. The state leaves you at liberty to do as you please, as long as you do not impede others in the exercise of their freedom. Note, though, that nothing says you will be *able* to fulfil your wishes.

Flapping your arms will not get you airborne, and applying for a job is not the same as getting one. Negative freedom provides only the minimum conditions for the achievement of your goals. It has nothing to do with whether those goals are achievable, sensible or in your best interests.

Negative freedom as an elaboration of the common sense view is, in effect, the **liberal** conception of freedom. There are two main strands to liberalism, which go by various names. Here we will call them **libertarian** and **social democratic**. There are important differences between them that we will look at, but they do have broadly the same understanding of what freedom is, and this has certain implications:

1. *Freedom to choose is more important than what is chosen.* Therefore the state must not attempt to promote any one conception of what it would be good for people to want. Instead, it must act as the enforcer of laws that will preserve the greatest amount of freedom for the individual. A consequence of this is the priority of 'right' over 'good'. Good is seen as a matter of free individual choice; right as the defence of that freedom. The only general good that the liberal state assumes is the value of this freedom to choose; the rest is up to the individual.

2. *An inescapable consequence of such freedom will be* **inequality**. The political economy of liberalism is the free market (capitalism), which is a competitive place. Competition means winners and losers, because people are not equal in their abilities or in the effort they are prepared to expend. So it is an important feature of a just society that individuals shall hold the goods that they have won by their own efforts, while others may fail to obtain some or all of such goods. Luck does play a role in one's success, of course, but it is not up to the state to correct the effects of this.

We now turn to a more detailed examination of libertarianism and, later in the chapter, social democracy.

Libertarianism 1

Libertarians are the strongest proponents of untrammelled negative freedom. They hold that we need only a *minimal* state. The strength of the libertarian argument arises partly from the way that it seems to connect to many people's intuitions about freedom and the individual. On this view, freedom is the one political good, a basic entitlement or 'right' of the individual that is not to be infringed upon by the state.

The world of the 'western' movie has many of the qualities most prized by libertarians, including lots of freedom for the individual and not much meddling from the law. The hero here is the cowboy or the drifter, going his own way, making his own decisions and living with the consequences. Larger social groupings appear as small towns, with their saloons, dry goods stores, livery stables and so on. In the town, with its various occupations (victualler, undertaker, blacksmith etc.), individuals meet in free relations of mutual benefit, buying and selling their wares in the market. In the average western this sort of unglamorous economic activity is rarely stressed, which is understandable, but we will keep it in mind as the essential background because it provides the main reason for anyone being there at all.

In this paradise for the strong individual, the law (or the state) is represented by the sheriff. His task is to use any force necessary to prevent marauders from depriving the townsfolk of their lives and property. It is in the townsfolk's interests to supply him with deputies, as they must support him if they want to live in peace. If he were not there, it is possible that after much bloodletting the most powerful gang would eventually seize control of the town and impose a protection racket, demanding something along the lines of 'pay us and we will let you keep your lives and most of your goods'. If this bought peace it might well be regarded as preferable to the alternative of anarchy. But preferable to either anarchy or gang-rule would be a contract between sheriff and people. Apart from anything else, it would provide conditions for exchanging the sheriff for a replacement if he fails to perform adequately in his job. We will return to this idea of a contract between state and citizen later.

Now, it is important to see what the sheriff does *not* do. It is not part of his job to advance money to the owner of the dry goods store to tide him over when business is bad, still less to ensure that the store owner's family is fed if the business fails completely. Nor will we find him redistributing recovered booty to pay the schoolteacher's wages in order that the town's children can learn to read. All that and more is left entirely to individuals and their families. Any assistance he does render will be strictly charitable and in a private capacity, just like any other citizen. The sheriff/state only has the role of defending the right to liberty and property; everything else is left to effort and luck. As the libertarian utopia places such importance on this concept of an individual **right** to freedom and property we will turn to examine briefly the meaning and significance of 'rights'.

Rights

We have already seen that liberals emphasize right over good. They seek to separate the just treatment of citizens from any conception of what might be the best kind of life for them to lead. 'Right' in this context refers to law in general. But the term 'right' can also have the more particular sense of *fundamental justified claim*. We say someone has a right to something if no one may be permitted to stop them from doing or possessing that thing.

Rights are supposed to be basic and inviolable, trumping other claims or considerations. So if one has a *right* to life, liberty, free speech or property, for instance, this is taken to mean that these claims are paramount even if they conflict with general welfare. Suppose that I have the right to free speech. This means that the government must allow me to utter or publish my views, no matter how unwelcome. If my government conducts delicate trade negotiations with an autocratic state, and I broadcast information denouncing the brutal policies of that autocracy at a particularly delicate moment for the deal, my government *cannot* silence me, however inconvenient my timing may be. Thus a right marks a limit to, or immunity from, interference by the government. It places a barrier between the freedom of citizens and their rulers, and protects minorities against the power of elected governments. Furthermore, rights imply duties: my right to free speech means that the government has the duty at least not to silence me.

It might seem that rights represent *absolute* freedoms for the citizen. This is generally not the case, however. If I further exercise my right to free speech by inciting fellow citizens to murder the visiting envoys of the autocratic regime and those who do business with them, my free speech will be curtailed and I may be punished. This is because the exercise of my right threatens to harm others. So my right has a *relative* rather than an absolute status, since there are circumstances where it may be removed. The 'harm to others' criterion limits rights, as it does freedoms in general, in a way that is fairly clear and unobjectionable in cases like this. But there are circumstances where the application of the criterion is less helpful. One example is the exercise of the right to property.

Property rights presumably confer on owners the freedom to dispose of their possessions as they wish. But consider the case of a landowner seeking to build on her property in an area of outstanding natural beauty. People living nearby may object to the destruction of a large and attractive part of the natural environment, and they may argue that she is harming the quality of their lives. This is a dispute that is harder to resolve in terms of the 'harm to others' principle, because the landowner is not threatening to assault her neighbours or deprive them of physical necessities such as drinking water. In exercising her property right she is 'only' annihilating something that they value. The question is whether this comes under the heading of 'harm to others'. The principle could be extended beyond that of narrowly defined physical harm, but this runs the risk of making it difficult to know which actions do *not* fall under that description. A very wide-ranging interpretation of 'harm to others' might make it impossible to do anything that others deeply dislike. Publications that deeply offended a group's religious sensibilities or public art that appalled some people might have to be banned. It looks as though we need another criterion for deciding the extent of our rights.

One suggestion, made by the legal philosopher Ronald Dworkin, is that we should distinguish between basic liberties, which are not to be infringed except in cases of particular and serious harm to individuals, and general liberties, which can be curtailed in the interests of general welfare. The right to free speech would fall under the former heading, property rights under the latter; but it remains unresolved how we are to decide which liberties are basic and which are general. Presumably, decisions would be reached through a political process in which the rival claims of different goods – such as liberty, equality and welfare – are assessed. If so, we have travelled a long way from the conception of a right as somehow just 'there' as an immovable block or boundary to the reach of the political authorities.

Where do rights come from?

Are rights just something we make up? It is possible to deny this and claim that we have **natural rights**, held by us just because we are human beings. On this view, all we need do is recognize that which is part of our very being, something that is earlier and deeper than politics and therefore beyond the reach of politicians or majorities. But if this is so it is unclear how we come to know of these rights, how many there are, and whether God or Nature meant us to have just these or also others we have not (yet) detected. Perhaps we are supposed to grasp their presence in a flash of intuition, or in the light of reason, but if so we must account for disagreements over the character and range of natural rights, or even whether they exist at all. If some people have better rights-detecting equipment than others, it is unclear what the criteria are for identifying the owners of this useful faculty. In any case, the assertion of natural rights does nothing to clarify the problem of what to do in cases where they clash or when upholding them is extremely damaging to the general good.

On the other hand, we could claim that rights derive from political decisions, customs or conventions rather than from nature. This clarifies their source, but opens them to debate and amendment and thus deprives them of the 'pre-political' quality that gave them much of their force. As something we have *invented*, they become subject to the very claims and considerations they were supposed to limit; the assertion of a right thus reflects pre-existing moral and political commitments, which are open to challenge. Dispute may centre on who is a bearer of rights, and what rights they are supposed to have. Rights have been ascribed to fellow citizens, property holders, all men, all humans, foetuses, rational beings in general, animals etc., and have included claims to freedom, life, votes, property, work, financial support and so on. Universal assent to such claims is not easy to find, to put it mildly.

The starting point of libertarianism is that of the supreme and self-evident value of individual freedom. It therefore tends to regard claims to individual freedom and property as if they were natural rights. But many have argued that this conception of 'rights' as narrowly concerned with the entitlement to get and hold property is actually a reflection of a political preference, not a neutral description of timeless truth. We could propose other rights claims, such as the right to work, rather than the right to own. The translation of political preferences into the language of claims and rights seems to be part of the problem rather than the solution, as it forecloses on the debates about values, ends and means that are the very stuff of politics. 'I have a right to this!' is an assertion, not an argument.

Perhaps rights are best seen not as self-evident truths independent of politics, but rather as a *political* way of entrenching fundamental claims of individuals and groups against the expediencies of power. This does not mean that rights can be completely divorced from morality. The right not to be tortured, for instance, seems an even more profound claim than many of Dworkin's 'fundamental liberties', perhaps because 'liberty' does not seem to be the word that best captures what is demanded. Such basic claims, among others, have been increasingly framed in terms that transcend national boundaries, led by the United Nations Universal Declaration of Human Rights. But what counts as a right and the nature of the duties that may be laid on parties continue to be subject to controversy. Should there be a right to clean water, for instance, and if so who has the duty to provide this water? It seems clear that claims about rights and duties can never be lifted entirely 'beyond' politics. So while some freedoms may be entrenched as rights we are not bound to accept the individual rights-holder as the foundation of an entire political philosophy.

Libertarianism 2

A libertarian society could be a pretty hard place to live in, especially if you are improvident, ill, poor or just plain unlucky. Being seriously ill and penniless will leave you applying for charity if your family and friends cannot or will not help, since the state and society are under no obligation to help you. On the other hand, the individual is not blocked by anyone in her efforts to better herself economically, if she so chooses. This may make the libertarian community particularly productive and economically efficient, at least in terms of providing prizes for the enterprising. But its hardy individualism can seem unacceptably harsh in its consequences for losers, because justice in such a state emphasizes merit rather than need – a merit understood as *successful effort*.

A major criticism of the minimal state is that, for a society supposed to maximize freedom, it is precisely freedom that is poorly distributed. If the dry goods business in our example fails, then the proprietor's children may not be able to afford medical care or even food. So illness and malnutrition may seriously limit their freedom to choose and to act. Compare them to their more successful neighbours' children who get all these benefits. Unequal access to education also limits freedom. Those who cannot afford to pay someone to teach them to read do not have the freedom to decide whether or not to study a book (assuming they can ignore their pangs of hunger). The minimal state does not deliver *equal* freedom, and the worry is that many will never have the wherewithal to exercise their choices. It can thus be criticized as a strangely *unsocial* view of society. It emphasizes the individual as the primary fact of human affairs, and has only a 'thin' account of social good, understood primarily as the individual's right to be left alone.

Real societies are marked by *social* phenomena. These include patterns of inequality. Different families, districts, ethnic groups etc. inherit greatly different life chances, irrespective of individual effort. Districts with poor housing, schools and health care provide less freedom than those inhabited by the better off. Individuals suffer from being born in the wrong social group as well as from the effects of their own unwise or unlucky decisions. Of course, libertarians may shrug at this, arguing that this kind of inequality of freedom is a price worth paying for a free society that promotes a strong individualism.

There are at least two kinds of objection to this view. The first, which might be voiced from within the liberal camp, is one that we have already encountered. It is that libertarianism is unjust in its distribution of freedom, and is therefore in danger of being a liberalism for the rich and successful, promoting autonomy and efficiency at the expense of distribution and participation. The other, made from a non-liberal perspective, criticizes libertarianism on the grounds that it fails to meet some important criterion of goodness or justice apart from the maximization of freedom. This is an important point that we shall return to later.

Social democracy

Faced with the libertarian offer of a robust liberty with no safety net, many prefer to opt for something else. Here is an alternative way of thinking:

> *Any society that I would want to live in must prize individual freedom, but not to the exclusion of social responsibility or of justice. Justice is fairness, equal opportunities for all to make something of their lives, and a way back up from the depths for those who fail.*

This sort of view often goes by the name of 'social democracy'. Social democracy brings the pursuit of social justice into the foreground. It aims to find a social arrangement that promotes a broadly liberal ideal of freedom, while providing a better provision for *equality* of liberty. It interprets justice not merely as leaving individuals to themselves, but also as providing them with *equal freedom*. It accepts the necessity of a market but assumes that there are some things the individual cannot easily arrange for himself if left to his own devices. Different social democrats draw the line in different places, but provisions they usually want to see include some kind of national educational programme ('state education'), assistance for those unable to find work ('social security', 'welfare'), and medical provision available for all, irrespective of their ability to pay. All these might be arranged in very different ways, of course, directly supplied by the state or through some kind of regulation of the free market. Either way, the aim is to ensure some sort of provision, however basic.

All this implies a much enlarged state, paid for by the citizens through their taxes. Taxation diminishes the liberty to dispose of one's wealth as one chooses.

The citizen consents to this decrease in individual freedom because it is in her interests to live in a society that promotes a more equal freedom. Such a society provides a safety net against the rigours of the market, ensuring that everybody's basic needs are met through the contributions of all but the poorest members. Taxation can thus be seen as both a kind of insurance policy for the individual and a way of maintaining social cohesion. If this is accompanied by a democratic political system, the citizen can participate in the selection of spending priorities as well as ensure that the government remains accountable for its actions.

The social democratic state is still distinctively liberal. Despite its active role in promoting equal freedom, it shares deep affinities with libertarianism in its conception of freedom as individual autonomy. Proponents of both views think the

John Rawls (1921–)

John Rawls taught at Harvard University for many years. He is best known for his seminal book *A Theory of Justice* (1971), which is perhaps the most written about philosophical work in English of the twentieth century.

Rawls is a defender of liberalism of the 'social democratic' type against libertarians and other critics. In his work he argues that the most basic rights, liberties and opportunities (such as the right to vote, the right to hold office, freedom of conscience, freedom of speech, freedom from discrimination, etc.) should be equally distributed. But he allows that some kinds of inequality may be justifiable if, by allowing them, everyone – including those at the bottom of the heap – are better off than they would be if wealth and other goods were distributed in a strictly egalitarian manner.

Rawls argues for this view by constructing a novel variation on the old idea of the social contract. He asks you to imagine that you are in what he calls the 'original position'; that is, you are about to be cast into a society, but you have no idea who you will be. So you do not know whether you will be male or female, black or white, rich or poor, Muslim or Catholic, clever or stupid. Rawls claims that the general principles of justice you would opt for if you were in this position are the ones that are most justifiable. Much of *A Theory of Justice* is devoted to showing that if we were in the original position we would choose Rawls's principles of justice.

state should be neutral on what the individual ought to choose as her good, and the greatest strength of both philosophies is this openness to a plurality of ideas, values and lifestyles. Both also accept, with differing degrees of unease, the persistence of material inequality as the necessary accompaniment to this freedom. Where they differ is in their response to this state of affairs. The libertarian is inclined to leave the market to its own devices on the assumption that this is the best way to maximize freedom and promote overall economic success, while the social democrat wants to intervene in order to promote a certain notion of justice as fairness.

Imagine a circular athletics track. The starting blocks are arranged in such a way as to give each athlete a fair – that is, equal – chance. The blocks are placed progressively forward as they approach the outer side of the track, so that the athletes on the inner tracks do not have an unfair advantage. This means that all athletes will have an equal start, though it does not imply that all will win, of course. Likewise, social democracy seeks to promote *equality of opportunity,* but assumes *inequality of result* as far as material rewards are concerned. Everyone is (ideally) equally free to compete in an unequal society, regardless of gender, race or wealth. The state is thus committed to intervene in order to soften the unequal effects of competition, but not to abolish it altogether. It cannot abolish inequality without abandoning its conception of individual freedom as the highest good. For there to be genuine negative freedom there has to be space for success *and* failure in the acquisition of goods; *free* individuals have to be left to make their essentially 'private' arrangements with each other, for good or ill. Real freedom must include the freedom to fail.

Liberal assumptions about freedom have not gone unchallenged. It is possible to argue that individual autonomy, private property and the market are not indisputable natural facts or rights but *social* arrangements, the products of history and culture. This means that we are entitled to change them if we wish. Our laws need not regard private property as sacrosanct if other considerations such as equality, solidarity or justice seem more pressing. Moreover, some social phenomena seem to have a meaning and a logic that cannot be understood in terms of individuals and their choices alone; these include patterns of work and unemployment, exploitation and poverty, global shifts of capital, feelings of civic pride, social class and identity.

The inequalities of outcome that are characteristic of liberal societies tend to entrench the disparities in people's life chances that the social democrat struggles perpetually to minimize. Imagine two lawyers, each earning £100,000 a year. Suppose they are hard-working individuals who have achieved what they have on the basis of pure merit, thanks to equality of opportunity. Now imagine two individuals in the catering trade, each earning £10,000. Each lawyer earns 10 times more than each of the caterers – a large disparity. Now suppose that the lawyers marry each other. Their combined income is now £200,000. If the caterers marry, their combined income is £20,000. What effect will this have on the different life chances of any children the two couples may produce? Both couples will want the best start in life for their offspring, but the lawyers can obviously afford to give their children a much better start. And not only will the better-off children get this advantage for themselves, but they are likely to pass this relative advantage on to *their* children, perhaps increasing it in the process. Inequality of outcome thus presents a perennial problem for social democrats who want both to intervene in the name of equality of opportunity *and* leave well alone in the name of freedom.

Social democrats recognize the social or public dimension – but only as a dimension. Their recurrent interventions are based on the centrality of the individual and her choices, and this makes them stop short of any very radical changes. The liberal wants to stress that the importance of freedom is paramount, and that the right to make choices (however irrational or damaging to the individual) and to acquire and hold goods (with the consequent inequalities) must be defended, indeed promoted. Right is still ascendant over good. If the liberal model is deeply flawed – as its critics insist it is – the problem may lie with the theory of the good that the liberal employs. This, as we saw, is the claim that the promotion of individual freedom is the highest social value. But this assumption can be challenged, as can the contention that the free market is the inevitable and best possible system of economic relations. Both claims rely on a conception of human nature that we will now consider more closely.

Political philosophy and theories of human nature

All political philosophies presuppose a theory of human nature. Some are explicit about this, some not. But all have an idea of what humans are basically like. If they did not, they would be unable to make much sense of what humans actually do, or what they would like them to do. For instance, an argument for the right to make unimpeded decisions assumes that people are capable of acting autonomously. And people who believe we are all basically selfish will probably incline towards a different political philosophy to those who hold that we are all 'naturally' altruistic.

Even the attempt to explain political behaviour relies on a theory of human nature. When we try to say why people do something (what motivates them) we have already brought into play an idea of what *can* motivate them. Any attempt to explain human behaviour involves an act of interpretation that allows the person giving the explanation to shape the facts in a way that is meaningful. These interpretations rest on ideas about what human beings are fundamentally like, and these in turn are enmeshed with the explainer's values and politics. The attentive reader will have noticed a circularity at this point: political philosophies presuppose theories of human nature, which are themselves affected by political perspectives. There is thus no neutral place from which we could add up the facts and pronounce on what the best kind of society must be, as 'best' is loaded with assumptions about what is or ought to be desirable.

Although interpretations give a shape and meaning to the facts, this does not mean that all interpretations are equally valid. Sometimes this is because the facts are not as the interpreter claims. It is just not true that the German people were threatened by a worldwide Jewish conspiracy in 1933, whatever the ideologues of the Nazi party claimed. Nazis have a view of people conditioned by their racial theories, and these can certainly be contested by historians and biologists. 'True' and 'false' are relevant to political argument.

Nevertheless, it is not easy to decide about general theories of human nature which state that people are basically selfish and aggressive, or altruistic and cooperative, etc. Such views of our 'nature' – including the idea that there *is* a human nature that is either fixed or changeable – underpin decisions about which facts are relevant or important. For this reason, the theories cannot be thought of as simply being either true or false. How to appraise them is thus a difficult question.

Perhaps the best approach is to examine any theory of human nature to see if it leaves out crucial aspects of our experience. If a theory seems to demand as a condition of acceptance that we ignore or abandon a considerable part of what we thought we knew about ourselves, alarm bells should ring. They should also ring if the theory strains our credulity by demanding that we imagine people acting or thinking in ways that are nothing like real people we know. So the best account of human nature needs to be comprehensive enough to do justice to our complex reality. Let us look at liberal presuppositions about human nature with these considerations in mind.

Positive and negative freedom

Negative freedom builds a model of the human as individual unit-with-desires, a 'wants machine' whose main problem is getting unimpeded access to the objects of those wants. This assumes (1) that I know what I want and (2) that the main obstacle to getting what I want is other people with *their* desires. The task is to get rid of as much unnecessary clutter from the state as possible in the war of each against the rest. So the human subject becomes a kind of dodgem, a bumper car thudding into others in its pursuit of satisfaction, with the state as a kind of umpire. One serious objection to this model is that it is too crude: it just stresses the space in which individuals should be left to make their choices. As the philosopher Charles Taylor puts it, negative freedom offers us an *opportunity* concept of freedom, emphasizing what we can do, what is open for us to attempt, whether or not we do anything to exercise these options.

Being an individual with desires is a lot more complicated than the negative freedom supporters credit. A different conception might start from two assumptions:

• What I think I want is not necessarily the same as what I *really* want (that is, what would be in my interests).

- Desires and interests cannot be understood if we only concentrate on the individual; we need to think about 'us' rather than 'I'. The emphasis is thus on the Common Good, on what is in the true best interests of men and women considered as social beings.

This way of thinking paves the way for the idea of **positive freedom**. Instead of being an opportunity concept this is an *exercise* concept. It stresses the degree of control one has over one's life, and the activity of shaping one's life, perhaps in the light of some ideal, however imperfectly articulated. An advocate of a more 'positive' understanding of freedom therefore attempts to provide a fuller account of the connections between desires, beliefs and ideals, since it is crucial to this view that we should have a notion of better and worse ways of exercising our freedom.

My desires and beliefs are intimately connected. I have to believe certain brute facts about the world in order to see something as desirable. For example, I would not see a glass of water as desirable if I did not think it would quench my thirst. Some beliefs are more complex, involving judgements about which of my competing desires I had better satisfy and when (for instance, the belief that it is better to work first and then have a drink). Other beliefs – and these are of particular interest to us here – are associated with my self-understanding, the kind of person I think I am or would like to be ('I'll never be happy without a more challenging job', 'I ought to be kinder to my students'). Note that these last involve making judgements about the self and others that accord with beliefs about what is important and of value to a self already embedded in an inescapable social context. To shape one's life in the light of an ideal is a particularly sophisticated thing to do, as it involves taking up a standpoint that allows one to criticize and seek to revise the beliefs that inform current desires. It means not only having desires, but also having 'higher order' desires *about* those desires (for example, I may desire to have fewer selfish desires).

Self-understanding is both social and dynamic. It is social because we are born into more than a physical environment of 'brute facts'. Our humanity is formed by a culture, interactions with others living and dead that shape our sense of what is really important and significant. This is the context of our desires, the higher order ones as well as the other kinds. Education, media, advertising all exert formidable pressure on the developing self, moulding a kind of person who will have particular beliefs and wants. Any struggle against this will also be done in the light of alternative ideals that already form part of a social reality. Desire is dynamic because we are capable of criticizing wants and aversions that seem founded on false assumptions about the world and our place in it; this allows us to develop a new perspective that rejects yesterday's outlook as too limited, selfish or immature. And this is not despite but *because of* our character as social beings.

Negative freedom leaves people pursuing their various goals based on their current desires. This is supposed to be freedom, but the philosopher Hegel contemptuously referred to it as the 'freedom of caprice'. Asking someone if she is free to satisfy her desires may not be a good guide as to whether she is truly free. Would we agree with a happy slave that she is free? A well treated slave might tell us she is happy with her lot because she has all that she wants, but are we bound to agree with her that she *is* free or genuinely happy? The slave's desires have been limited by her narrow experience of choices, so all she wants is servitude: she has come to be comfortable with her chains. Would we be wrong to break her shackles if we could? If we can contrast the obviously enslaved in this way with 'freedom', we might carry the point further: inequality, poverty, even consumerism may have a similar effect on people. They can narrow the imagination, thus stunting conceptions of what we can achieve or be. If people's self-expectations are pitched very low, then meeting their current desires is a seriously inadequate way of ensuring their freedom.

The critics of the liberal model of freedom often emphasize the social conditions for the exercise of freedom along with the dynamism of human desire, noted above. This marks a shift of priority from the *right to choose* to *choosing rightly* (that is, choosing that which is good). This understanding of free choice is part of what we have called 'positive freedom'. Let us further our understanding of this notion by looking at two ways in which it could be interpreted.

Positive freedom 1: a new start for humanity?

Suppose that a group of people, rejecting the competitiveness of liberal society, set up a new kind of community based not on individualism but on a shared vision of the common good. They move far away from the nearest town and begin to live a life based on ideals of equality and self-realization. What this means in practice is the abolition of private property and the commitment of all the members of the community to working for the good of all, not for the enrichment of one at the expense of others. We can imagine them working out a rota of tasks and pooling any goods (money, tools, food etc.) for the use of all.

To make our discussion clearer, let us concentrate on four members of the group: Jill, Jack, Sid and Nancy. On Monday, Jill harvests the apples in the communal orchard, Jack prepares dinner, Nancy mends a broken tractor and Sid writes poetry. On Tuesday it is Sid's turn to work in the fields, and Jill's to do the dinner, and so on for all of them throughout the week. It takes quite a lot of organizing but they all feel enthusiastic about the new world they are building. More important than the physical details of how their commune flourishes are the new selves they are developing as people who see others not as potential enemies but as brothers and sisters. The free development of each is the business of all, for the common good means that none may flourish at the expense of another. Of course, they still have to overcome the 'old self' that they had in the world they left, the slavish self that was trapped by its own compulsions, desires swollen by the lure of consumerism, hatreds inspired by the law of the jungle (in other words, the market place). But they are optimistic. They will make a start, and then they will bring up a new generation in the truth that to be a free human is to be one that renounces selfish advantage. This new generation will not need to be coerced to follow rules, since it will realize that what one wants to do should be the same as what one *ought* to do. They will realize the ideal of harmonizing desire and reason.

But the old selfish self is hard to slough off. Jack, tempted perhaps by the abundance of consumer goods available in the nearby town that he glimpses on market days, starts to skim off a little of the commune's produce for his exclusive use. Perhaps he hoards apples in a secret place for later sale. He is discovered and is made to explain himself to the others. Whether he claims to have struck a blow for individual freedom or hangs his head repentantly need not detain us. Instead, imagine the view that the collective would have of him. They would be less likely to see him as free spirit or courageous entrepreneur than as an *unfree person*. In the light of their collective aspiration for a new start, Jack is a backslider, someone who has given in to *mere appetite*. The lower self, the 'old Adam' as St Paul calls it, has (temporarily?) reasserted its control over him. Whether they choose to expel, punish or re-educate him, they will not see him as someone who has just used his freedom differently, but rather as someone who has acted unreasonably, and thus unfreely. This is because in stealing the apples he acted as if his interests were opposed to the others. In fact, his true interests lay in acting in concert with the commune. The way they see it, to act in accord with the dictates of Reason is to act for the Good of all, not for oneself alone. Jack is to be pitied, and if possible reformed.

The version of 'positive freedom' sketched here starts from an assumption that there *is* a Common Good, which can be known and aimed at by all. It is a general approach that has taken different forms in history: religious, nationalist and utopian-political. In each of its forms the citizens strive to realize the identity of their individual goods with the Common Good. As the need to compel individuals to respect the freedom of others disappears, the distinction between state and society withers away, along with the need for law and its enforcers. Since the individual must want what is in his own best interests, which is the Good of all, it is simply unreasonable for the individual to pursue any other goal. If he does pursue such goals, they are only apparently good − in other words, they are false goals that are not in his true interests. Advocates of this view often compare this kind of disharmony between the individual and the collective with a supposed disharmony between the 'lower' or bad desires of the individual and his 'higher' or rational ones. The truly free − that is, rational − citizen realizes that what is right for one is identical with what is rational and Good for all.

All this talk of harmonizing the interests of the individual and the collective sounds very fine, but there is a problem. What we have just outlined may be a blueprint not for 'positive' or 'true' freedom but for oppression. One reason is that the view we have just described finds it hard to give a proper account of diversity and disagreement. If the Truth is known to all, why do so many ignore or reject it?

And what is to be done with these dissenters? The very fact that there is disagreement about the nature and even the existence of the highest Good may push the proponent of the 'higher way' to the assumption that some of us are more enlightened than others, who are (perhaps wilfully) blind. So these others must be educated, or compelled, to want the right things.

This attitude, thinking one knows what is in a person's best interests better than they themselves do, is known as **paternalism**. Once this attitude comes out into the open, an unappealing picture emerges of the new society as a re-education camp, with Sid, Nancy and Jill as tutor and leader to a less enlightened Jack. This means trusting Sid, Nancy and Jill a great deal. It means assuming that they know the truth about the Good and are themselves so far advanced on the path of sweet reason that they can be trusted with all that power over Jack. The history of the last two centuries might disincline one from making such a leap of faith.

The difference between this conception of how we should live together and the ones we discussed earlier is stark. The 'positive freedom' we have just described would not be recognized by liberals as freedom at all. In trying to avoid the excesses of individualism, the supporter of positive freedom seemingly sacrifices diversity and dissent in the pursuit of One Big Truth. But many would be sceptical of the existence of such a thing, or unclear about the credentials of those who claim to have become enlightened about it, or unconvinced by a society devoted to the pursuit of One Big Truth (whether or not there is such a thing). It looks as if we have not found an adequate alternative to liberalism.

A defender of the negative or 'common sense' notion of freedom might point out that true freedom includes the opportunity to make wrong decisions about what to do with one's freedom. While liberals are not committed to approving the satisfaction of all possible desires, they do keep open a space for the diversity of human aims, unlike the proponents of full-blooded 'positive freedom' who seem damagingly committed to the idea that there is one overarching Good for people, in contrast to the liberal diversity of goods. This is enough to tempt us back to the ideal of maximizing negative freedom. But to do so would also mean returning us to a crude model of human beings as 'wants machines' and an acceptance of major inequalities as inevitable and endemic. Before settling for that, let us look at another way in which the idea of positive freedom might be constructed.

Positive freedom 2: freedom to flourish

One possible alternative to the liberal/free market approach is *egalitarianism* or democratic socialism. A case for this has been put forward by Richard Norman. According to Norman, equality need not be the opposite of liberty. In his view, the main problem we face is the concentration of power, wealth and educational provision in the hands of a privileged minority; so what we should aim for is greater equality. But unlike the utopians, a democratic socialist like Norman need not interpret equality as uniformity (that is, the same life for all) but instead as *equal access to freedom*.

This view may look pretty similar to the social democrat position, but it differs in its critical response to the slogan of 'equal opportunities for all'. If these are opportunities merely to compete in a hierarchical society, says the democratic socialist, they are a false promise of freedom because, as we saw, even a liberal meritocracy reinforces privilege based on inequality of outcome. Societies in which the inequalities in power, wealth and education are deeply entrenched will be very difficult to reform in an egalitarian direction; for those who currently enjoy wealth, power and privilege tend to use these advantages to bolster their position. Meanwhile, the people at the bottom enjoy what can only be described as a nominal freedom. Only concerted action to change the structures that deny people a worthwhile life will genuinely increase freedom in this situation.

Worthwhile lives are led by those who have the power to exercise their freedom. This is less possible if one is poor, powerless or ignorant. Poverty, apart from any physical suffering it brings, breeds low self-esteem and shrunken expectations. Powerlessness encourages apathy and hopelessness. Ignorance keeps people in the dark about their possibilities and capacities. Take the example of education. The minority of adults who return to full-time education often experience this as a life-changing event, and not just because their earning power is enhanced. Access to knowledge, intellectual stimulation, mastery of new skills, and the habit of critical thinking encourages a new confidence. As their sense of their own possibilities expands, they change, and so do their desires. But the 'free' society of the liberal fails to deliver to most people the equality of well-being or flourishing that such transformations exhibit. Too many people are prevented from exercising genuine ('positive') freedom in their lives, as distinct from merely satisfying a few of the desires they happen to have already.

This problem cannot be resolved by concentrating only on opportunities for individuals to compete in the market. The egalitarian approach favours social changes that would eliminate structures that perpetuate inequality. These could include such measures as a widening of political participation through democratization, greater social and democratic control over the market, and the elimination of unequal access to the best education.

One objection to those who urge such a set of political goals is that it would diminish the freedom of some people. If we just consider education, the implications of an expansion in education for all along with a genuine attempt to remove entrenched privilege would probably include higher taxes and the closing of private schools. An increase in equality is thus created at the expense of freedom. Against this, supporters of change could argue that a move in this direction would lead to a greater overall increase in freedom for the majority. Only the privileged few would lose out, and they would be ceding a freedom that others should share in. Nevertheless, doubts would persist as to whether the massively increased public spending necessary, presumably supported by redistributive taxation, would be acceptable to a society composed of individuals who value the freedom to spend their income as they choose.

Making real this second kind of positive freedom would thus require a massive commitment to social change based on commonly agreed ideals. Its opponents will question its economic viability (it may simply prove too great an infringement on the effective functioning of the market) and its moral authority (it restricts at least some people's negative freedom). So the argument is batted back and forth between the two conceptions of freedom to no decisive conclusion. The debate is not helped

think critically!   Straw men and slippery slopes . . .

These are dubious strategies adopted in order to discredit the arguments of an opponent by distorting an argument in order to make it seem weaker than it is. Unsurprisingly, they are prevalent in any area of controversy, especially politics.

How to attack straw men

Here you construct a weak version of your opponent's position and then attack that — which is always an easy target — instead of your opponent's real position, as they might set it out themselves.

For example, a proponent of positive freedom might characterize negative freedom as an approach that countenances any kind of action and any kind of policy, no matter how much inequality or unhappiness results, just as long as no one's rights are violated. They can then attack this 'straw man' and achieve an easy victory. But this apparent victory is worthless, because the straw man does not represent the opponent's true position.

Sliding down the slippery slope

Imagine your opponent in an argument proposes or advocates X. You then reply that if we accept or allow X it will lead inevitably to Y, and once we have Y it will only be a matter of time before we end up with Z, where Z is chosen to be something terrible or shocking or implausible.

Here is an example: 'Proponents of positive freedom want to constrain the free working of the market. But if we do that we take a big step towards a centralized command economy. And this inevitably takes us down the road to tyranny.' The weakness here is that each step down the slippery slope, each claim that one thing leads to the next, can be questioned. If any of the steps is unsound then all subsequent steps are seriously weakened. (But if each step *can* be shown to be sound, then the slippery slope and its dangers may be real.)

by the fact that quite often the two sides attack caricatures of the opposing positions ('straw men') rather than the more complex, thoughtful views of their best philosophical representatives, and see any departure from their own principles as the beginning of a slippery slope towards perdition (see the box).

Perhaps the real distinction between the various political philosophies is best captured not by the pair 'negative' and 'positive' freedom, but by the attitude towards the notion of the human good that each embodies. What is really distinctive about theories employing versions of positive freedom is that they provide a fuller description of what the good is like instead of leaving it as a blank space for individuals to fill in for themselves. As we have seen, the problem is how to ground such a theory in a conception of the good that can provide a basis for justice ('right') without losing the possibilities of dissent and pluralism that are such distinctive (and valued) features of the liberal state.

The good

A more fully worked out conception of the good might provide the moral authority to challenge the market-driven freedom of liberalism. It would represent a decisive move towards a 'good before right' approach. Terms like 'worthwhile life' or 'exercise concept of freedom' lead us in this direction. But there is always the danger that a *substantive* conception of the good (a 'thick' theory of the good, as it is sometimes called, as opposed to the 'thin' theory underlying the libertarian approach) will be used to justify interfering with people's negative freedom.

The oldest and most obvious approach is to develop a theory of the good based on a factual description of what human beings are actually like. From this we can then try to construct a conception of the good life for a human being. The ways of life that would then be recommendable for individuals would be the subject of ethics, with the preservation of social conditions conducive to living a good life being the task of politics. This approach also serves to ground a theory of justice in which the purpose of law would be the promotion of *human flourishing* rather than the preservation of abstract property rights and freedoms.

'Flourishing' is rather a vague word. A notion of the good would have to be more fully spelled out to be useful. It might include a basic set of essential goods such as *meaningful work, basic subsistence, leisure, art, social relationships* and, crucially, the demand for basic *autonomy* in the exercise of freedom. This set of goods has to be coherent and plausible, and it must also be practical – that is, it should be an effective guide to our decisions about what is just. Such a thing may be possible. For instance, the recognition of the need for meaningful work as a basic social good could provide a criterion for rejecting the libertarian ideal, on the grounds that it leads to and tolerates unemployment.

However, a theory of justice based on an articulated conception of the good poses problems of its own, especially for dissenters and minorities. Orthodoxies grounded in notions of the collective good can be conformist, bigoted and dangerous to individuals. For example, some would say that the good life for both individuals and society cannot involve homosexuality; they might then try to use this aspect of their view of the good to justify the denial of gay rights. To avoid this, a society organized around some central notion of the human good needs to distinguish between things that the individual can be left to decide, such as sexual preference, and things that society has a legitimate interest in promoting (like participation in elections) or preventing (like poverty). If this is so, then it looks as if we cannot do without some conception of rights after all.

'Good' may be tightly or loosely defined. If it is definite, detailed and highly prescriptive, it threatens to oppress those who differ from the paradigm it has established, since freedom of choice in areas like religious worship, occupation and taste might be taken out of the hands of the individual. But if it is very broadly defined it risks vacuity. To affirm that meaningful work is a constituent part of human flourishing, for instance, offers no guidance where goods conflict. According to many economists, maximizing economic efficiency inevitably produces some unemployment. So which should take priority here: employment for all, or a higher general level of material prosperity (which is presumably also part of the good)? Nor is it clear where the promotion of the good by a state may be limited by the rights of the citizen. These are difficult problems, but are not necessarily insuperable. What remains crucial is the attempt to clarify the values that underpin social institutions and inform conceptions of social justice, equality and liberty. What role such values might play in founding the authority of the state is our next consideration.

Authority and power

From where does the state derive its authority? Here is one quite widespread view:

> *It is the strongest who rule. Whatever anyone says, it is the ability to use force that compels obedience. Look at history: when power fails the state collapses.*

This position can be supported by a simple argument. Any state must be able to ensure that its laws are respected by the citizens. Thus, a state must be seen to have the power to *require* compliance. Power is thus the essential prerequisite for authority. Without power there is no authority. It is not merely that authority needs to be able to coerce in order that its writ shall run, but that finally it is power that is the truth of authority, the reality that lies behind appearances. It thus worthwhile to investigate what we mean by power.

We can relate the claim that 'power is the truth of authority' to our earlier example of the 'wild west' town. There we described people living together for their mutual benefit. The peace is kept by a powerful agent, the sheriff. Without him to protect them they might fall prey to bandits – call them the Clancy brothers – so they pay him well and support him when the bad guys come to town. Then everything will depend on the sheriff being better at gunplay than his opponents. If he is not and they overwhelm him, the marauders will impose their will on the townsfolk. Force, not sentiment, is decisive. So the moral seems clear: it is the most powerful who rule.

'Power' is the ability to make things happen. In political and social contexts, it means getting people to do one's will. This could be achieved by sheer physical force, in which case the people being coerced have no choice because an external agent overrides their independent ability to act. But more often the mere knowledge of what power *might* do is enough to ensure compliance. This is true even in cases where very violent and unwelcome power establishes itself – as in a Nazi style occupation or at the hands of our Clancy brothers – since most people choose to preserve their lives and property by doing what they are told. The laws of authoritarian regimes like the Nazi government in Germany simply derive their authority from the power (meaning in the end, force) of those who promulgate them, and the citizen has the choice of complying or suffering the consequences, which is not much of a choice at all.

Nevertheless, power established by and relying exclusively on brute force is apt to be resisted at the earliest opportunity. Suppose the Clancy brothers decide to stay on in the town as a kind of robber aristocracy (a 'kleptocracy') in order to live off the inhabitants. It would then be in the bandits' interests to develop some kind of *modus vivendi* with the townsfolk, rather than just kill and ravage at will. Quite apart from the fact that long-term extortion only pays if enough of the prey are left to live and prosper, life could become quite insecure for the town's new masters with only terror to keep the people docile. So the Clancy brothers need to offer a positive reason to the townsfolk for putting up with them, as it is clear that the imposition of tyrannical force on a permanently resentful population is not a safe prospect for the ruler in the long term.

In practice, the citizens – or rather, subjects – need a positive reason for obeying beyond the fear of unpleasant consequences should they transgress. So a sovereign who wants to avoid deposition will usually offer the people something, even this is only more security than they would enjoy under conditions of anarchy. This peace is kept by a combination of fear and hope: the subjects' fear that something unpleasant will happen to them if they transgress, and their hope that a similar fear will inhibit others. The sovereign power says, in effect: 'Always keep a-hold of Nurse / For fear of finding something worse', and the prudent subject does not stray. In this situation, then, authority rests not only on brute force but also on the consent of those ruled – even if it is only a tacit and somewhat fearful consent. We can call this kind of consent *prudential consent*. To secure prudential consent it may be enough to be the lesser of two evils, the logic resembles that of the protection racket.

The existence of something approaching consent in the exercise of even the rough kind of authority we have been discussing suggests a distinction between *authority* and sheer *power*. The word 'power' here refers to brute force; one party calls the shots and the weaker party has no say in the matter. The word 'authority', by contrast, has a more bilateral sense; there is a degree of mutual recognition between ruler and ruled, and some assent on the part of the latter. When we *recognize* the authority of laws or leaders, we thereby acknowledge their legitimacy. This means that, in principle at least, we might withdraw our consent, leaving the sovereign power with nothing other than force to support it. The precariousness of such a state of affairs for the sovereign power is graphically illustrated by the fate of regimes that have to send tanks into the street to shore themselves up: it is usually the beginning of the end for them.

Why do I let others rule me?

Authority thus needs power, but power without authority rests on force alone, which is unlikely to serve in the long run. Even the most egregious usurpers have usually recognized that a ruler needs to claim to have right as well as might on his side. Instead of saying 'I am the law' they prefer to say 'I am lawful.' This suggests that we all, rulers included, tend to think of genuine sovereignty as meaning rule by law rather than by force, and that we attribute an independent authority to law. If this is so, we need to examine the grounds on which this authority stands. We need to know what can confer sovereignty on law apart from force. The clue may lie in the role of consent in the establishment of authority. We are thus led to a very basic question: Why do people ever consent to be ruled?

> *People generally consent to something if they think it is in their self-interest. Without government there would be no laws; and if there were no laws everyone would live under just one law – the law of the jungle. No one wants that, so we have governments.*

We have already touched on this view, first at the beginning of the chapter, and again when we discussed the distinction between authority and power. The basic idea is that the state is the defender of the liberty and property of the citizen in a kind of 'social contract' between rulers and ruled. The laws are allowed to diminish the otherwise absolute freedom of the citizen in order to ensure the liberty and security of all. Without such laws we would return to the violent anarchy of the 'state of nature' that preceded the establishment of society. The contract is taken to exist even where the citizenry are unable to express their preferences at the ballot box, because what is crucial is the trade off between freedom and the security of the private individual. All that is necessary is a *tacit* consent arising from the self-interest of ruler and ruled – an entirely prudential basis for rightful authority. This is the sort of thing that developed in our wild west example, tacitly between the robbers and the townsfolk and more explicitly with the sheriff.

However, this account may still not do justice to the full sense that a term like 'rightful' carries. The presence of consent indicates an ethical dimension, since a contract is taken to involve a promise (even if it is implicit), and promising is usually thought to create moral obligations. The moral dimension in any social contract is generally clearer when the government is chosen by democratic means. This is because the promising involved is more explicit: people who seek political office say that if they are elected they will do this, that and the other. But apart from any explicit promises that a democratic politician might make or break, standing for office under a particular constitutional arrangement usually implies a commitment to the preservation of this arrangement. Voting itself can be taken as a kind of promise on the part of the electorate to respect the authority of the state. Both 'sides' are expected to play by the rules, and moral language is invariably used to condemn them if they do not. Office holders – like the sheriff in our example – can be accused of betrayal, selling out, taking advantage of their position, and so on; those they govern can be branded as criminals or rebels if they fail to abide by their side of the contract. Contrast this with the relationship between a dominating ruler and a terrorized population; here, the ruler issues threats rather than promises, and 'rights talk' counts for little against the brutal realities of power.

Thomas Hobbes (1588–1679)

Thomas Hobbes is often regarded as the first great modern political philosopher. Writing at the time of the English civil war, Hobbes's guiding concern was to lay down what was necessary in order to avoid the kind of social chaos and widespread misery that is characteristic of society in which law and order has broken down.

Hobbes's greatest work is *Leviathan* (1651). In it he imagines what life would be like in a hypothetical 'state of nature' where there are no laws and no central authority. His view is that in these conditions life would be 'solitary, poor, nasty, brutish, and short'. To escape from the state of nature people agree upon a 'social contract'. They agree to give up some of their individual liberties, handing them over to a 'sovereign' whose job it is to make sure everyone keeps to the contract – that is, obeys the law. In this way, stability, peace and prosperity are secured. The subjects of the state are then free to pursue their various ends, secure in the knowledge that they do not stand in danger of becoming prey to the greed and aggression of other men

There are a number of fairly standard objections to social contract theory. One is that of historical inaccuracy. There never was a time when state and citizens actually signed up for such an arrangement – so neither can be parties to a contract that has the odd characteristic of being fictional, and the even odder characteristic of being impossible to refuse. But this objection can be fairly easily countered. We can concede that there never was a historical contract but still argue that viewing society *as if* it were based on a contract helps us better understand the relation between state and citizen. It is *as if* such a deal had been made; the effects are the same, whatever the historical details.

Another criticism often levelled against the theory is that it is tied to a simplistic model of human nature. Self-interested, asocial individuals, apparently alone in the state of nature, are supposed to come together to make the social contract. Since contracts are relatively sophisticated products of human society, it is unclear how 'natural' man and woman could ever take the first step out of anarchy. But this objection can be overcome in the same way as the previous one. What is at issue is not the historical origins of human society, but whether certain political arrangements can be illuminated, and perhaps justified, by this model. It is a model whose purpose is to account for political rather than social relations. Thus it is not, nor need it be, committed to claiming that before they lived in political society human beings were asocial.

However, the critics might want to press their point. The idea of a contractual relation as the basis of a political relation is, they might claim, dominated by a historically specific and overly individualist model of politics. The 'contract' is the bond of *homo economicus*, of relations that obtain between buyers and sellers in a market; its transference to the political sphere presupposes that our political relations resemble capitalist ones. It is thus unsurprising that it fits the libertarian model so neatly, springing as it does from a typically libertarian view of human nature.

Whatever the strength of this objection, we might still think that there is something valuable in the notion of the social contract. First, its emphasis on promises that ought to be kept underlines the importance of consent in modern political affairs. Consent of the ruled is nowadays often viewed as a *moral* demand that must be met if the state is to possess legitimate authority, and this is often taken to be a strong argument in favour of democracy. Secondly, social contract theory explains how and why the state has certain obligations to its citizens, such as the promotion of justice. Contemporary notions of legitimate authority founded on consent have thus developed beyond the purely prudential conceptions with which we began. Libertarians may see the state's job as simply that of protecting each individual's basic rights, but other theorists have extended the idea of the contract. Social democracy, for instance, writes into the contract an obligation on the part of the state to promote equality of opportunity. And once we accept the general idea that the state has a contract with its citizens to deliver more freedom than they enjoyed in the state of nature, the door is open to expecting that the state should do all it can to ensure that everyone enjoys the full benefits of freedom.

This leads naturally to the idea that a further justification for the state's authority lies in its ability to promote the common good. We saw in our discussion of 'positive' freedom that there may be goals that the state should aim at for intrinsic, moral reasons, and not only because they promote freedom or security. For instance, the state may set up, fund or subsidize health care, education, welfare, invalidity benefits, libraries, museums, art galleries, music festivals, national parks, wildlife sanctuaries etc. on the grounds that they make possible or positively promote what we referred to earlier as human flourishing, and not because they protect anyone's rights or promote equal opportunity. As we saw, this is a conception of the good that includes but exceeds the good of individual freedom. But as we also saw, it is difficult to articulate a theory of the good that is wide enough to ensure diversity and pluralism yet specific enough to act as a guide to social policy.

Utilitarianism

> Why complicate everything with all this talk about 'human flourishing'? The concept is either too vague to be useful or too determinate to guide the policy of any state committed to protecting freedom and respecting diversity. Moreover, the concept is not needed, since we have a simpler, better concept to hand: happiness. The state's job is to promote everyone's happiness. This is what we want from it, and as long as it tries to do this its authority is legitimate.

This identification of the good with happiness (which includes the alleviation of suffering) is the basic tenet of utilitarianism, a doctrine we also considered in the chapter on Ethics. Stated simply, the utilitarian view is that the state should aim to promote the greatest happiness of the greatest number. This is the end, and the state is essentially a means to this end. So too are all its laws. It is this purpose of promoting general welfare that gives the state and its laws authority, and only a state that pursues this goal can rightfully demand our consent.

It is important to understand that utilitarianism first defines the good, happiness, and then determines what is right – whatever promotes the good. On this view, the state is not protecting anyone's 'natural rights' or 'God given liberties'. Nor do the laws correspond to moral laws that exist prior to or independent of human society. The reason we are justified in having a law that prohibits murder is not because murder is inherently wrong but because if we did not have that law there would be less happiness in our society. We may, of course, sometimes make mistakes about the effects of laws. We might think that prohibiting the sale of alcohol during the day will reduce drunkenness, absenteeism, street violence, traffic accidents and alcohol related diseases, when in fact these things are made worse by having licensing laws than by not having them. But occasional mistakes of this kind are to be expected. It is sometimes very hard to know what the full, long-term consequences of passing a law or implementing a policy will be. Laws against the sale and possession of narcotics, for instance, are usually justified on utilitarian grounds: it is held that the social problems associated with narcotics would increase if the drugs were legalized. But some people dispute this, arguing that the legalization of narcotics would actually have beneficial long-term consequences.

The way the laws are intended to promote general happiness is analogous to the way the highway code promotes safety on our roads. There are particular occasions where following the highway code decreases rather than increases happiness: for instance, if you miss an exit and have to choose between driving five miles out of your way or disobeying the 'No U turns' sign. But this is not a good argument against codifying the laws and enforcing them. In order to maximize happiness overall, the code needs to be respected by all of us in just about all situations: short-term happiness is sacrificed for the sake of greater happiness for everyone in the long term. The existence of traffic regulations that are obeyed by all creates exactly that predictability that is so important for road safety. If we can safely assume that the habit of following the rule is ingrained in everyone, we need not worry that the driver of the car coming towards us is making a private decision about whether or not it is worthwhile to indicate his intentions. We do not want that driver to have developed the bad habit of treating all rules as provisional, and we should not encourage such habits by our own example. The same goes for laws in general. Universal observance of the laws has a general beneficial effect. If a law fails to deliver such an overall effect, it should be removed by the legislators; but while it stands, it ought to be obeyed.

However, this line of reasoning is more questionable when we come to consider matters of conscience. A citizen who agrees with utilitarianism may think that a law fails to promote the greatest happiness. She may, in fact, think that it causes real suffering and, moreover, that this suffering is so great that it would be unethical to keep obeying it until it has been changed. People who refused to pay the poll tax that the British government introduced in the 1980s often used this argument. Or she may want to break a law that does maximize happiness in order to protest publicly against a government policy that, in her view, does not. Anti-war demonstrators, for instance, have sometimes damaged property illegally in order to publicize their disagreement with their government's policies. She may even regard the government that frames such laws as a bad one that must be overthrown in the interests of everyone. As a utilitarian, she will have calculated that in these circumstances the right course of action is to break the law, or even to challenge the state.

The larger issue here is the ethics of civil disobedience. Under what circumstances, if ever, and for what reasons might citizens be justified in breaking the law? From a utilitarian viewpoint, our allegiance to the state and its laws is always conditional. True, a 'rule utilitarian' – one who advocates regulating our conduct by reference to general principles like 'Don't steal', which have proved to promote the general happiness if obeyed – could argue that 'Never break the law' is a principle we should always follow. Any law breaking, the argument goes, undermines the authority of the law and hence threatens social stability and the general happiness.

But surely there can be *exceptional* circumstances in which defying the law really does promote the greater good? A good example would be the situation in parts of the United States in the late 1950s, at a time when state governments and many public and private institutions actively discriminated against African-Americans. Those protesting against this situation often employed the tactic of non-violent civil disobedience, and they could plausibly argue that a long-term utilitarian calculation would justify their actions. But this creates a new difficulty; for what counts as an exceptional circumstance? It looks as if this is something that people are going to have to decide for themselves, and we can expect there to be different opinions on the matter, even among utilitarians. In practical terms, what often proves decisive is the view of the majority of the citizens; the more people agree with you, the more likely your civil disobedience will be effective and promote the general good. But if this is so, then the utilitarian approach has not solved our problems about authority, for now we are once again appealing to the principle of *consent* as conferring authority to the laws. When conscience clashes with the law, the principle that we should promote the general happiness will not, by itself, provide a way to resolve the conflict.

Consent may confer authority, but it does not itself provide a *purpose* for government or for legislation. Utilitarianism tries to do this by justifying the state together with other ends the state tries to secure (like justice, fairness and freedom) as means to the general happiness. But if justice, freedom and the protection of rights are thought of as means to the higher end of happiness then, presumably, it may sometimes be acceptable to sacrifice them to this higher end. The same problem also arose in our discussion of utilitarianism in the Ethics chapter. It is certainly a problem, but to be fair to utilitarianism, it is can be just as much a problem for the non-utilitarian. Consider, for instance, the debate that has been raging in South Africa ever since the end of apartheid over whether police and army personnel who illegally harassed, beat, tortured and killed people under the apartheid regime should now be brought to justice. Devotees of justice at any price say yes; but many others, worried about how this might seriously hinder the process of building a stable, united, prosperous society, take the more pragmatic, utilitarian view that the future happiness of everyone matters more than righting past wrongs. It is a tough dilemma.

One other obvious problem for the utilitarian view that the state should concern itself with promoting happiness is that there are many different ways in which people seek happiness. Are some kinds of pleasure or happiness better than others? Is enjoying opera or walks in the countryside somehow 'better' than enjoying children's comics or the effects of marijuana? For this reason, some theorists talk of 'preferences' rather than happiness. The attraction of doing this is that one keeps away from any hint of an evaluation. 'Preferences' are simply what people want, as expressed by what they say and what they do. But this term brings its own problems. What people want is sometimes not the same as what is in their best interests. So the question arises as to whether it is better to give people what they actually express a wish for – giving them what they *say* they want – or to correct their preferences – giving them what they *would* want *if* they were better informed, cleverer, free from prejudice, etc.

If we follow people's declared wants, the utilitarian state is in the paradoxical position of possibly lowering real utility because it is intent on giving people what they want, no matter how misguided and no matter how unhappy it may make them in the long run. Conceivably, following this path could eventually lead to what some people would view as a diseased, ugly culture, dominated by consumerism, pornography and drugs. And the critics of this culture would unhesitatingly assert that the people wallowing in it are not as happy as they would be if they had been encouraged to seek other satisfactions. However, if the state opts for promoting what the masses 'really' want – that is, what those in power believe the masses would choose were they more enlightened – we are back with the problem of paternalism that we encountered in our discussion of positive freedom. Who is to decide what people *should* want?

This last question has not been answered; but the implications of how we answer it have become clearer in the course of the chapter. Let us conclude by linking this question to what has been said. Clearly, there are dangers in the state allowing people's preferences to hold absolute sway; and there are dangers in deciding for other people what is in their own best interest. Those who are inclined to give what is right priority over what is good tend to identify freedom with negative freedom. They will lean towards giving people absolute freedom to do as they please, as long as this does not harm anyone else. If that means giving some people a rope to hang themselves with, so be it. This is the *libertarian* view. On the other side, those who give priority to the good and then define what is right by looking at what promotes the good will be more comfortable with the concept of positive freedom. *Democratic socialists* are usually in this camp. They will be more willing to risk the dangers of paternalism by allowing the state to go into the business of actively promoting people's well-being.

The main danger of *paternalism* is fairly obvious: it can become oppressive. The slippery slope from not allowing people to possess heroin to requiring them to attend re-education camps may not be very steep, but it is nonetheless a source of legitimate concern. There does seem to be a continuum of degrees of state interference in people's lives, and it is hard to know where to draw the line. Libertarians, of course, argue that the line is drawn by the harm principle: you let people do whatever they please as long as they do not harm anyone else. But this view has dangers that are equally serious and in many ways more real. The main danger is that if the state does nothing except protect people's negative freedom, then the social inequalities that will result, and the consequences of these inequalities (such as poverty, crime, fear and depression), will mean a much less fulfilling life for large numbers of people – perhaps even for the majority. This lack of fulfilment could be exacerbated if crude market forces are allowed to determine what is attempted and produced within a society, resulting in a pervasive and shallow consumerist culture.

Social contract theory, which is often the preferred political philosophy of social democrats, takes a middle road. In a sense, it too makes the right dependent on the good. The contract establishes what rights people are to enjoy and what the basic principles of justice are to be. Even when conceived as a merely hypothetical contract, it is usually taken to have as its main aim the general good – peace, stability, opportunity, prosperity and so on. But the rights and laws are justified on the grounds that they would be agreed to by anyone entering into the contract, and this gives them a firmer foundation than they enjoy on, say, the *utilitarian* point of view.

The idea of the social contract can also justify more extensive state intervention than a libertarian would allow. For if the argument can be made that people entering the contract would authorize a welfare system, public education, municipal libraries, government-run regulatory agencies, and so on, then these things have their justification. But at this point the familiar debate starts up again. Would those entering the contract be mainly concerned to ward off any threat of dogmatism, intolerance, elitism and other similar evils by insisting that there are many conceptions of the good life and it is not the state's job to prefer some to others? Or would they agree on a reasonably determinate ideal of what constitutes human flourishing – a framework within which all more specific notions of the good life will be found – and thus sanction measures taken by the state to promote this ideal?

7 Philosophy of art

Everybody who reads this book already has some idea of what the word 'art' means. We can best clarify what that meaning is not by looking for the 'essence' of art but by investigating why art is valued. So we will concentrate on the *value of art for us*, rather than hunt for some overall definition – in other words, we will be asking '*Why* art?' rather than '*What is* art?' This has the advantage of taking us straight to some of the most important and interesting debates in the field. And it is a natural place to start, since some people do place a very high value on art. Evidence for this might be the millions spent on it every year, and the thousands of hours and masses of paper devoted to producing, consuming and analysing it. Even those who claim to be entirely uninterested in art pay taxes that go to keep this vast process going. So it seems reasonable to ask what it is that we want from it.

Art and pleasure

Here is a short, simple answer to the question of what we are looking for in art:

> *We value art if it gives us pleasure.*

This looks like an attractively straightforward and common sense answer. If pleasure is the criterion of aesthetic value, it is easy to say why we value some art above others. Moreover, we have a ready answer to any question about the worth of a particular piece of art. We can simply apply the 'pleasure test': if it gives pleasure it is good; the more pleasure it gives the better it is; and the art that is most enjoyable is thus the best. Unfortunately, this sort of approach is not as helpful as it first seems.

One problem is that connecting pleasure with art fails to pick out anything specific about art. There are lots of things that can give us pleasure that are not works of art – a walk in the countryside, an ice-cream, a hot bath. Some of these may even give us more pleasure than art. Since we want to know what would justify the value placed on art as opposed to ice-cream, the claim that art gives pleasure is unhelpful. Another objection to the pleasure test is that even if art can give pleasure, it is not clear that it always does this, or that where it does give pleasure this is its main purpose. Some works of art, generally held to be extremely successful, do not seem to be pleasurable at all within the usual meaning of the word: examples include Goya's *Horrors of War*, with its mangled corpses and scenes of abjection, or some of Paul Celan's poetry, haunted by the Holocaust. So it seems unlikely that the pleasure test can really account for the value of art over non-art, or that some art has more value than other art.

A way of saving the pleasure test might be to posit a special type of pleasure found only in art. We could use the term 'aesthetic pleasure' to distinguish this special type from pleasure in the sense of 'entertainment' or 'amusement'. Works of art like the *Horrors of War*, which are not conventionally entertaining, might offer the spectator a distinct kind of pleasure. If so, our next task will be to identify what it is in the picture that produces such an effect. Not the content, presumably, with its severed limbs and anguished faces. It might lie in the form, the way in which the artist has composed the pictures, his use of shading, line and so on. Perhaps there is a way of seeing these features that evokes this special kind of pleasure in the spectator.

But the difficulty here lies in saying precisely what this special pleasure reaction is, and in identifying how form triggers it in the spectator. If the experience is recognizably similar to 'ordinary' pleasure, then we need some way of knowing when a spectator is experiencing 'aesthetic pleasure' and not the common-or-garden variety. If it turns out to be quite *unlike* what we normally call pleasure, we might be better off calling it something else – the x factor, perhaps. And this still leaves unanswered the question of how it is that the form of a work of art produces this effect. To say that the experience, whatever it is, is evoked by special or significant form explains nothing. We can only identify the form as significant through the response it evokes, and the response as special because of something about the form – a perfect example of circular reasoning. So any account of this kind needs to connect something in the art with the reaction in the viewer or listener without becoming vacuous and circular. As we shall see later, 'arguments from form' are especially prone to just this kind of problematic circularity. But whatever the merits or drawbacks of this kind of approach, it does not succeed in establishing a clear link between pleasure and the value of art.

Using pleasure as the *sole* criterion for aesthetic value also makes it hard to account for differences of opinion about the value of particular works of art. Suppose we go to see a film. You feel immense pleasure in watching it, while I feel none at all. Now, it might be that you are one of those people who can tune in to the special property in the film that causes 'aesthetic pleasure' but that I am not. In that case, spotting really good films, music, books and pictures seems to be a matter of having a special kind of *intuition*; and some have it and some do not. Analysis and discussion is therefore irrelevant. The obvious problem with this account of the pleasure–value relation is that it too fails to explain anything; the idea of a special kind of intuition is a *mystification*, not an explanation.

We thus seem to be left with one other possibility. If pleasure is the only guide to aesthetic value, and we differ in what gives us pleasure, then aesthetic value is *entirely* a matter of personal taste. In other words, if the film gives you pleasure, but not me, then it has value for you, but not for me. But this turns us away from our task of trying to explain aesthetic value in terms of the qualities of the work of art and replaces it by the identification of 'value' with whatever gives the individual pleasure. This is evidently a dead end, as it still leaves us with no idea as to the specific qualities of art that lead us to value it so highly, nor the grounds for our discriminations and differences, nor why it is that we value at least some art for reasons unconnected with its capacity to give pleasure. To answer these questions we have to turn back to the work of art itself.

Art and imitation

A large part of the value much art has for us seems to come from its capacity to represent or imitate reality. At least part of the appeal of Monet's paintings of water lilies and poplar trees is that they represent something that occurs in reality. The artist is praised for having somehow 'captured' naturally occurring effects of light, texture and colour. And this is also true of much literature. A novel such as George Eliot's *Middlemarch* can leave the reader with the impression that this is a particularly successful evocation of provincial life in 1830s England. More than that: we may put the book down thinking that characters such as Bulstrode, Casaubon and Rosalind are somehow like people we have met in our own lives. These are fictional people, we know, but the novel seems to have 'caught' something real about certain kinds of character. Other art forms like film, drama and sculpture also strive to achieve an accurate representation of reality. We could even make a case for a kind of representationality in 'abstract' painting and instrumental music. Whatever the truth of that, it seems indisputable that the idea of imitating reality has long had and continues to have great importance for most art works. Let us see if we can clarify what we mean by 'representation in art' by focusing on the visual arts, since they most obviously aim at some sort of representation.

> *Art, as they say, holds a mirror up to nature. We enjoy most paintings because they actually look like something in the real world. We are only going to praise a portrait if it looks like the person who sat for it. If it does, it's a success ('a good likeness'), if not, then we call it a failure. The same goes for landscape, still life and most other types of painting. Inexpert painters fail to render shape, colour and size accurately; good ones get it right. The history of at least Western art bears this out: compare Roman, medieval and modern paintings, and you will see a steady development of technique in the service of making better and better resemblances.*

This seems to be true for much of the visual art produced for many centuries, at least in the West, whose aim seems to have been to reproduce as accurately as possible the way things actually look. The history of art could be viewed as a long struggle to refine the techniques for doing just that, with the development of the rules of perspective as a significant step in this direction. On this account, *accurate representation* is the central aim of visual art. Discussions about exactly what this means have been much influenced by the writings of Plato and Aristotle. However, they used the term *mimēsis*, which has been translated as 'representation', 'imitation' and 'copy'. These three words do not all mean the same thing in English, and exploring how they differ may prove enlightening.

Let us start with the idea that paintings are *copies* of reality. If the production of accurate copies was the aim of the artist, we might suppose that the most successful examples would be those that create the illusion of reality in the viewer. Paintings like this do exist; there is an example of one in Chatsworth House, Derbyshire, England, in which the artist has painted a violin hanging from the wall. It looks so much like a violin in its position on the wall that the viewer briefly takes the copy for the thing itself. The name for this sort of painting is *trompe l'oeil*. They are certainly very skilfully executed, but do we want to say that they are the very best examples of Western art? Probably not. After all, when we have realized our mistake, we are left with, at most, amusement at our momentary confusion combined with wonder at the artist's skill in bringing about the illusion. The effect is similar to that of a successfully performed conjuring trick. But this has not been the aim of the vast majority of paintings in the history of art. Art does not in general aim simply to make perfect copies of things.

Yet we do value the power of art to represent (literally, re-present) aspects of our world. Think again of how we respond to a portrait: the picture is valued for the way in which it has 'caught', as we say, something of the sitter. But this does not mean that we are likely to confuse the picture with the person. If we look at one of Rembrandt's many self-portraits, we do indeed see that the painter has exerted himself to convey the effects of skin tones in a realistic manner ('a good likeness'), but we also see that this has not been done in the service of visual trickery (he makes no attempt, for instance, to conceal the effects of brush strokes). What has been achieved, instead, is a sense of the sitter/artist's character, his presence. People are not moved by Rembrandt's portraits because they think they have gazed on an exact copy of how he looked at a certain

The Iveagh Bequest, self-portrait c1665 by Rembrandt Van Rijn (Kenwood House © English Heritage Photo Library)

age, nor just because this is the famous Rembrandt. If something of the 'real Rembrandt' comes over to us in those portraits, it is surely more a matter of *character* than physical resemblance; what impresses us is the way in which his character is there, *in* the effect of ageing flesh. The success of the representation has to do with the artist's skill at conveying what we see when we see a human face, which is not just shapes, lines and colours, but something more than the sum of them: a person. To do this so successfully demands a certain insight on the part of the artist, along with other qualities such as honesty and courage. The picture eschews the illusion of reality in pursuit of the truth of character.

When we look at portraits we seem to be drawn both to what is represented and to how this has been done. We 'see' a face in the swirls of paint on canvas without forgetting the paint and the canvas. The art work re-presents something external to itself without confusing us about how the two things – the art work and the thing it represents – differ. We know we are not looking at Rembrandt, and yet an old man of that name is 'visible' in the oils. So even if we discard the idea that mimesis is about producing illusions of reality, we still seem to be confronted with a likeness, a kind of imitation. If imitation is central to at least some art, our next task is to investigate how this is achieved.

Representation in visual art

Here is one way of understanding how mimesis works:

> *Figurative art aims, through careful observation and application of technique, to render as accurately as possible what the artist saw.*

We can imagine an artist who wants to paint a country scene taking her easel out to the place that she wishes to depict. Having selected her scene, she places herself advantageously and begins to paint. Her powers of observation and artistic skill will be devoted to making a picture that resembles as much as possible what is before her. This seems to be a kind of copying without the aim of deception. Note that there are two key stages: first the artist looks at what is before her, and then she makes a picture that resembles what she sees as closely as possible. This has been called the 'innocent eye' account of how art is made, because it assumes an initial passivity on the part of the artist as viewer followed by an active stage where what has been has been received is put onto the canvas.

The problem with this account is that it makes dubious assumptions about every stage of the process of making a painting. The artist supposedly 'sees' the world as it is, without adding any interpretation of her own, before transferring what she sees to the canvas using her best technique. But it is hard to believe that this is what happens. We would not expect to find a different artist who painted the same scene producing an identical picture, even if his technique was equally accomplished. We would be more likely to think that different artists would interpret what they saw in different ways. Of course, the defender of the innocent eye account might concede that there is room for different styles and personal idiosyncrasies at stage two of the process, but still insist that each artist *sees* the same thing in the same way. But even this implies a rather crude distinction between 'seeing' – which is viewed as essentially passive – and interpretation, which is taken to be active. Few artists would go along with this attempt to separate out the different moments of the creative process. Most would say that 'seeing' is in some ways very active, while an 'interpretation' of what is seen can sometimes just 'come to them' or emerge in the course of their work.

It is perhaps more helpful to think of seeing in terms of 'seeing as'. 'Seeing as' implies that our imagination is modelling what is before us: we see clouds shaped like animals, or a shadow on the ceiling as resembling a face. What and how we see is also driven by our needs: city life demands that the pedestrian, the cyclist and the car driver attend to the meaning of what is happening in the street – assessing possible threats and opportunities. Mood too plays a role: joy and depression 'colour' how we see our world. The upshot of all this is that tones, textures, lines and shapes – the 'elements' from which pictures are made – show up for us *as* houses, trees, friends, policemen etc. Our interpretations continually shape what we see, and vice versa. Our perception, our awareness of the world through our senses, is not merely passive. To see, hear, feel, smell and so on *is* to interpret. All of us, artists or not, are perpetually engaged in trying to make sense of the world – a world made up of shared interpretations, with cultural and individual variations.

Each of us is born into a culture, a shared pattern of behaviour and belief. This pattern or web of conventions is itself the product of a long period of historical development – a *tradition*. Culture and tradition thus provide the inescapable context for individuals, whether they conform or rebel. The relevance of culture to an individual artist's interpretations seems clear, even if its extent is open to debate. For example, the ways in which Western European artists came to represent nature were very different to those characteristic of Japan and China. But whether or not culture is the decisive influence on how an artist interprets her world, it is clear that producing an 'accurate rendering of what the artist sees' is not a simple matter of copying reality. Further evidence of this is the uncertainty many artists have about what they will create. They seem to work out what they want to say through a struggle with their materials. All this is a long way from the artist as passive recorder of an independent reality.

Is representation merely convention?

Nevertheless, it remains the case that some art seems to represent something outside itself. The question is: How is this possible? How is it that we 'see' Rembrandt in one of his self-portraits? We have already seen that representation is not simple copying. It is a process of selection and interpretation that the artist partly shares with all perceivers, partly inherits from artistic traditions, and partly introduces in an original manner. Much debate about the nature of representational art, especially in painting, has revolved around the question of how much the conventions of representational art are rooted in pure convention alone and how much they are grounded on 'objective' or 'natural' principles that determine the accuracy of a resemblance. In other words: Is our conviction that a portrait captures something external to itself well founded, or is it an illusion? Here is a radical view:

> *Our ideas of what it is for a painting to represent anything depend on the codes we develop in our culture. This is why we 'read' a set of shapes, lines and colours as representing chairs, persons or trees. But these codes are purely conventional: they aren't based on any actual resemblance 'captured' by the artist.*

This view denies that an art work must in some way *resemble* the thing that it is representing. At first sight this may seem absurd. Surely the portrait of Rembrandt in some way looks like the man as he actually was? Yet this view, which we shall call 'radical conventionalism', argues that the route to representation in the arts does not run from the thing being represented to the viewer via the production of resemblance by the artist. As we saw, there are reasons to reject the 'innocent eye' theory of art as copying. The artist is not a passive receiver of reality who merely gets down on the canvas what she sees, but a perpetually active interpreter; and, as we also saw, her interpretations are largely influenced by the culture in which she lives. Remove 'largely' and replace it with 'totally', and you arrive at radical conventionalism. Let us examine the case for this view.

Defenders of radical conventionalism argue that what any picture most resembles is other pictures. Pictures are flat objects that have had paint, ink, charcoal etc. smeared, daubed or inscribed on one side. Even a few intersecting lines and scribble can 'represent' a human being: a 'matchstick man'. We see a person in these lines not because of resemblance but because the conventions make us see it *as* a picture of someone. The way that these materials are arranged represents people or things only by *convention*; they actually look nothing like anything real.

A given culture has certain conventions of representation, but there is nothing that says that any other past or present culture must use the same ones. Very often they do not. One of the key conventions of Western art is that of perspective, the representation of depth in pictures. The eye of someone brought up in Western culture experiences perspective as 'natural', but there is no reason to suppose that someone used to the traditions of Chinese, Inuit or Persian art must experience it in the same way. It is no answer to claim that perspective is obviously 'right', a discovery of the West, for we are concerned here with the development of artistic conventions and not advances in the science of optics. It is no surprise that perspective looks 'right' to people influenced by the tradition of Western art; other conventions also look 'right' to the inheritors of other traditions.

Conventionalists think of these conventions as operating like a language. Words generally have an *arbitrary* relation with things. The word 'dog' has no resemblance to the animal that wags its tail when I take it for a walk. We just use it in accordance with a convention understood by speakers of English. It would be naive to ask what part of the word looks like the thing to which it refers. And just as there are other languages that have other words (like *chien* or *Hund*) for this same furry referent, so there are cultures that do not share Western codes of representation. Representation, then, is about convention, not resemblance.

There are difficulties with this view, however. One problem is that it makes it hard to distinguish representational art from art that does not aim at representation at all. The following thought experiment is particularly telling. Imagine two pictures, one of blue clouds in a white sky, the other of white clouds in a blue sky. Would you say that each was equally representational? If the conventions of painting really did operate like languages we would be able to say yes. The *words* 'blue' and 'white' can be reversed unproblematically, as long as we have been made aware of the new meanings, since the relation between a word and the thing it stands for is arbitrary. It does not seem reasonable to say this of the colours used by a painter.

For this reason, it is probably more convincing to hold that representational art *combines* resemblance with convention. We must know what the conventions of representation are in order to see an art work as resembling something, but this does not mean that resemblance is *purely* a matter of convention. Mimesis is correctly understood as imitation, provided we do not naively imagine the artist to be passively copying an independent reality. Radical conventionalism reminds us that our perceptions are shaped significantly by cultural and psychological factors, but it takes this idea too far.

We want a lot more from art than copies or conjuring tricks. The arts of selection, intensification, heightening and so on can challenge us to be better perceivers, helping us to shed stale and habitual ways of seeing. This process requires two parties, and ideally both parties will be creative. The artist stimulates the faculties of the spectator, prompting him to a more active engagement with what he sees. The spectator in turn responds creatively (or recreatively) to the vision of the artist. When this happens, the viewer may see things in the picture that others, even the artist, do not. However, none of this implies that all interpretations of a work of art are equally valid. The recreative response, if it is to be more than private fantasy, must be genuinely authorized by something in the work of art.

We have seen that representation is not the same thing as mere copying, and that a representation can be 'truthful' without attempting to be anything like a photographic copy. Its truthfulness resides in the way it captures something about its subject and enables the viewer to become newly aware of facets of the things represented. This is a much more significant criterion of the success of a representation than its merely being 'a good likeness' in a mechanical sense. However, we have reached this conclusion by reflecting almost entirely on mimesis in the *visual* arts. We have not established whether it applies to any of the other arts. What, for instance, is the place of truth in literature?

Representation in literature

Here is one view about the place of representation in literature:

> *It's no use looking for truth in literature. The last thing we should ask of, say, a novel is: 'Is it true? Did it really happen?' Novels are fictional, either in whole or in part; and fictional means 'not real', or 'not true'.*

We might immediately object to this that novels very often do convey a great deal of true information about the world: the works of Balzac or Dickens, for example, are noted for their accurate depictions of personalities, places, periods and events. When Dickens was criticized for getting rid of one of the characters in *Bleak House* by having him spontaneously combust, he indignantly defended himself by citing several well-documented instances of this actually happening to people. Thus novelists may certainly be concerned with getting the facts right.

However, this point is not being denied in the view above. Literature may accurately convey information about clothing, social attitudes or coal production in a given period, but then so do monographs written by social historians or economists. If I want to know about the state of the people of England in the middle of the nineteenth century, I might go to the novels of Mrs Gaskell or Charles Dickens, but I would probably look elsewhere for the bulk of my data.

A large part of most novels is taken up by the delineation of characters (imaginary people) and plots (events that did not occur), even when the setting is conveyed authentically. To enjoy Balzac or Dickens for the social history is not to engage with what they essentially write – namely, literature. A novel or a poem may contain a wealth of information, but the point of the works themselves lies beyond the literal truth of that information. Literature is not the pursuit of social history or science by other means. To pursue literature in search of facts is to miss the point, as Charles Babbage (pioneer of the calculating machine, the forerunner of the modern computer) did when he wrote to Tennyson to complain that the poet's 'Every moment dies a man / Every moment one is born' was misleading. If it were correct, he pointed out, the population of the world would remain static. He suggested that Tennyson alter the line to 'Every moment dies a man / Every moment one and one sixteenth is born.' Babbage conceded that one-sixteenth was still an approximation, but considered it close enough for literature!

It is easy to dismiss Babbage as a philistine, and to conclude that literature has only an incidental relationship with the merely factual. However, there does seem to be something odd about expelling the need for truth from literature entirely. It is hard to imagine someone understanding the opening line of Keats's *To Autumn* – 'Season of mists and mellow fruitfulness' – without knowing anything about mist, or about its association with autumn in some parts of the world, or about the place of autumn in the seasonal cycle, or about the connection between autumn and harvesting, or about this season's common metaphorical associations with death. The opening line, like the whole poem, presupposes that certain things about the world are true, or are believed to be true. All literature must connect with the network of beliefs that writers and readers have about the world or no one would be able to understand it. This is even true of the wildest fantasies. If a book uses a language understandable by a human, then that language will carry with it the common beliefs that human beings have about the world.

But even if we concede this, as surely we must, it is still possible to criticize the idea that literature has truth in it. After all, the beliefs we just considered in connection with the first line of *To Autumn* are what the poem presupposes: we are not getting this *from* the poem. Similarly, in a novel, the world of the fictional characters generally resembles the one we *already* know. Of course, a novel might contain a good deal of factual information that we did not already know. *Moby Dick*, for instance, gives a detailed account of whaling techniques in the nineteenth century. But this information could be obtained from a work of non-fiction. For the most part, novels tend to present a world that accords with what we know already as a setting for the fictional drama. And fiction, by definition, is *not true*.

But if this is correct, it leaves the reader of literature – and the viewer of plays and films – in an odd position. What are we to make of our responses to literature? It seems irrational of us to get upset or joyful at something that has not actually happened, yet the end of the film *Casablanca* and the death of Cordelia at the end of *King Lear* typically provoke strong emotional reactions in audiences. If we are to believe the 'no truth in literature' argument, all this emotion is just a response to something unreal. But few of us who have been moved by a play, film, poem or novel would accept this argument. Furthermore, it leaves us with no real basis for saying that a work of literature is somehow praiseworthy because it is truthful, except in the relatively trivial sense of 'accurate' we discussed above.

Perhaps the argument that the fictional cannot be truthful is unsatisfactory because it misses the central point of literature. We noted earlier how a work of art's success might be judged in terms of its truthfulness. But we also saw that this truth was more than the production of an effective illusion. If we turn to the novel, it is surely possible to distinguish between texts with very different ambitions. There is a sort of novel which aims at verisimilitude in order to encourage the reader to accept the reality of the invented plot and characters. Historical events, actual locations, period detail and technical information may all be called upon to add credibility to the invented characters and plot. The reader is thus able to escape more easily into 'another world'. The works of John Grisham, Frederick Forsythe and C. S. Forester are examples of this kind of writing. This emphasis on factual accuracy may remind us of *trompe l'oeil* painting, which aims to produce effective illusions. On the other hand, there are novels whose main aim is quite different. The truthfulness they seek is connected to insights into the human condition. Here, imagination is the crucial factor, and as with some painting and sculpture, representing rather than copying is the goal: they do not attempt to produce a simulacrum of reality.

Take George Eliot's *Middlemarch*, for example. The character Casaubon announces, with startling certainty, that he is disappointed with the reality of love, as it is nothing like the passionate experience he had heard it was. He is in love, but he experiences none of the pulse-quickening excitement that others speak about. So he concludes that love is not such a wonderful thing after all. What Eliot gives us here is more than just a description of a dried-up scholar and his delusions. What is of permanent interest in the characterization lies neither in the cleverness with which the character is drawn and fitted into the plot, nor in the possible resemblance of Casaubon to anyone who really existed. If there was a real model for Casaubon (and it seems there was), he is long dead. What is Casaubon to us, or us to him? Yet the question of truth does arise in considering the delineation of this man.

The power of Eliot's presentation of the scholar lies in the way that Casaubon's story is true to a more general human reality. Through him, a part of the human condition is held up for our examination. If we experience a sense of recognition when we view Casaubon it is because Eliot has 'caught' something we can relate to: *he is like us.* So in the end we are learning less about nineteenth-century provincial life than about ourselves. This may seem impossibly didactic, with the novel operating as a kind of moral tale, a vehicle for George Eliot's views on the proper attitude to one's fiancée, and so on.

Many Victorian novels in fact have just this sort of flaw: to read them is to experience the numbing effect of literature as sermon. Fortunately, George Eliot avoided this sort of sermonizing. Neither story nor character in *Middlemarch* can be treated as a vehicle for a separable message about life. Imaginative literature can present characters and events in ways that provide prompts for the reader's imagination without prescribing exactly *what* to think. We 'see' Casaubon, and we grasp why his egoism is expressed just as it is. His lack of insight into himself and his limitations may strike us as having moral significance; but how this is so and the nature of this significance are left to us, the readers, to decide. We are left able to think about him, about why he is as he is, and beyond that about what sorts of failings this fictional man may share with the real people that we know, ourselves included.

If we undertake this kind of reflection, we may come to think that we have deepened our understanding of what literature and life can be. But this may not happen. Imagination is an *enabling* faculty – a necessary but not a sufficient condition for a deepened grasp of self and others. The novel provides its readers with cues, but it is up to them what kind of response they can or will make. Indeed, in some ways it is the work of art that puts the reader in question, demanding that the ideal reader bring to the reading all the insight, imagination and honesty of which she is capable. If this is so, it might help to explain why the same work can elicit different responses from different people, or from the same person on different occasions.

We saw that the Greeks' *mimēsis* could be rendered as 'copy', 'imitation' or 'representation', and that of these 'representation' seems to be the best term to describe the relation between art and reality that is most important to us. We have also seen that although truth in art is important to us, we are more interested in some kinds of truth than in others. The kind of truth that is most relevant to us is the kind that carries general significance rather than merely communicating accurately some particular fact. Art can make us look again at our world, to see it as strange, questionable, inspiring, or even cosmically funny. Part of the power of art lies in its ability to suggest the universal in the particular, whether or not that particular ever actually existed.

Art and expression

Many people value art above all for its expressiveness. Usually, though not always, the term 'expressiveness' refers to its capacity to convey emotion. Here is a fairly typical view:

> *A work of art is the artist's way of achieving self-expression,*
> *particularly the expression of feelings. This is what we feel and*
> *respond to when we attend to an art work, and this is what gives*
> *it its value.*

We might imagine the process happening something like this: an artist has the emotion of anger, and she paints a picture that has the effect of making those who view it feel angry as well. So the artist has 'expressed' her emotion in the painting, and the spectator has 'caught' the anger by attending to the picture. We can call this the 'contagion' model of expression. A painting might be judged successful because we approve of the feelings involved, or because of the sincerity of the artist, or because the picture is effective in conveying the feeling.

This claim for the expressiveness of art presents us with the artist, the work and the audience. The claim is that some x, originating with the artist, is passed via the work and is somehow received or picked up by the audience. That x is most often described as *emotion* or *feeling*, though this is not always the case. In addition, it is claimed that it is this quality of expressiveness that confers aesthetic value. We will consider these claims by looking at our example of the expressive painting in more detail.

Let us start with the artist. We have supposed her to be angry, and to have somehow expressed this anger in her painting. We could ask whether it is important for her to be feeling the emotion as she paints the picture, or whether she might be expressing the way she felt at some other time. The former seems unlikely, as it would imply that artists work only as feeling grips them. But there might be long periods spent waiting for the rage to strike! So we may want to allow our artist to remember her anger as she paints. Now, if we can accept this, we can surely also accept that a painter could express not her own previous anger but the anger of some other person. After all, Shakespeare is able to put words into the mouths of all kinds of people to express diverse feelings – envy, ambition, guilt, pride and so on – which he may not have felt himself, or at least not felt in the same way. Similarly, a painter can convey all sorts of feelings that she may not have experienced. This seems to be correct. But it moves us away from the idea of art as *self*-expression in the originally intended sense of expressing feeling actually experienced by the artist.

These reflections seem to make the personal sincerity of the artist less crucial. Of course, we can still call the painting a piece of expression – but now it is her expression of what it is like for someone else, real or imaginary, to feel angry. Her feelings may be quite different. Here we can make the useful distinction between expression *in* a work, and what a work expresses. The figures in a painting or a character in a novel may be presented as angry, greedy, joyful or whatever, but this does not mean that the work is *expressing* anger, greed or joy. In the Sistine chapel, Michelangelo portrayed damned souls howling in rage and fear, but we do not suppose that Michelangelo felt like howling in rage. It is more likely that the painting is intended to express his pious feelings at divine justice. George Eliot conveys Casaubon's etiolated emotional life, but this does not mean that she actually feels like him or endorses his viewpoint. Quite the opposite.

The question of sincerity in art is a difficult one. We tend to think of it as having to do with the artist being truthful in her art about how she feels or has felt. But just as we distinguish between the personal feeling of the artist and what the art expresses, so we can separate personal sincerity from *artistic* sincerity. The former has to do with the feelings of the artist, the latter with what is expressed through her art. Personal sincerity is no guarantee of artistic worth: think of all the atrocious poetry written by people in love. But we need not condemn the art as a lie just because the artist does not have the feeling expressed in the art work itself. As Stravinsky said, 'most artists are sincere, and most art is bad, and some insincere art (sincerely insincere) can be quite good'.

The question of sincerity is further complicated when art expresses meanings that are at odds with the conscious attitude of the artist. Some artists manage to say more in their art than they seem to know in their lives. They may even show sympathy with feelings and views quite alien to them in their 'normal' lives as citizens. Dostoevsky, for instance, was an anti-semitic, slavophile supporter of the Russian Orthodox church. One might expect his novels to be vehicles for his politics or his prejudices. But this is not usually the case. In *The Brothers Karamazov*, Dostoevsky created the attractive, articulate atheist Ivan. It may have been that Ivan was intended simply to be part of Dostoevsky's larger plan of writing a novel that would discredit atheism and further his own political and religious ideas, but it does not read like that. It is not a didactic novel of answers but a novel of questions and different points of view, none of them entirely triumphant. Artists may not be fully aware of all that their work expresses and thus may say more than they know.

Problems for the 'contagion' theory

The issue of sincerity thus poses difficulties for the 'contagion' model of artistic expressiveness, though the objections are not necessarily insuperable. A more serious problem with this model lies in its apparent devaluation of the art work itself. If the only point of the work is to be a vehicle for an emotion, then its value lies only in how effective a vehicle it is. This suggests that one expressive work could be exchanged for another without loss, provided that the emotion was equally well communicated. The expressive content would make the *form* of expression irrelevant.

However, this is not what actually happens in even the most obviously 'expressive' arts. Take soul music, for instance. Bobby Womack's song 'Across 110th Street' seems to be highly charged with feeling, a combination of compassion, disenchantment and indignation. If we limit ourselves just to the feelings expressed we may be able to quote other songs by performers working in the same broad genre – Marvin Gaye or Al Green, for instance – yet no lover of this kind of music would regard the Womack song as exchangeable with any other, however similar in feeling. Moreover, finding a 'feeling equivalent' may well prove impossible, since real works of art often involve quite complex feelings. Simple emotions like 'anger' and 'joy' are easier to find in theory than in practice. The work of the major soul artists is not in fact regarded as interchangeable. What is valued is specificity: how one singer phrases, the timbre of another's voice, those horns at that moment, etc. And if such an exchange is hard to imagine within soul music, it is even less imaginable between different genres.

A further question concerning expression in art has to do with the relation between the art work and the thing expressed. It is unclear what makes, say, a painting expressive. It cannot be the choice of subject matter, for then all similar subjects would present the same feeling and we know by experience that this is not the case. One painting depicting a battlefield may express patriotic pride whereas another may express disgust at war's barbarity. Presumably, then, it lies in the artist's treatment of the scene. But it still remains a mystery how an emotion like anger can be 'read off' from the lines and hues of a composition. Certain colours do seem to have standard associations in people's minds: red might connote anger, for instance. But the idea that there is a colour code for emotions, with a colour standing for each affect, is implausible. Some colours are associated with several different things (red, for instance, is associated with sexuality and danger as well as with anger). Some colours may have no obvious feeling connected to them (yellow, for instance). And the complexities of emotional life outstrip by far the available colours. It is hard to imagine a colour combination capable of expressing the 'feel' of 'Across 110th Street'.

The difficulties faced by the contagion theory do not diminish when we come to consider the role of the audience. The idea seems to be that the spectator of the 'angry' painting experiences a relevant emotional response – anger itself, perhaps. So how do feelings aroused by looking at a painting compare to emotion in ordinary life? Presumably, plays, novels, poems and television soap operas can all be expressive in this way. An emotional response certainly plays a crucial part in most people's experience of art. Yet it would be strange if someone watching *Othello* felt the same at the death of Desdemona as he would if he saw a real murder. In the case of the play, he knows that no one is actually being harmed. So to think of a spectator as simply 'having' an emotion in the usual sense may be misleading. Instead, we should perhaps describe the response as involving an *imaginative grasp* of what it is like to feel a certain way. Clearly, the role of emotion in art is a lot more complex than the contagion model suggests.

If catching emotion from art were as easy as catching a cold there would be no need for any knowledge, skill or training on the part of the spectator, whatever the art form. One would simply look at a painting to trigger the relevant emotion. Furthermore, if our appreciation of art were entirely a matter of having a certain emotional response, then anyone who did not catch the 'right' emotion would not be truly appreciating the art. But this account again fails to appreciate the complex relationship of feeling to knowledge and belief. Imagine a work of art made by a deeply religious artist, full of images of suffering intended to evoke feelings of piety. Some spectators who do not share the beliefs of the artist may not feel any emotion. Others might dismiss the beliefs but still have an intense emotional experience of some kind. Yet both groups of spectators might be highly skilled and knowledgeable art lovers, so it is unreasonable to say that they are entirely failing to appreciate the art. If we do claim this, it makes it particularly hard to understand the way in which we seem able to appreciate art made in the past by people whose beliefs we do not share. Not everyone who responds to Bach's 'St Matthew' Passion is a Christian, and not everyone who enjoys Shakespeare's *Henry V* is an English patriot.

The contagion theory implies that the criterion for judging a work of art is based on either the *quality* of the feeling involved or the *effectiveness* of the medium in infecting (affecting) the audience. The 'quality' criterion is likely to lead to what is

---

think critically!   Reductio ad absurdum

The Latin phrase *reductio ad absurdum* means reduction to absurdity. It is the name given to a very common kind of argument that is used to refute a claim that one disagrees with. The basic idea is that if a statement logically entails another statement that is absurd or contradictory, then the first statement must be false.

Here is an example. Suppose that during a discussion over the nature of art you define art as whatever is exhibited in art museums. I then point out that, on your view, if a curator takes a chair from the coffee bar and places it in an exhibition spot, the chair – that moment an uninteresting functional object – suddenly becomes a work of art. But it is absurd, I argue, to suppose that objects can just change their status in that way. Therefore, your definition must be false because it implies that they can do this. I have reduced your position to absurdity, at least in the eyes of anyone who accepts my other assumptions.

essentially a moral judgement: if the feeling is approved, the work is good. Art is then judged on its capacity to produce moral uplift in the audience. An example of this sort of thing might be Victorian didactic painting, much of which seems to have been designed to produce the 'right' feelings in the viewer. Unfortunately, fine feeling may lie behind a wretched daub, just as a brilliantly painted picture may have no sincere or socially redeeming feeling behind it. Recall Stravinsky's remark about sincerity. The 'effectiveness' criterion is even cruder. If the worth of a work is judged by how successful it is in communicating emotion to a large number of people very quickly, then dance music is surely one of the highest art forms. It is no criticism of disco music to suggest that any theory of art that entails such a conclusion must be mistaken. (The form of argument employed here is known as a *reductio ad absurdum* – see the box.) Even among aficionados of rock music, distinctions are usually made on grounds other than its capacity to stimulate waves of emotion in crowds of listeners.

The contagion theory thus runs up against many objections. The emphasis on feeling over everything else seems overly irrationalist:

- it raises difficult problems concerning the place of sincerity and the meaning of truthfulness in an artist's work;
- it offers an oversimplified account of feeling; and
- it clashes with the way we normally think about art.

This last objection has to be taken seriously. If a theory that purports to explain what art does goes against too many of our intuitions, it is the theory rather than the intuitions that probably has to go. We need a better theory of expression. It ought to avoid, if possible, the tendency to under-emphasize the particularity of the specific art work, and it should try to stay closer to what artists and audiences actually do.

Art and expression revisited: the case of music

In spite of these difficulties, it still seems reasonable to believe that expression is important to art, even if art is more than just expression. Any approach that seeks to discard or marginalize this view has to produce a better theory of how art is produced and consumed, and also has to explain why many people think that the art they love is somehow expressive. The plausibility of the art-as-expression thesis is particularly strong where the mimetic arts are concerned, where words and images evoke the lives and experiences of human beings. It is a harder case to make when we consider those arts that do not employ such features, such as non-figurative art or purely instrumental music. These art forms are not so easy to relate to the kind of expression we have been discussing, because without the presence of words or forms taken from life it is often hard to say just what is being expressed. In the case of music, for instance, one is unable to say just what the link is between tones and rhythms and feeling. Yet it is music that people most often describe as conveying particularly strong emotions. How is this supposed to happen? How can wordless and imageless tones and rhythms express anger, grief, happiness or contentment? Here is one possible view:

> *The relationship between music and expression is like a language with purely musical features that indicate the 'feel' to the audience. Minor keys are generally experienced as sad, certain chords express assertive or positive feelings, other chords suggest melancholy, and so on. Together with rhythm, tempo, timbre and other elements, we can elaborate a sort of 'language of music'.*

But there are problems with this view. One interesting but troubling question is how non-Western musical styles are supposed to fit into this 'language'. More fundamentally, it is not clear how the language is supposed to work. Music can often leave listeners with different opinions about what is expressed. All the 'language of music' approach can say to this is that some of the listeners are not listening properly. But it is obviously circular to say that differences of opinion arise from failure to 'read' the language. Once again, the question arises: How do we know when an interpretation is correct?

If music really is a language of emotions, we lack any kind of precise explanation as to how the elements of music have the expressive powers that they do. The very complexity of some music, its use of melody, harmony, rhythm and texture, leaves open the question as to how the composer can achieve the desired effects. And if this is the way in which music 'speaks' to us, are we to suppose that all composers are speaking the same language? Bach, Stravinsky and Duke Ellington are very different composers, and if they are expressive they are surely not expressive in the same way.

Formalism

The above considerations have often led to the denial that music is truly expressive of emotion. Rather, we should prize it for its *formal* qualities: the combination of purely musical elements that make it beautiful. The appreciation of form – the way in which elements like tone, pitch and tempo relate to each other as shapes or patterns – deepens the listener's understanding and appreciation of a piece of music. There is a particular delight to be had in attending to the way a melody in jazz is revisited in ever more imaginative and remodelled, or to thematic transformation in a symphony by Brahms or Beethoven. This emphasis on form – the way in which certain features of the art work relate to each other in various satisfying ways – is certainly not limited to music. Painting, dance, sculpture, poetry and even the novel can be appreciated in these terms.

Yet it is questionable whether it is always possible to separate the purely formal from other aspects of such works. Some art forms, as we have already seen, seem to be essentially *mimetic*. A novel may be well proportioned in its handling of themes, for instance, but the reader will usually expect it to be 'about' something, to have a subject other than itself. And in the vast majority of novels this is indeed the case. However, this has not stopped some critics from answering our initial, guiding question – What is it we value in art? – with the thesis that all the arts gain their real aesthetic value from formal qualities. The argument for form as the central or only aesthetic value in art is likely to be at its strongest when we consider abstract painting or instrumental music, because there need not be any 'subject matter' to get in the way. Conversely, any serious objections to the 'form' argument with these works are likely to raise doubts about its applicability elsewhere as well.

To see how this sort of argument might proceed, we will turn first to an influential account that claims the value of music resides in its form alone. Here is a bold statement of this view:

> Instrumental music is beautiful because of the ways in which the composer has used the elements available to make something beautiful. It is not 'about' anything but itself: the subject of music is itself. Anything else – 'joy', 'fear' or what have you, is projected onto the music by the listener.

This position can be supported in the following way. If we say that music somehow expresses emotional states, we are showing that we do not understand what emotions are. Emotions involve beliefs, and this means they are always *directed* in some way. If I am angry, I am angry because I believe something to be the case, I am angry *about* something, or *with* somebody. But as music does not contain concepts, it cannot be directed at or be about anything. The most music can do is convey things like a sense of acceleration, waxing, waning, slowing, rising etc. It may be that audiences associate these features with certain emotions and are thus led to think that music expresses emotion. But although a listener may be aroused or lulled in some way by tempo, rhythm, crescendos and so on, it does not follow that the music is about anything or expresses anything. Music, unlike language, does not contain signs that point to anything beyond itself. It is entirely possible to use words that describe emotions – 'joyful', 'eager', 'sad' – to describe music, but all we are doing here is using figurative language. We could just as well use words descriptive of the weather, or nature generally – 'fresh', 'warm' etc. But the most accurate description will always be purely descriptive, such as 'This music is allegro in C minor.'

In many ways this formalist position is attractively sensible. It seems to say something true about the emotions, while accounting for the tendency most of us have at times to sink into a reverie when we hear music, embroidering our own feeling on the experience rather than actually attending to what is going on. It also avoids the problem of pinning a feeling on a sound. And its account of the role of belief in emotions is certainly plausible.

One phenomenon not mentioned by the account is that of *mood*. Mood, unlike emotion, need not be directed at any particular thing, so could it be this that is expressed by music? Just as I can be in a sad or happy mood without thinking about a person or event, so music can just be sad or happy. The formalist might reply that although moods are not 'directed', they are ascribed to people on the basis of characteristic forms of behaviour; and while they may not be connected to propositions, they do characterize our judgements about things. You know I am sad because I behave sadly; and if I am sad my experience of the world is coloured by that mood, thus affecting my judgements. Mood, like emotion, is a public thing rather than just a floating inner sensation. What this means is that the use of mood terms like 'sad' or 'happy' cannot be separated from human behaviour and attributed to adagios and modulations.

The importance of metaphor

But there is a fundamental problem with the formalist account of music: it does not accord with our *experience* of music. Listening to music, as distinct from hearing sounds, means attending to a kind of imaginary object. Integral to the experience of listening to music is to hear it as movement. Music rises, falls, accelerates, decelerates etc.; themes pursue, generate and transform each other. We might think that if there is movement, there must be a space in which it can occur – but in fact nothing is *really* moving, and there is no real space in which such movement could happen. There are just vibrations in the air, physical events that the eardrum picks up as sound. Yet hearing sound is not the same as perceiving music: we hear music *as if* there were such a thing as musical space, with forms made of tones moving through it. It is a kind of *metaphorical* grasp of aural events, in which the listener hears music in the sound. If this account is correct, then what we have described is not just one way of listening to music. Rather, this perception of an imaginary object (a space in which movement occurs) *is* 'hearing music'.

This means that metaphor is at the heart of even the most 'formalist' account of a piece of music – a dynamic form in which themes generate other themes, return in new guises, 'rise to a climax', echo one another, and so on. These features are not optional extras, projected onto music by lazy listeners. It is true that we can limit ourselves to purely technical description, saying that a piece is in C minor or that it is played *andante*. This kind of information can be interesting and useful; but it is an illusion to suppose that this technical description is of something that is 'really' there, in contrast to a metaphorical description that involves a projection on our part.

This is an important point that takes us back to the problem of how music can express meaning. Once we see that metaphor is fundamental to the experience of listening to music, we see how further metaphors – of journey, struggle, triumph, defeat and so on – can lead us into an imaginative identification with the movement of the music. And this happens in spite of the fact that in music, unlike in a play or a novel, there is no subject experiencing emotions and no object at which the emotions can be directed. We can, in life or in art, recognize the expression of an emotion even when we do not know its object. A painting of a face contorted with grief, looking at something outside the frame of the picture, is still expressive. Similarly, there is no real person or real object in music, but there is something that somehow lies between them: the expression of feeling. As for how this affects the listener, the point made earlier about what we believe when we engage with fiction applies here: the listener does not feel exactly as she would if the emotion were aroused by a real event, but she does *imaginatively entertain* what that feeling might be like. It is not a matter of holding a real belief but of having a certain kind of experience – one that relates to, and is reminiscent of, an emotion but is not the emotion itself.

We have seen that the full-blooded formalist position runs into difficulties even as an account of a 'non-mimetic' art like instrumental music. These difficulties are compounded in mimetic arts like the novel and cinema, where there is obviously a definite subject matter. For example, Jean Renoir's film *The Rules of the Game* certainly has formal qualities, but its aesthetic value does not lie solely or even principally in its form. The film can be enjoyed for its virtuosic use of the camera, a deep focus style giving great visual depth to the scenes, or for the way the plot weaves together the fortunes of various individuals in patterns that are enjoyable in themselves. There are other features we could name – *mise-en-scène*, use of sound, and so on; but it is clearly misguided to regard such formal features as the main point of the film. When it was first shown in 1939, some of its audiences rioted in the cinema. What they were seeing (and not liking!), in and through the style, was a socio-political content – a scathing critique of a self-absorbed society oblivious to the abyss that was opening up beneath it at that time.

However, while these observations may reveal the limitations of formalism, nothing we have said proves that subject, theme or truthfulness have aesthetic worth. It might be that viewers and readers are *distracted* by non-formal features. A proponent of formalism might claim that this distraction is the result of working in an impure medium, that art made out of words or pictures tends to lead the untutored away from the formal qualities. This approach is encapsulated by the critic Walter Pater's famous statement that 'all art aspires to the condition of music'. For the formalist, the art work has various properties that derive from the arrangements of tones, shapes, masses and so on, to which the viewer, reader or listener ideally responds. So if we are to give formalism a fair hearing, we must examine the way it answers two further questions:

- What, exactly, do we value in form?
- What kind of response is the audience supposed to be having?

Form and beauty

Here is one very traditional answer to the question of what we value in form:

What we value in art is beauty.

It would be convenient if we could leave it at that. If asked what we meant by beauty, we could answer that the nature and presence of beauty in a work of art is obvious, something anyone can recognize. But this would make the identification and appreciation of beauty a matter of *intuition*. And the problem with intuition as a basis for the detection of beauty is that it forecloses on all discussion, disagreement and debate, making it impossible to understand why we agree or disagree about which things are beautiful and what we think we are doing when we discuss our judgements. If the 'beauty intuitionist' is correct, when we look at the ceiling of the Sistine chapel or listen to Beethoven's Pastoral symphony, there is nothing to say but 'This is beautiful.' And if someone disagrees with us, no dialogue or discussion is possible because *we* have intuited beauty and *they* have not.

This is not what really happens, of course. In practice, we do say why we think one thing beautiful and another not, and we try to support our judgements by invoking features of the art work under discussion. Instead of just pointing at a beautiful thing and gasping, we use words to convey, convince and dispute judgements. But which words?

Part of the problem is that the word 'beautiful' is used in English to cover an enormously wide range of things: a sunset, a trumpet solo, a child, a poem, a motor cycle, a horse. Almost anything, it seems, could be called beautiful. If the word points to something that all these things possess, it is not clear what that something is. It is difficult, perhaps impossible, to say what a beautiful child and a beautiful trumpet solo by Miles Davis have in common. So we need more specific terms than 'beautiful'. Many of them, like 'majestic' or 'elegant', are fairly general and therefore need to give way to more specific terms in particular cases. If the shape in question is elegant, a term like 'slender' might be employed to describe why it is elegant. But it is unclear how elegant relates to slender. Does either imply the other?

As soon as someone lays down a set of rules for determining what is beautiful – and there have been plenty of attempts to do this – something comes along that breaches the rules. Botticelli's *Primavera* is called beautiful by many, art critics and lay people; but so is Jackson Pollock's *Autumn Rhythm*. Are they both beautiful but for different reasons (in which case it seems that the meaning of 'beautiful' may be too wide to pin down)? Or is one not beautiful at all (suggesting that we prize the unbeautiful in art)? 'That's beautiful' appears to have more to do with the spectator's or listener's response than anything we can identify in the specific art work.

The aesthetic attitude

If what we just said is right, then it might be better to investigate the nature of our responses to art instead of looking for an '*x* factor' possessed by all beautiful things. There might be a particular kind of experience identifiable as the 'aesthetic response'. If so, we would have to be able to distinguish it from other, non-aesthetic responses. Here is a possible account of what this response might involve:

> *An aesthetic response is one of distance and detachment. When I see the gangster in the film, I don't flee. I don't act as if I'm having a real experience. I contemplate the thing before me for what it is, for itself and not as something that represents a threat or an opportunity. I respond to it as an aesthetic phenomenon.*

The claim is that the aesthetic response is marked by a certain distance from our usual concerns. We contemplate the aesthetic phenomenon as it is in itself, rather than for the use it might have for us. The exact nature of the experience remains unclear, as do the precise conditions that bring it about. Unless anything whatsoever is capable of triggering the aesthetic response, it would seem to be caused by some special feature or property of an object.

We seem to be back with the mysterious x factor. Presumably, we know we are having the reaction because we are in the presence of beauty, or x, and we know this because we are having the special response. This is not much of an advance on pointing and gasping, and it may inspire the suspicion that aesthetic judgement is an arbitrary, subjective reaction. Unless it can be shown how this response differs from just saying 'I like it' or 'It moves me', aesthetic experiences are of the same kind as experiences of ice-cream and rollercoasters. Furthermore, while this account emphasizes the non-instrumental, contemplative side of aesthetic experience, it neglects an important dimension of our *engagement* with art. Far from being detached and disengaged by drama, for instance, we find our emotions stirred by what we see and hear. We care about what is before us. Our capacity to 'entertain imaginatively', as we discussed earlier, means that we can be moved by the sufferings of a Lear, Cordelia or Desdemona without confusing what we see with a real experience of death and loss.

We need a better account of aesthetic response. Accounts that characterize our reactions to art in terms of emotion or intuition alone are inadequate because they neglect the role of the intellect. We feel *and* think when we encounter art, otherwise we would be unable to communicate our experience beyond pointing and gasping. A good account would be one that combined this 'gut feeling' aspect of our response with the evaluative one. Without it, we cannot break out of the wordless and mysterious circle of 'form–special response–form'. Let us therefore consider one of the most influential attempts to give such an account.

The nature of aesthetic judgement

The account we will look at is the one given by Immanuel Kant. It is put forward mainly in his *Critique of Judgement*, which is itself part of a larger undertaking, the 'critical philosophy'. What Kant has to say about aesthetics is fairly complex and involved, and we do not have the space to pursue it far here. But we can review briefly some of the important and suggestive claims that he makes.

An aesthetic response involves a *judgement*. It is a special kind of judgement that must be sharply distinguished from two other ways of interacting with things in our world. First, aesthetic judgements are not like what Kant calls 'logical' judgements, which are about whether something is the case or not. 'That is a blue dress' and 'This is a dog' (and not a tree, or a cloud) are examples of logical judgements. They claim the status of knowledge; so if the judgement is correct, anyone who disagrees with it is wrong. It is not a matter of personal preference: either that *is* a dog, *or* it is something else.

Aesthetic judgments are like logical ones in that they communicate something to others, but what they communicate is special. They are not simple claims about what is the case in the world 'out there'. They signify that the person speaking is having a certain kind of experience. But here it becomes important to distinguish aesthetic judgements from the 'private' judgements we make when something gratifies us. Private judgements merely express an individual's pleasure. I like pistachio flavoured ice-cream, but you may not. If I say 'This tastes nice' and you say 'It's disgusting', neither of us is 'wrong'. We just differ. With an aesthetic judgement the situation is different: I listen to Miles Davis and say 'This is beautiful', and by this I mean that the music is affecting me *and* that you ought to be similarly affected. The reason I think you should be affected in a similar way is (1) because the music is beautiful, and (2) because this *matters*. If I didn't think this, I might as well just listen and gasp: the experience would be mine alone, like that of the ice-cream. As it is, if you say 'It's ugly' I think you are wrong, because here we are talking about certain qualities the music possesses and not, as with the ice-cream, just about the pleasure or the disgust felt by you or me.

For Kant, the pleasure we experience before a work of art is *disinterested*. He means by this not that we do not care about the art, but that we care in ways not motivated by our needs or desires. We contemplate colours, melodies, dialogue and so on for what they are, and not for what use we can make of them. The upshot here is that, for Kant, the kind of delight we experience when we say something is beautiful is *qualitatively different* from the kind that prompts us to say that the ice-cream tastes nice; the former has a kind of universal validity, whereas the latter just expresses my personal gratification. I think everyone who hears Miles Davis playing 'So What?' ought to respond to it as I do; I do not think everyone ought to like pistachio ice-cream. This is not to say that the aesthetic judgement is of the same order as 'This is a dog.' Logical judgements give us knowledge and do not admit of dissent. I can demand that you agree that the furry barking thing with a wagging tail is a dog and not a tree or lamp post. It is not like that with the trumpet solo I so admire. I cannot expect my judgement to compel your agreement this time. But I nevertheless say that you should agree with me. I am not saying 'Trumpet solos of this type are invariably beautiful', or 'Anything by Miles is good.' I am judging this specific recording of Miles Davis playing the trumpet as something beautiful, and I demand your agreement.

The question is: What entitles me to make such a demand? To understand Kant's answer we need to look again at the difference between logical and aesthetic judgements.

As we saw in the Metaphysics chapter, Kant does not view the mind as a passive recording device that simply registers input from the senses. He argues that it actively orders our experience, so that seeing is always 'seeing as'. Having an experience means experiencing a world composed of things (that birch tree, this little brown dog) that are grouped by us into classes of things (trees in general, dogs in general). We do this because of the mind's capacity, and also its need, to shape and classify experiences. Without the resulting structure there would be no shape or regularity and thus nothing we could call an intelligible experience. This shaping of the thingness of the world is the work of the imagination; the job of classification is the work of the understanding. So when I say 'This is a dog', the imagination has shaped experience to let us perceive a discrete, yapping, furry thing, while the understanding applies a concept ('dog'); we can then grasp that the particular object offered by the imagination belongs to the class of dogs rather than to the class of cats or trees. This means that we can know the object and communicate that knowledge to others. The imagination has been 'disciplined' by the understanding. That is how we form 'logical' judgements; but it is not how aesthetic judgement works.

Aesthetic judgement does not give us knowledge in the sense that an object presented by the imagination and classified by the understanding is known in the manner just described. The peculiar thing about aesthetic judgement is the way it blends the discriminating and evaluative work of the understanding with the shaping activity of the imagination. The result is a feeling of delight that demands to be communicated. I cannot enforce my feeling on another: no one can be coerced into feelings of delight. I am, nevertheless, responding to beauty in a way quite different from the way in which I relish pistachio ice-cream. That relish was a matter of personal gratification, whereas aesthetic delight arises from a *disinterested* response to beauty. My rapture has an impartial quality that makes me want to share it with others. When we talk about art we have something significant to communicate, something that is not personal advantage, appetite or propaganda. Because it is important to us, we resist any attempt to put it on the same level as a liking for ice-cream or burgundy. And in attempting to communicate our experience to another person, we affirm that there is a community, at least potentially, to share the things that matter. It is as if deciding what things in the world are worth caring about and caring for prepares us for living together in the world as citizens or as friends.

This delight at beauty arises through what Kant calls the 'free play of the understanding and the imagination'. Exactly what Kant means by this is unclear. It seems that the beautiful thing – in my example a trumpet solo – provides me with enough form or structure for the understanding to grasp it as a shape of a certain kind, but not enough to pin the imagination down under a definite classification (or 'concept'). My imagination is stimulated to 'play' – to make associations and to roam. Perhaps this accounts for the essentially metaphorical way in which we grasp music – we hear courage, resolution, melancholy and so on 'in' the sound of the instrument, both as it plays and then later as it lingers in the memory. The understanding keeps the listener close to the actual music being played, and provides a kind of limit to the rhapsody of the imagination. We are listening to *this* music (or reading these words, or looking at this picture) here and now; this limits our possible responses.

Kant's account is undoubtedly illuminating. Nevertheless, it still leaves us with the mysteriously circular effect of 'form': we know we are in the presence of beauty because we feel disinterested delight; disinterested delight occurs in the presence of beauty. This is not very informative, and it is not clear how it will help us to justify our aesthetic judgments. Consider again my delight at a particular performance of a piece of music. I urge my friend that she should judge and feel similarly. But what if she does not? Aesthetic questions generate controversies at least as much as they uncover agreement. Our experience of aesthetics is often that of dispute and discussion, not of a community of tasteful aesthetes all pointing and gasping at the cause of their collective delight. Kant seems to leave us with the notion that people who have taste will have the right response, while those who do not will not. The fact that they do not respond correctly shows they are without taste, or are judging in the wrong way.

This is obviously unsatisfactory. Moreover, it is a view that makes taste appear to operate in a crudely binary way. The object is held to be either beautiful or not with no gradations; you either have the experience or you do not. There seems to be no notion of response waxing or waning as the subject re-experiences the supposedly beautiful thing. But here, once again, the theory does not accord with our actual experience of art in its different forms. Of course, it might be that some encounters with art are marred by the wrong approach on the part of the viewer or listener. We may come seeking gratification or moral elevation or knowledge, and only later attune ourselves to the vibrations of pure form. But there is surely more to be said on the matter than this. Most people's experience of art and beauty, whatever we conceive that to be, is not a simple case of just tuning in to a mysterious x factor.

The problem lies in the strangely ineffable nature of what Kant refers to as delight. As we have remarked, it has that peculiarly self-validating circularity and lack of gradation that characterizes the aesthetics of form and beauty. The elite are attuned to the unique vibration of the beautiful form and the rest are not. The elitism inherent in this attitude is probably enough to rule it out for many, but in any case it has a strangely unreal quality to it as an account of what is supposed to happen when we encounter art. And it has the effect of leaving sceptics with the suspicion that all the talk about significance and communicability conceals the fact that aesthetic judgements really express nothing more than personal preferences.

Subjectivism

These doubts bring us close to what may well be the most common view on the value of art:

> Good art is whatever one says it is. As the proverb has it, 'Beauty is in the eye of the beholder.'

We touched on this attitude earlier when we considered the idea that what we value in art is beauty in form. The attitude expressed here is based on the familiar distinction between the subjective and the objective. The account draws a distinction between two kinds of thing. There are objects in the world, like trees, mountains and apples, which have properties like size, shape and weight; and there are subjects who have attitudes, preferences, feelings and so on. If I tell you that an ice-cream cornet weighs such and such an amount I am making an assertion about something objective; if I tell you that it is delicious I am making a claim that has only subjective validity.

Subjectivism holds that aesthetic judgements are subjective and therefore tell us nothing about the work of art; they only tell us about the work's effect on the person making the judgement. It follows from this that two contrary judgements about a work of art do not really conflict. If I say that a certain piece of music is beautiful and you say it is dull, neither of us is wrong. And just as it would be unreasonable to call someone 'wrong' who did not share my liking for pistachio ice-cream, so my liking for that Miles Davis solo remains entirely a matter of how I just happen to respond.

Such a view is attractively uncoercive. No one can be bullied into thinking that their reactions are less valid than anyone else's. It looks like an anti-elitist alternative to the view that there are those who just 'know' that something is of aesthetic value and who therefore possess a membership card that shows they belong to the class of tasteful persons. It also avoids misty and unsupported claims about objective aesthetic value founded in some x factor. But is it a well-founded view?

Aesthetic subjectivists sometimes support their view with the following argument:

> *Premise*: There is great disagreement over aesthetic questions.
> *Conclusion*: Therefore, aesthetic judgements are subjective.

This is a very widely touted argument, but it is nevertheless quite weak. The premise is not obviously true; and even if it were true, the conclusion would not follow from it. Against what the premise asserts, we can point to the large amount of *agreement* in aesthetic judgements. When we look at the history of painting, drama, the novel, music etc., what stands out is the extent to which there is a consensus. How many people champion the merits of Hummel over Beethoven, or Beaumont and Fletcher over Shakespeare? When re-evaluations do happen, they occur against this background of general agreement. Effective challenges to the canon are usually based on arguments about the aesthetic value of particular works, not on the denial that such arguments are possible. As for the conclusion, it is simply not the case that disagreement by itself implies subjectivity. People disagree about all sorts of things: for example, the causes of poverty, the age of the earth, and whether there is intelligent life elsewhere in the universe. We do not suppose in these cases that the lack of agreement indicates that no one can be right or wrong. As we saw in the Ethics chapter, mere disagreement is not evidence of subjectivity.

However, we could argue like this:

> *Aesthetic judgements lack objectivity because they are not factual but evaluative. Factual judgements are objectively true or false. There either is or is not intelligent life in the universe. Even if we never discover the truth about this we can say what would count as evidence and proof. The same thing cannot be said about aesthetic judgements.*

Behind this argument lies the assumption that objectivity belongs only to things 'out there'. In the case of art works, the only objective claims we can make are those that describe the facts about the work: its duration, size, colour etc. To these could be added other statements conveying information about when and by whom it was created, who owned it, and so on. Disagreements about these matters are in principle resolvable. Subjectivity, on the other hand, concerns what is 'in here', the attitude a subject takes to the art in question. So if I make an aesthetic judgement, I am merely giving a report on what I like or how I feel. A disagreement here is not amenable to resolution, because it is impossible to be right or wrong about such matters.

The problem with this line of reasoning lies in the false dichotomy between the two poles of objectivity and subjectivity. The view that facts are somehow just neutrally 'out there' while our values are 'in here' is seriously misleading. It leads to the view that we project our values onto an outer world of neutral fact. However, all facts are not equal, and this inequality is not a matter of individual choice. I may have 2,198 freckles on my arm; I may also have two children. The difference is that the former is not a significant fact, but the latter is. I cannot make the number of freckles more significant just by *willing* it. Imagine someone saying 'Today, the number of freckles on my arm will be the most important thing in life *just because I say so.*' What could this possibly mean? For someone genuinely to believe this, they would need some kind of reason. Perhaps they think that some hitherto unknown hereditary illness threatening their children could be diagnosed in this way. Now it becomes an intelligible claim, open to investigation and criticism. But the shift in importance is not due to just feeling that it should be so; and the significance of the facts is not separable from what matters to someone.

Things stand out as important against what the Canadian philosopher Charles Taylor calls a 'horizon of intelligibility'. Judgements and choices only make sense and only possess meaning because of things that we already view as significant, which here means *true* and *important*. Since this is also what we mean by 'value', it should be clear that values belong here and not in some inner world of the self. Values are part of the horizon of intelligibility against which the reasons for choices (such as whether to save one's children or not) become understandable.

The aesthetic object

The claim just made obviously has important implications for the question of aesthetic value. It means that we can only grasp what art is about by seeing it against the horizon of intelligibility. A painting, for example, is a physical object that is thoroughly saturated by meaning and value: it is an *aesthetic object*. Consider again the self portrait of Rembrandt described at the beginning of this chapter. It is a two-dimensional physical object with certain dimensions, weight and mass, and reflects light. We also see it as a representation of a three-dimensional object (a man, probably the painter Rembrandt). Beyond that, it is an aesthetic object, something designed to satisfy aesthetic interest, which engages our imagination and possesses meaning and significance. When we look at the painting we see this third (aesthetic) level 'in' the other two. This is why the language of criticism or judgement does not confine itself to a neutral description followed by a report on the critic's feelings.

The language of criticism attempts both to articulate the critic's personal experience and to justify it with reasons. If our critic is to do more than merely point at the art and gasp (or sigh), she has to justify her response by referring to the art work. Her account will generally have three components.

- *Basic information*, such as duration, dimension, characters and instruments. Selection will be at work even at this level, since not everything will be deemed to be of equal relevance or importance.
- Deciding what is of importance brings us to the indispensable role of *interpretation*. Some aspects are more significant than others. While there may be broad agreement on some of the things indispensable to an adequate description (an account of Hamlet without any mention of the prince is obviously inadequate), the critic's sense of what is of central importance plays a crucial role.
- Finally, there is *evaluation*: the critic's judgement on the relative success of the piece. To be able to offer a convincing appraisal of any work, she must be an informed critic who can give an adequate description guided by a credible interpretation.

The role of description is to prompt another person to imagine what sort of experience prompted the critic's evaluation: this is why the critic needs to be informed and not merely intense. Most judgements are probably neither entirely positive or negative, but *mixed*: 'the movie's opening sequence used sound effects very effectively'; 'some of the dialogue was a bit wooden, but on the whole the plot was ingenious and effective'. Here, attentive consideration is more important than a simple thumbs up or down. An ideal critic might be thought of as opening a dialogue about the art work in which judgement and criticism invite response rather than simple acceptance.

The guiding question throughout our enquiry has been: Why do we value art? We have looked at some of the main possible explanations:

- the pleasure it gives;
- its capacity for making representations that renew and refresh the way we see and hear;
- its expressive qualities, through which we seem to enter into the experiences and emotions of imagined others;
- the delight that it can trigger in us;
- the way it inhabits a shared world of meaning and significance.

We found that any attempt to *reduce* the value of art to any one of these things is untenable. But even as we examine the possibility of doing this and come to recognize the objections to such a reduction, we also come to appreciate more fully the importance of each of these features.

We also saw how the difficulties in giving an adequate account of why we value art can lead to a sceptical, subjectivist view of aesthetic value. Perhaps part of the appeal of this position is that it appears to release us from any obligation to justify our aesthetic judgements. But why should we have any less of an obligation to justify our aesthetic judgements than we have to justify our factual or moral judgements? Perhaps the hidden assumption here is that art is somehow less important than the domains of scientific knowledge and morality because it is basically a form of recreation. But while art may certainly have a recreational dimension, this does not entail the conclusion that art is somehow not serious, or not genuinely important. It is a form of serious play that can stimulate us to the fullest possible exertion of our imagination and understanding. Art matters because these things matter.

8 Philosophy of religion

The concept of religion, like many other important but complex concepts, is hard to define. Things would undoubtedly be simpler if we could go along with the definition offered by Thwackum in Henry Fielding's novel *Tom Jones*:

> When I mention religion I mean the Christian religion; and not only the Christian religion, but the Protestant religion; and not only the Protestant religion, but the Church of England.

But Thwackum's definition is useful only as a warning against defining religion too narrowly, in a way that reflects a particular cultural heritage. It is especially easy for people steeped in the traditions of Judaism, Christianity or Islam to fall into the assumption that religion has to involve belief in a single, personal God. But even a slight acquaintance with other religious traditions reveals that there are religions that do not fit this description. Some religions are polytheistic; others, like Buddhism or Taoism, do not posit a divine being equipped with intelligence, feelings or personality.

For this reason, most proposed definitions of religion tend to be extremely general to the point of being uninformative. The American philosopher William James, for instance, defines religion as 'the feelings, acts and experiences of individual men in their solitude, so far as they apprehend themselves to stand in relation to whatever they consider the divine'. But even this definition perhaps unwittingly reflects an individualism that is not present in those religious traditions where the primary focus is the community rather than the individual. A well-known contemporary philosopher, Paul Tillich, offered a famous and even more general definition. 'Religion', he said, 'is ultimate concern.' This captures the idea that religion has to do with the most basic and important issues in a person's life – it is what anchors their values and their belief (or hope) that what they do is of genuine and lasting significance. But it is also so general as to cover things that are usually viewed as secular rather than religious: for instance, a deeply held commitment to a particular political system and its ideology.

Coming up with a good definition of religion is thus not easy, and the reasons for this are fairly obvious. First, as we have already noted, there is the great diversity of actual religions that are or have been practised by different peoples. These differences manifest themselves most obviously in the different rituals and ceremonies associated with each religion. But they also concern the most fundamental doctrinal questions, such as:

- How many gods are there?
- What is the nature of the divine?
- Can there be more than one true religion?

A second reason for the difficulty is that the concept of religion is very broad; metaphysical beliefs, moral teachings, psychological attitudes, legends, traditions, written scriptures, habitual practices, ceremonies, poetry, song, music, art, dance and theatre can all be constitutive elements of a religion. Finally, scholars disagree over whether certain so-called religions really should be thought of as religions. Confucianism, for instance, is sometimes said to be not a religion but a moral code. Certain small, culturally marginal, historically unsuccessful forms of life or systems of belief that contain many religious elements are classified by some as 'cults' rather than as religions. But how are we to draw a sharp distinction between a cult and a religion? And should we even try to do so?

One thing that nearly all religions, however defined, seem to have in common is a *soteriological* interest. The term 'soteriological' is derived from the Greek word *sōtēriā*, meaning salvation. The salvation in question may not necessarily be that of the individual, nor need it involve an afterlife. In the Hebrew bible, for instance, what is at stake most of the time is the future well-being of the community, not the everlasting happiness of particular people. But most religions embody the idea that subscribing to or participating in a certain way of thinking and behaving moves us towards a better state than the one we enjoy at present.

One would hesitate, though, to write this concern with salvation into the definition of religion. The underlying idea of some religions – for instance, some of the indigenous tribal religions of Africa and the Americas – is not so much to secure salvation as to ensure the continuation of things as they are through good harvests, good hunting, success in battle, fertility and so on. Moreover, certain secular enterprises, particularly political movements, could also be viewed as aiming at our salvation in the sense that they seek to lead us from our present less than ideal state toward a 'promised land' of affluence, security and justice. In the end, therefore, we may be forced to conclude that the concept of religion, like many other important concepts, cannot be clearly defined. But this realization should not inhibit the study of religion or the philosophical examination of religious beliefs. The fact that a concept has blurred edges does not necessarily make it useless or even suspect; after all, it is only occasionally that we are unsure as to whether the predicate 'religious' should be applied to some belief or practice. But the difficulty of defining religion does bring home the diversity and the complexity of the phenomenon we are dealing with.

What is philosophy of religion?

Philosophy of religion is very different from religion itself, just as philosophy of science is quite distinct from actual science. The goal of philosophy of religion is not to preach, or convert, or comfort, or save, or take over any of the functions of religion. Its goal is, rather, to deepen our understanding of a certain sphere of human existence – namely religion, and particularly religious concepts and beliefs – through philosophical enquiry. It also subjects these concepts and beliefs to rational criticism.

Philosophy of religion should also be distinguished from **theology**, though the two can overlap in places. The theology accompanying a particular religion consists of the theoretical elaboration of that religion's essential premises and what they imply. Hindu theologians, for instance, might discuss the question of how soon after the death of the body the soul is reincarnated. Jewish theologians might discuss the exact meaning of and reasons for the injunction in the Torah against boiling a young goat in its mother's milk. Theologians thus tend to conduct their enquiries within a 'circle of faith'; they accept the basic tenets of a religion and proceed to work out their full meaning and implications. Philosophers of religion, by contrast, do not take any religious claims for granted but evaluate such claims in the same way that they evaluate any other claims that might be made about the world, using the usual methods of rational enquiry. Naturally, therefore, they devote most attention to the basic questions raised by religious belief, questions such as:

- Is there a God?
- Can the existence of God be proved or disproved?
- Is religious faith reasonable or unreasonable?
- What difference does the existence or non-existence of God make to our lives?

According to some philosophers, this is all that philosophy of religion can or should do – analyse religious concepts and evaluate particular religious claims. Others, however, allow it to include a discussion of matters that overlap with (critics would say properly belong to) questions raised by anthropological, historical, sociological and psychological approaches to religion. For example:

- What social functions has religion served in the past?
- What functions does religion serve today?
- Why is some sort of religious belief found in all known cultures?
- What psychological needs does religion satisfy?
- Can human beings flourish, psychologically and socially, without religion?

Clearly there are innumerable interesting and important issues that the philosophy of religion can address. Here, though, we will have to content ourselves with examining just a few of these, concentrating on those that have traditionally been central to this branch of philosophy.

The nature and existence of God

Is there a God? This is surely one of the most fundamental questions we can ask. How we answer it presumably has massive implications for the way we view the world and our place in it. But as is so often the case in philosophy, before we can tackle the question we need to clarify what it means. Here that means clarifying what we mean by the term 'God'.

Obviously, there are different conceptions of God. Taoists conceive of ultimate reality, the ground of being, as a single unchanging, non-personal, dynamic principle that gives rise to and contains everything that exists, even things that we think of as opposites or as contradicting one another. Christians have usually thought of God in highly personal terms as a being who is in some ways like us, capable of thought and feeling, but who differs from us in having no limitations or imperfections. Since we cannot possibly deal separately with all these different conceptions of God, we will restrict ourselves to the conception of God that has been dominant in Western civilization for more than two millennia. This is the idea of God with which many readers will be most familiar.

The conception of God in question is one that arose within ancient Judaism roughly three thousand years ago and was embraced later by Christians and Muslims. Orthodox adherents of all three religions would thus describe God in very similar terms. All would see the following attributes as being essential to God:

- *Uniqueness*: There is only one God.
- *Omnipotence*: God is all-powerful.
- *Omniscience*: God is all-knowing.
- *Moral perfection*: God is loving, benevolent, merciful and just.
- *Necessary existence*: Unlike the world and everything in it, God did not come into existence; nor could he cease to exist.
- *Creativity*: God created the world and sustains it in its existence.
- *Personality*: God is not a mere abstract force or source of energy; he has intelligence, understanding and a will.

We could extend this list, adding further attributes such as incorporeality or indivisibility; but if we did we would begin to enter troubled waters. Whether or not these qualities should be predicated of God has been questioned by theologians within the traditions mentioned (as has the appropriateness of calling God 'he'). But the overwhelming majority of believing Jews, Christians and Muslims would agree that the qualities listed above are defining attributes of God.

However, the God of the philosophers – that is, the God whose existence philosophers of religion have sought to prove – is generally conceived in more abstract terms. Nor does he necessarily have all the listed attributes. Some proofs of God's existence, for instance, only try to prove that the world must have been created by an intelligent being; other arguments merely try to show that the 'first cause' of the world must be very powerful indeed and must depend for its own existence on nothing other than itself (that is, it must exist necessarily). As we look at the main arguments for God's existence, we will thus have to pay attention to exactly what kind of God is under consideration.

It is an interesting feature of the Bible that none of its authors ever try to prove the existence of God; his existence is simply assumed throughout. The idea that our beliefs should be justified by logically structured arguments is one that comes from the Greeks. These two great tributaries of Western civilization – the Hebrew and the Greek – eventually came together in the middle ages as Christian thinkers, benefiting from the work of Arabic scholars, became interested in Greek culture, particularly Greek philosophy. The result was a flowering of philosophy and theology that sought to work out ways in which the claims of the Bible could be harmonized with the truths arrived at by rational reflection. It is during this period that we first encounter sustained and sophisticated attempts to prove God's existence. Here we shall consider three of these, each of which still has its defenders among contemporary philosophers.

The ontological argument

This argument was first developed by Anselm (1033–1109), an Italian monk who eventually became Archbishop of Canterbury. It is called the 'ontological' argument for rather unobvious reasons: ontology is the branch of metaphysics concerned with the ultimate nature of being, and the argument tries to show that it is part of God's essential nature to exist.

Anselm asks us to compare two kinds of idea:

• the idea of a thing that actually exists;
• the idea of the same kind of thing, except that in this case it does not exist.

Clearly, he argues, the first idea contains something that the second idea lacks: namely, existence. For this reason, the first idea is of something greater or more perfect.

Now, the concept of God is the concept of a being who is infinitely great: in other words, a being who is so great that it is impossible to think of anything greater (that is, more perfect). This is part of the very definition of the word 'God'. Suppose we try to conceive of such a being. The 'fool who sayeth in his heart that there is no God' thinks it is possible to think of God while at the same time denying that God exists, just as it possible to think of a unicorn while denying that unicorns exist. But according to Anslem, the fool is fooling himself, for you cannot coherently think of God as not existing. If your idea is of a being that does not actually exist, then you have not really formed the idea of the greatest or most perfect being possible. *That* idea, as we established above, would be of a being that, in addition to all its other qualities, actually exists. In short, if you try to think of God and think of him as not existing, then you have not really thought of God. And if you do think of God in the correct way, then you will be thinking of a being who necessarily exists. Thus God cannot exist merely as an idea in our minds; he must exist in reality too.

A somewhat simpler version of this argument was later defended by Descartes in his fifth Meditation. Pared to its essentials, Descartes's version could be laid out as follows:

1. God, by definition, has all the perfections.
2. Necessary existence is a perfection.
3. Therefore, God necessarily exists.

What are we to make of this famous argument? The first thing to note is that the argument can be presented in two forms. One version leads to the conclusion that God exists, the other to the conclusion that God exists *necessarily* (that is, it is impossible for him to not to exist). In either case, the argument is a remarkable attempt to deduce a claim about what exists from premises that are supposed to be a priori truths (necessary truths that can be known independent of any experience).

A contemporary of Anselm's, a monk known as Gaunilo of Marmoutier, responded with an objection that many have found convincing. Imagine a perfect island. The perfect island, by definition, has all the insular perfections: pleasant climate, clean beaches, fine food, free drinks etc. Now, if existence is indeed one of the perfections, then the perfect island must have the property of existence. After all, you would certainly prefer to book your holiday on an island that exists in reality rather than on one that only exists as an idea. Thus, if the ontological argument is sound, it follows that Gaunilo's 'proof' that the perfect island exists must also be sound. Since the perfect island does not in fact exist, there must be something wrong with the argument. The question is, what?

Let us focus on Descartes's simpler version set out above. The *logic* of the argument seems to be impeccable – if one accepts the premises, then one *must* accept the conclusion. In the jargon of the logicians, the argument is formally *valid*. So if there is a problem, it must lie with one of the premises. At least one of them must be false.

The first premise states that God, by definition, has every perfection. This is just another way of making Anselm's point that God is a being who is so great that we cannot conceive of any being who is greater. Now, one could try to dispute this definition, arguing, perhaps, that God as he is represented in the Bible is actually less than perfect. (He does, after all, advocate and participate in some rather brutal 'ethnic cleansing'.) But this objection would be misdirected. Proponents of the argument could reply that the idea of God that matters here is the one that they are describing: namely, the idea of an infinitely perfect being. It is the existence of *this* being that they are trying to establish, not the character who talks to Abraham and Moses.

We might also question whether the idea of an infinitely perfect being is one that we can really form. It is, after all, extremely abstract. But this in itself should not be a problem. The issue is not whether we can form a mental *image* of an infinitely perfect being, but whether we can grasp the *concept* of such a being. And unless it contains a contradiction, it seems reasonable to suppose the concept is intelligible in the same way that abstract mathematical concepts like pi or infinity are intelligible to mathematicians.

The first premise, then, is difficult to argue against. It simply brings out something that is contained within the definition of God. What about the second premise? This states that existence – or *necessary* existence in Descartes's version – is a perfection. Not surprisingly, this is seen by many critics as the weak point in the argument. One objection is that there is no good reason to view existence as a perfection. To be sure, a real island paradise is better than an imaginary island paradise; an actual gold ring is better than the mere idea of a gold ring. But these are loaded examples. Is a real serial killer better than one who lives only in the mind of a detective story writer? Is actual pain better than the mere idea of pain? At the very least, defenders of the argument need to explain further what is meant by the term 'perfection' and justify the claim that existence is a perfection.

A second, somewhat more sophisticated objection was first put forward by one of Descartes's critics, Pierre Gassendi, and was later developed by the eighteenth-century German philosopher Immanuel Kant. They argued that it is a mistake to think of existence as a property of things on a level with other properties such as wisdom or incorporeality. If you first think of a thing – say, a house – and then think of that thing existing, you are not altering the idea that you began with. To think of a thing, and to think of that thing existing, is to form the same idea. This is because existence does not belong to the *content* of the idea. When I say that a house is large, made of wood, has seven gables, and is over two hundred years old, I am fleshing out the idea of a particular house. But if I then add that in addition to all these properties the house exists, I am not adding another detail; rather, I am asserting that the idea corresponds to something that exists in the material world. The ontological argument starts out analysing the idea of God and concludes, on the basis of this analysis, that the idea stands in a certain relation to something outside itself (namely God himself). But this is not a conclusion that conceptual analysis alone can support.

These are powerful objections. Nevertheless, the ontological argument still has its defenders, among them some very well-known contemporary philosophers of religion such as Charles Hartshorne and Alvin Plantinga. One interesting feature of these more recent proponents of the argument is that, like Descartes, they focus on the idea of God's *necessary* existence and seek to explicate what this means and what it implies.

One argument that has emerged from these reflections runs as follows. The contrary of necessary existence is contingent existence. A contingent being is a being who could either exist or not exist. Another way of putting this is to say that one can imagine a possible world in which it did not exist. This is not true, though, of a necessary being. A necessary being, by definition, would exist in every possible world. From this, a surprising conclusion follows. If there is even one possible world that contains a necessary being, then that being must exist in every possible world (which includes, of course, the actual world we inhabit). Since we can easily enough imagine a world in which God exists, such a world is presumably possible. But in that case, God must exist in every possible world: in other words, he exists necessarily.

This reasoning is certainly ingenious, but it is fair to say that critics of the ontological argument remain underwhelmed. Apart from anything else, the premise that God (that is, a necessary being) exists in *some* possible world can be challenged. This claim has a prima facie plausibility; but the concept of a necessary being may be incoherent. If so, such a being belongs with square circles and married bachelors – entities that exist in *no* possible world. For this reason, the critics maintain that the most the argument can prove is that *if* God exists then he exists *necessarily*.

The cosmological argument

There's clearly something fishy about trying to prove the existence of God simply by unpacking the definition of God, which is what the ontological argument tries to do. Surely, a more plausible approach is to argue that the mere existence of the world is evidence for there being a creator. In other words, if God didn't exist, we wouldn't be here.

This form of argument – from the existence of the world (or of something in the world) to the existence of a being causally responsible for it – is known as the cosmological argument. It has been put forward in many different forms, most famously by the great medieval theologian Thomas Aquinas.

A simple version of the cosmological argument runs as follows:

1. The world exists.
2. Everything that exists has a cause.
3. Causes precede their effects.
4. The chain of cause and effect cannot go back in time indefinitely.
5. Therefore, there must be a 'first cause' that is not itself an effect.
6. Since everything has a cause, this first cause must be the cause of itself.
7. This self-caused first cause is God.
8. Therefore God exists.

There are probably many people who accept something like this as a reasonable justification for belief in God. But if we subject the argument to critical scrutiny it soon becomes evident that it is really quite weak. Premise 4 is not obviously true. It is perfectly conceivable that time and the chain of causal relations extends back into infinity. Even the theory of the big bang favoured by most contemporary cosmologists is compatible with there being an infinite recurrence of big bangs. Premise 5, which posits a self-caused being, contradicts premise 3, which states that causes precede their effects. And the identification of this self-caused being with God at step 7 seems gratuitous. There is nothing in the argument to suggest that the 'first cause' is alive, intelligent, omnipotent, omniscient, just, merciful, incorporeal or endowed with any of God's traditional attributes other than being causally responsible for the universe.

Thomas Aquinas (1225–1274)

Thomas Aquinas is generally regarded as the greatest philosopher and theologian of the medieval period. He was born near Naples, and studied at the University of Naples and in Paris and Cologne. In 1252 he began teaching theology in Paris and spent the rest of his life either there or at various places in Italy teaching and writing on philosophy and theology. Aquinas was a prolific writer. He produced numerous translations of and commentaries on the works of Aristotle as well as various short treatises and commentaries on other thinkers; but his best-known works are the *Summa Theologiae* and the *Summa contra Gentiles* (against the infidels). He was made a saint by Pope John XXII in 1323.

Aquinas was trained as a Christian theologian. At the time he lived, the main intellectual challenge to Christian theology and philosophy came from Aristotelian scholars, particularly Islamic philosophers such as Averröes (1126–1198). A good deal of Christian doctrine was based on scripture and as such was regarded as truth revealed directly by God. Aristotelian doctrines, on the other hand, were generally supported by rational arguments; they thus exercised a pull over the minds of many scholars, and were seen by some as a threat to the authority of the Church.

Aquinas's major intellectual achievement was to create a philosophical system that synthesized Christian theology and Aristotelian philosophy. In doing so, he had to work out the exact relation between reason and revelation. As he saw it, there are some truths that we can demonstrate rationally without relying on revelation (for example, that the soul survives bodily death), while there are others that we only know through revelation (for example, that Jesus was God incarnate). In many cases, though, reason and revelation provide two routes to the same conclusion. For instance, following Aristotle, Aquinas argues that the existence of motion and change in our present world indicates that there must be a 'first mover', by which he means some being that is ultimately responsible for the phenomena in question. Reason also tells us that this first mover must itself be unmoved (and hence unchanging), otherwise it would not bring the regress of explanations to an end. Reason thus leads us to posit what Aristotle termed an 'unmoved mover', and Aquinas naturally identifies this being with God.

This is one of five ways in which Aquinas thinks the existence of God can be demonstrated. But for those who are either not acquainted with or unable to follow this sort of reasoning, belief in God can be based on the revelation provided by the Bible. Moreover, scripture fills out our knowledge of God by revealing some things that reason is not able to prove: for instance, the fact that God created the world at a point in time, or that God is three persons in one.

Although Aquinas held that the ultimate end of philosophy is to attain knowledge of God, his philosophical system is comprehensive, offering a fully worked out metaphysics, theory of knowledge, philosophy of mind, ethics and political philosophy. Since his death he has exerted an enormous influence on later philosophers. In part, this has been due to his exalted position within the Catholic church. But even today, Catholic and non-Catholic thinkers alike continue to draw inspiration from his writing in all areas of philosophy.

Clearly, if a cosmological argument for God's existence is to be at all persuasive, it needs to be more sophisticated than the one laid out above. Often, the more sophisticated versions that have been advanced rest on what is known as the **principle of sufficient reason**. This principle asserts that there is a reason for anything being the way it is. Included within this idea is the principle that there is a reason for the existence of anything. The principle of sufficient reason is assumed all the time in science and in everyday life. Why is the earth tilted on its axis? Why did my tomatoes flourish? Why are there tigers but no dinosaurs? We assume that all such questions have answers. The complete answer might be fantastically complicated, and it might be beyond our ken now and for ever; but we nevertheless assume that any and every state of affairs has an explanation.

It should be fairly obvious how the principle of sufficient reason might be used to support a cosmological argument for God's existence. Put simply, if the principle of sufficient reason applies to everything, then it applies not only to every entity *in* the world but also to the world as a whole. In other words, if there is a complete explanation for the existence of anything, then there is a complete explanation for the existence of everything. It would be odd to say that the principle is true of everything with one exception: the whole world.

But is it really so odd? Why should we expect that what applies to every particular thing in the world must also apply to the totality? Every physical object exists in space, but the whole universe does not exist in space. It is space. A similar point can be made with respect to time. All events occur within time; but the entire temporal sequence of events that constitutes the complete history of the universe is not itself a temporal event. So, in an analogous way, everything in the universe may have an explanation, but the universe itself may not.

That is one powerful objection to the cosmological argument. There is another and even more basic problem with most versions that have been put forward, the one above included. At some point they all assert that what cannot be true of the world is nevertheless true of God. For example, we are told the world cannot exist necessarily; it is contingent. But it is said to be created or sustained by God, who is not contingent. Or again, the world cannot be self-caused; so it must be created by a God who is self-caused. But this move is always suspect. If God can exist necessarily or be self-caused, why can't the world?

> The fact that positing a God over and above the spatio-temporal universe is not a necessary step does not prove that taking that step is a mistake. Perhaps the world was created by a self-caused being who exists necessarily.

This point is perfectly correct. But most metaphysicians subscribe to a principle known as **Occam's razor** (see box on next page), which urges us to avoid making our theories unnecessarily complicated. The hypothesis that there is a God who created the world may be a perfectly legitimate hypothesis. But for it to be justified, even as a mere hypothesis, it must be able to do some work: it must reduce the number of unanswered questions that confront us, or at least give us a deeper insight into why the world is the way it is. It cannot claim to reduce our stack of unanswered questions, since for every question about the world that it claims to answer it leaves us with an identical unanswered question about God. As for its claim to offer insight into the nature of the world, this can only be taken seriously if the hypothesis is true. After all, if it is false then we have error and illusion, not insight. Obviously, though, the truth of the claim that there is a God cannot be assumed in order to give credibility to an argument that is supposed to prove that there is a God.

The argument from design

The ontological argument and the more sophisticated versions of the cosmological argument have been much discussed by professional philosophers and theologians, but it is probably fair to say that to most lay people they are less interesting and less persuasive than a third 'proof' of God's existence usually referred to as the **argument from design**. Like the cosmological argument, the design argument comes in more than one form. In all versions, the starting point is not the mere *existence* of the world but its *character*, or the character of certain things in it such as living organisms. The basic thrust of the argument is that the world, or parts of it, exhibit evidence of intelligent *design*.

One version of the design argument might be labelled the 'argument from the interconnectedness of things'. It takes as its datum the marvellous way in which the different elements within nature work in harmony to produce a simple, glorious system. The laws of physics; the position and angle of the earth relative to the sun; the succession of the seasons; the geography of the continents and the oceans; the earth's meteorological patterns; and countless other such variables all work together to produce the wonderful, varied and complex carnival of life that we witness all

think critically!

Occam's razor

Occam's razor is a methodological principle that is employed in the natural and social sciences as well as in philosophy. It is named after the medieval thinker William of Occam. Basically, it is a principle of economy. It says we should try to make our theories simple, avoiding needless complexity. Of course, complicated phenomena sometimes require complicated explanations. But Occam's razor does not say that everything has a simple explanation. Rather, it says that if we have to choose between two theories that are equal in other respects (such as consistency with the data, predictive power, coherence with our other beliefs and so on) we should prefer the simpler theory.

What does it mean to say that one theory is simpler than another? The most obvious kind of simplicity has to do with the number of things it says exist. Thus a theory in physics that requires us to posit such things as the ether or dark matter will be rejected if there are other theories available with equal explanatory power that avoid positing such entities. But theories can also be simpler in other ways: for instance, they can make fewer unproven assumptions, or they can require a smaller number of general laws.

A good illustration of why we might want to accept this principle is provided by the Indian myth that the earth rests on the back of an elephant that in turn rests on the back of a turtle. The phenomenon to be explained is the fact that the earth does not seem to be falling through space. To explain this, two further entities are posited: an elephant and a turtle. But the obvious question arises: What supports the turtle? We could respond as one of Bertrand Russell's interlocutors did by saying that the turtle rests on another turtle and so on *ad infinitum* ('It's turtles all the way down, Professor Russell!'). But this promiscuous willingness to multiply entities seems absurd.

The other option is to say that the turtle needs nothing to support it. But that invites the question: Why not say the same thing about the elephant and thereby simplify the theory? And if we can do that, the obvious next step is to eliminate the elephant too and say that the earth needs nothing to support it. When we think this way we are using Occam's razor. And this same way of thinking can be used to criticize the cosmological argument for needlessly positing entities beyond the world to explain the world's existence.

around us and in which we participate. How likely is it that such harmony and organization could arise by pure chance? Certainly, much smaller and simpler productions staged by human beings require a great deal of rational planning beforehand. On these grounds there are many who would echo the psalmist's words:

> The heavens tell the glory of God
> and the firmament proclaims his handiwork.

A second version of the design argument might be called the 'argument from organisms'. It focuses not on the whole of nature but on its most peculiar and interesting parts: namely, organisms. Organisms are remarkable systems of interconnected parts, each part functioning in cooperation with the others to enable the whole being to live, grow and reproduce in its environment. For example, a cat's retractable claws, its specially adapted eyes that enable it to see in the dark, its incisive teeth, acute hearing, padded paws, speed, strength and balance, all combine to make the animal a highly effective hunter.

The way the parts are so perfectly suited to the ends of the whole organism is analogous to the relation between parts and whole in a human artefact like a car or a washing machine. Since we know that artefacts like these only came into existence as a result of intelligent design and purposive activity, it is surely reasonable to believe that this is also true of organisms. After all, organisms, with their cellular structure, DNA coding and, in the case of animals, central nervous systems, are vastly more complex than anything human beings have designed or made so far. Furthermore, close examination reveals the parts of an organism to be just as remarkable as the whole being. Take your skin, for example. It is not just a remarkably strong container for your bones, blood, muscles and internal organs; it is also supremely flexible, completely waterproof, an excellent insulator, a means of absorbing vitamins, and able to convey detailed tactile information to the brain about the things it comes into contact with. It heals itself when cut or bruised, it produces its own protection against the sun; it helps an overheated body to cool, it provides some of our most cherished sensual pleasures, it is beautiful to look at, and it even serves (through blushing, blanching and other reactions) as a means of expression and communication. How could something so remarkable have come about by accident or by chance?

Both versions of the design argument assert an analogy between the world, or a part of the world, and things we know to be the product of purposive design. For this reason the argument is sometimes called the **argument from analogy**. In both versions, the key claim is that it is highly improbable that the natural phenomenon in question – whether an entire ecosystem or an individual organism – was produced by chance. If one accepts this premise then it seems reasonable to conclude that behind nature there lies some sort of intelligence which is, at the very least, very powerful and ingenious.

As we noted earlier, the design argument has always been one of the most popular proofs of God's existence. Perhaps one reason for this is that it chimes with the view of nature shared by Judaism, Christianity and Islam. In Genesis, God gives man 'dominion over the fish of the sea, and over the birds of the air, and over the cattle, and over every living thing that moves upon the earth'; he goes on to say, 'I have given you every plant yielding seed which is upon the face of the earth, and every tree with seed in its fruit; and you shall have them for food.' On this view, nature clearly exists for our benefit. To anyone steeped in this tradition it is therefore natural to view the workings of nature as purposive. This is especially true in the case of organisms. Even today, scientists still describe organisms using purposive language, talking about the 'function' of the liver or the 'job' performed by the lymphatic system.

Nevertheless, the design argument is open to a number of serious objections. To begin with, we can question the idea that the system of nature is particularly beautiful or harmonious. After all, avalanches, forest fires, earthquakes, hurricanes, plagues, droughts, ice ages and the extinction of entire species all occur naturally. And in the animal kingdom, nature is, in Jack London's famous phrase, 'red in tooth and claw'. It is also a very big jump from saying that nature exhibits evidence of intelligent design to saying that the designer must be God as traditionally conceived. This is a point made with great force by David Hume in his *Dialogues Concerning Natural Religion*. When we try to explain the appearance of design in nature by positing a certain kind of cause, we cannot justify going beyond what suffices. (Here, once again, we encounter something like Occam's razor.) Perhaps there are grounds for positing a very powerful and highly intelligent designer. But nothing in nature requires us to assume that this intelligent designer is *all*-knowing, *all*-powerful or morally perfect.

Hume wrote a century before Darwin and felt forced to concede that it was reasonable to view nature as the work of some kind of intelligent designer (or designers), though he repeatedly stressed that nothing more definite than this could be inferred. But when Darwin's theory of evolution through natural selection came along, it really torpedoed the design argument, at least in the eyes of many scientists and philosophers. The reason for this is simple. Darwin's theory offers a very convincing explanation of how and why nature *appears* to exhibit design without appealing to any supernatural entities (such as a God) that are responsible for nature without being part of it. Take the retractable claws and excellent night vision of the cat, for example. To be sure, these are admirably suited to the cat's goal of catching mice. But the theory of evolution shows how these features were simply 'selected in' over millions of years. The cats (or proto-cats) that developed these features through random genetic mutations tended to be better hunters and therefore became stronger, lived longer, mated more frequently and produced more offspring than their rivals.

The theory of evolution also offers a 'naturalistic' explanation – that is, one that only refers to scientifically observable entities and forces – of the *harmony* of nature. An ecosystem consists of many diverse organisms living and reproducing while interacting with each other and with the non-organic environment. The harmony it exhibits, with each organism having its niche in the system, is also the result of an evolutionary process. Organisms that 'fitted in' survived; those that were not able to fit in either went elsewhere or died out. The long-term result of this process when undisturbed by external forces is a balanced ecosystem.

> *Does the theory of evolution really undermine the argument from design? It may explain many phenomena without appealing to a designer, but it doesn't explain everything. In particular, it doesn't explain how living organic things arose out of inorganic matter, nor how beings endowed with sentience, consciousness or free will could emerge from a world in which these did not already exist.*

This defence of the design argument deserves consideration. If we focus just on the problem of how living organisms first arose, it can perhaps be fleshed out a little more along the following lines:

> *For the process of evolution to get started, a first organism capable of reproducing itself must be formed. But even the simplest organism is more complex than the most intricate and complicated machines made by human beings. We find it quite absurd to imagine that bits of inorganic matter could come together by chance to form something as complicated as a car or a washing machine. So, by the same token, we ought to reject as absurd the idea that bits of organic matter came together by chance to produce a living, reproducing organism.*

This is a clever argument. But dyed-in-the-wool Darwinists have an answer. Certainly, they can say, the emergence of living organisms out of inorganic matter is an exceedingly unlikely event. But the universe is an exceedingly big place. There are billions of galaxies, each containing trillions of stars, many of which presumably have planets orbiting them. Thus, the odds of life emerging on any given planet could be fantastically low – many trillions to one against – and yet, because of the immensity of the universe, the odds of it occurring *somewhere or other* may be quite high.

The emergence of life may thus be incredibly rare without being an unfathomable mystery. To see the long odds against it happening at any *particular* time and place as an objection to naturalistic explanations is to be the victim of a certain kind of illusion. An analogy might make this clearer. Suppose you watch a film of two people playing cards in which the entire pack is shuffled and dealt out three times in succession, each player receiving 26 cards. If, after each shuffle and deal, one player has all the red cards and the other has all the black cards, you would assume that this result was not due entirely to chance. Somehow, the deal must have been rigged or the film edited. Normally this assumption would be quite justified.

But now suppose that the film you saw is, in fact, only a small segment of a very long (and boring) film, one that runs continuously for millions of years and consists entirely of a pack of cards being repeatedly shuffled and dealt. Throughout the film it only happens very rarely that the deal separates the pack perfectly into red and black piles. Even more rarely does this occur twice in succession. And only once in ten million years does it happen three times running. If all you see is the segment of the film in which this happens you will assume it could not be a chance occurrence. But if you see that segment in context – that is, as a tiny fraction of a very great whole – then you will readily accept the possibility that it came about by chance.

We have considered in some detail three arguments for the existence of a God: the ontological argument, the cosmological argument and the argument from design. These are by no means the only ones that philosophers have put forward. Immanuel Kant developed an 'argument from morality'. Our lives have a moral dimension, he argued; we have a sense of duty, sometimes feel guilty, and cannot avoid applying moral concepts to people and their actions. And this fact is significant, for it only makes sense if there is something like a God. That is, unless there is something more than the reality described by natural science, our moral notions can have no objective grounding, in which case our moral life rests on an illusion.

William James argued that mystical experiences, which are both more common and more consistent than is often recognized, should be taken seriously as indications that some such reality does indeed exist – something beyond what we encounter in everyday experience, beyond the reach of scientific observation and measurement, but somehow holding the answer to our deepest questions about truth, meaning and value. These are just two of the many arguments that have been proposed in addition to those discussed above. Nevertheless, the three we have examined are by far the most widely discussed in the history of philosophy. How persuasive they are is something the reader must judge for him or herself.

The problem of suffering

Perhaps it is easier to disprove rather than prove the existence of God. Isn't the fact that there is so much suffering in the world good evidence that God does not exist?

Without question, the existence of suffering poses a serious problem to anyone who wishes to defend the traditional Judaeo-Christian conception of God. To many it has seemed to be an insuperable objection – hence Stendhal's quip: 'God's only excuse is that he doesn't exist!' Although the problem is often called 'the problem of evil', a better label is the problem of *suffering*. 'Evil' can be used in a general sense to refer to anything that is harmful, but its more common and specific meaning is that of moral depravity; an evil person is one who intentionally prefers the bad to the good. The existence of this sort of evil certainly represents a difficulty for some religious outlooks. (If God created the world, is he not ultimately responsible for the presence of evil in it?) But the occurrence of physical pain or emotional distress, which in many cases neither afflicts nor is caused by those who are morally depraved, poses a yet more obvious difficulty for the traditional view of God.

Recognition of the problem of suffering goes back to biblical times; indeed, the presentation of this problem in the Book of Job remains one of the most profound and intense ever produced. Job, according to the story, is an upright and prosperous man who, through no fault of his own and with God's full knowledge, is visited by a succession of terrible afflictions including pain, disease, impoverishment and the loss of his family. Although at first he responds to his misfortunes stoically – 'the Lord gave, and the Lord hath taken away; blessed be the name of the Lord' – he is eventually driven in his anguish to question and protest against the ways of God. But after God appears in response to his challenge, and through a series of unanswerable questions makes Job realize the limitations of his own understanding, he 'stops up his mouth', resolved never again to be so presumptuous as to doubt God's wisdom or justice.

The Book of Job presents the issue with great literary and dramatic skill. But we do not need to go to literature to be impressed by the depth of the problem: the daily news will suffice. Each year, millions of people suffer in a variety of ways from a variety of causes. Famine, disease, war, poverty, injustice, neglect, abuse, crime, and natural disasters such as earthquakes, floods and droughts result in death, injury, pain and distress for huge numbers of people. The question obviously arises: What kind of God would allow all this to happen?

That people (and other animals, for that matter) really do suffer is surely an incontrovertible fact: a datum that can be neither ignored or denied. If God is omniscient he must be aware of this. If he is omnipotent then presumably he could prevent it if he so desired. And if he is omnibenevolent and morally perfect he would presumably *want* to prevent it. It is a strange kind of love that would not wish to alleviate the suffering – in some cases the truly agonizing, unbearable suffering – of the beloved. And it is a strange kind of justice that metes out such misery in what appears to be a perfectly indiscriminate manner. The problem for anyone who accepts the traditional Judaeo-Christian idea of God is how to reconcile these four statements:

- There is widespread suffering.
- God is omnipotent.
- God is omniscient.
- God is morally perfect.

Obviously, this is not a problem for an atheist. The atheist has a simple explanation for the existence of suffering: unpleasant things happen to people because human beings are not powerful enough to prevent them from happening and there is no other force that is trying to do so. Nor is it a problem for religious believers whose conception of the divine differs significantly from the orthodox Judaeo-Christian conception. It did not arise for the ancient Greeks, for instance, since they did not consider the Olympian gods to be either omnipotent or morally perfect. And modern monotheists can easily evade the problem by the simple expedient of denying one or more of the relevant attributes to God. They can say, for instance, that God is not all-powerful, so although he knows about our suffering and grieves for us, he cannot lessen it any more than he already does.

For the orthodox believer, however, the problem is a pressing one. Because the history of Western philosophy is entwined with Christianity there have been many attempts to solve it. Any such attempt is known as a **theodicy**, since it typically defends the idea that, appearances notwithstanding, God is just. (The word 'theodicy' is derived from the Greek terms for a god (*theos*) and justice (*dikē*).) Here we will look at three main lines of argument.

Theodicy 1: it doesn't really hurt

In Humes *Dialogues concerning Natural Religion*, Cleanthes advances a very simple theodicy:

> The only method of supporting divine benevolence . . . is to deny absolutely the misery and wickedness of man. . . . Health is more common than sickness; pleasure than pain; happiness than misery; and for one vexation we meet with, we attain, upon computation, a hundred enjoyments.

In other words, we do not suffer really – at least not very much. The obvious objection to this argument is that the description of the human condition it offers is flatly contradicted by many people's experience. In addition, the philosophical problem of evil does not go away if it turns out that there are fewer evils than we supposed. *Any* evil, any suffering, poses a challenge to the believer and calls for some kind of theodicy.

A more sophisticated attempt to deny the reality of suffering was put forward by St Augustine (354–430). He argued that the evils of the world have no positive existence; rather, they are privations. For example, blindness is the absence of sight; sickness is the absence of health; poverty is the absence of wealth. Everything created by God is good, just as the account of creation in Genesis explicitly affirms. But since evils are merely privations they have no real existence and God cannot be held responsible for them. This argument may be more sophisticated, but it also looks suspiciously like a piece of sophistry. The question can surely still be asked: Why couldn't God, if he is omnipotent, make a world with fewer evils? As one critic has put it: if evil is to be thought of as a lack of something, like the hole in a doughnut, it still seems that God could have done better by making less hole and more doughnut.

Theodicy 2: it's our own fault

Stated crudely, this theodicy says that human beings are responsible for their sufferings. Because God made us in his own image and intended us to live on a higher plane than all other creatures, he endowed us with free will. This is a genuine blessing; it allows our lives to have moral significance and value. But the blessing comes at a price. Since we are not morally perfect, and since we do make free choices, we sometimes make mistakes and must then suffer the consequences.

Taken in its simplest and most literal sense this explanation of the world's evils is clearly inadequate. For one thing, a good deal of human suffering is caused by natural disasters, not by people making poor choices. For another thing, even where the suffering is caused by human actions, the people who suffer are often not the ones who are misusing their freedom; rather, they are the victims of what others do. Consider rape victims, for instance, or the people targeted by practitioners of ethnic cleansing. Of course, we could interpret suffering as just punishment for earlier wrongs committed. But this interpretation seems neither plausible nor fair when the individuals who suffer are young children or morally praiseworthy people.

One way of trying to meet these objections is to extend the concept of moral responsibility so that every individual can be held responsible for whatever happens to them. The idea that prosperity must, at some level, be a reward for virtue while suffering must be a punishment for some kind of failing goes back a long way. We find it, for instance, in the reasoning offered by Job's comforters, his three companions who insist that Job's misfortunes must be in some sense deserved ('Who ever perished, being innocent?' asks Eliphaz). It appears in another form in the Hindu notion of *karma*, according to which there are hidden laws that ensure good deeds will have good consequences for the agent and bad deeds will lead to bad consequences. This may not be apparent in this life, but over many reincarnations the law will make itself felt.

Perhaps the most radical extension of the concept of responsibility, however, is the doctrine of original sin developed by Christian theologians like Augustine. According to this doctrine, no human being is ever perfectly innocent. A mythological explanation of this idea has it that when Adam and Eve disobeyed God in the garden of Eden they rendered not only themselves guilty but all their descendants too, the 'sins of the fathers' being passed on to later generations. A more abstract version holds that it is simply part of the human condition to be in some way contaminated with sin; this is part and parcel of having a physical body and a partially animal nature. In either case, though, the conclusion to be drawn is that since every human being is sinful, no suffering is ever entirely undeserved. On the contrary, as Hamlet puts it: 'Treat each man after his deserts and who shall 'scape whipping?' This view was taken to an extreme by the Calvinists, who held that God would be perfectly justified in condemning every human being to an eternity of torment; the fact that a few were saved from this fate was testament not to their virtue but to God's benevolence.

However, all these attempts to justify suffering by seeing it as in some sense deserved suffer from the same defect. They all rest on crucial presuppositions that most people not already committed to the religious outlooks they support would find unacceptable. The a priori assumption made by Job's comforters – that suffering is always a justified punishment – is just that: an *assumption*, and a most dubious one. There seems to be plenty of evidence against it, and in the case of young children it seems to make little sense. To meet these objections, we can introduce the idea of karma or the doctrine of original sin. But both these rest on specific metaphysical beliefs for which we have little evidential support and which, in addition, give rise to theoretical difficulties of their own. What does it mean, for instance, to say that a person was another person or animal in a previous life? And how can a newly born child be held responsible for the actions of his or her ancestors? Unless these difficulties can be met, the theodicies that view human beings as somehow responsible for their sufferings cannot be sustained.

Theodicy 3: it's good for us!

This line of argument also comes in more than one flavour. What has been called the 'cosmic harmony' defence calls attention to the fact that our perspective on the universe is extremely limited. If, however, we could see the big picture the way God sees it, then we would understand how what we call evil plays an important and valuable role in the great scheme of things. To complain about these so called evils is to be like children who complain about the rain that prevents them from playing, not recognizing how valuable it is in other respects. To wish that life were full of pleasures and completely free from pain is as misguided as wishing that we could have only days and no nights, forgetting that we are part of an ecosystem that requires the alternation of day and night. This way of dealing with the problem approaches the outlook characteristic of Taoism, an ancient Chinese philosophy, which views the light and the dark, the negative and the positive, as equally essential to a basically harmonious universe in which they balance each other out.

The idea that our perspective on the world is necessarily partial and limited is undeniably true. It follows that our understanding of particular things or events and how they relate to the whole is also bound to be imperfect. Moreover, to be reminded of this is surely healthy. In the Book of Job, God himself responds to Job's complaints by providing just such a reminder:

> Where was thou when I laid the foundations of the earth? / declare if thou hast understanding.
> Who hast laid the measures thereof, if thou knowest? / or who hath stretched the line upon it?

God's magnificent catalogue of things that the creator alone could possibly understand is sufficient to silence Job. But as has often been pointed out, God does not actually give a straightforward answer to the question: Why do innocent or virtuous human beings like Job suffer? Claiming that even apparently undeserved suffering is necessary, even if we cannot grasp how or why this is so, is all very well. But the suffering remains real and undeserved, and must therefore be viewed as an irredeemable imperfection in the world God has supposedly created. In a famous passage in Fyodor Dostoevsky's novel *The Brothers Karamazov*, Ivan Karamazov makes this point with great force. He relates the true story of a six-year-old boy who, because he threw a stone at the local landowner's dog, was stripped naked and, in front of his mother, was made to run before a pack of dogs who quickly chased him down and savaged him to death. In Ivan's view, nothing can ever justify or redeem this kind of suffering; and any God who chose to create a world that contains such suffering cannot be considered morally perfect. Examples such as this forcefully resurrect the initial dilemma: either God is incapable of eliminating innocent suffering from the world, in which case he is not omnipotent; or he could eliminate it but chooses not to, in which case he cannot be morally perfect.

How might one try to deal with this dilemma while holding onto the traditional conception of God? One way would be to deny that God's omnipotence implies that he can eliminate innocent suffering. This is a difficult argument to make, but it has been made, notably by C. S. Lewis. Another, perhaps more promising way, is to deny that God's willingness to let us suffer implies that he is not entirely good. This theodicy has been defended by the contemporary philosopher John Hick, drawing inspiration from an early Christian theologian, Irenaeus (130–202). According to Hick, those who see the existence of suffering as incompatible with the existence of God misunderstand God's purposes. In creating humankind, God's purpose was not to create a world in which everyone is happy and contented all the time. His intention was, rather, to create individuals endowed with free will who are capable of realizing themselves as moral beings. A world containing such beings has more value than a world in which everyone simply basks in easy, innocent contentment. But to achieve self-realization as a moral being is necessarily a process in which one must make difficult choices, learn from one's mistakes, overcome difficulties, struggle with adversity, and, on occasion, suffer. To be sure, God could have made us so that we always make the right decisions; but then we would not really be exercising free choices, and the moral selves we cultivate through our choices and experiences would not be our own achievement.

On this view, to argue that if God loved us he would never let us suffer is like arguing that parents, if they love their child, should try to ensure that the child's desires are never frustrated. Obviously, being a good or loving parent does not mean that one always tries to minimize a child's sufferings. Wise, loving parents regularly refuse to let their kids watch too much TV or eat too many sweets; indeed, they consistently and systematically deprive their children of certain pleasures! They also allow their children to learn some things through bitter experience; and they even deliberately impose suffering on them in the form of punishments. They do this because they believe there are things that are important besides short-term pleasure: for instance, self-control, wisdom, moral virtue and self-realization. From the child's point of view, the actions of the parent often appear incomprehensibly cruel. But this view is false, and the child only holds it because he or she cannot understand the broader perspective of the parent.

According to this theodicy, then, instead of seeing our world as a 'vale of tears' we might instructively view it as a 'vale of soul-making' (to use John Keats's phrase). The sufferings we experience and observe help build character by providing us with opportunities for spiritual growth and for the exercise of virtues such as fortitude and compassion. As a justification of God's ways, this approach seems to be one of more plausible options for those holding traditional Judaeo-Christian beliefs. Nevertheless, like most other theodicies, it is highly speculative. To explain certain phenomena it offers an account of God's plan for human beings, an account that seems to be arrived at by a combination of traditional religious ideas and speculative inferences and analogies. However, this objection will not trouble theologians and religious believers, whose religious commitments already indicate a willingness to speculate about things that lie beyond experience.

Harder to deal with are the problems posed by Ivan Karamazov's account of the six-year-old boy who was thrown to the dogs. How could the terrible fear and excruciating death of this child in any way help build his moral character? For that to be possible we would not only have to posit a life after this one; we would also have to assume that in this future life moral development was still possible. This is not usually part of the traditional view of the afterlife in Judaism, Christianity or Islam. The supposition also takes us even further along the path of unconstrained speculation. One could, of course, argue that the boy's sufferings helped the moral development of other people: the landowner might experience remorse; onlookers might have their capacity for compassion extended; the boy's mother might be better able to empathize with another person's grief and to cope with adversity in the future. But then it is hard to see how God can keep his reputation for justice intact. In effect, the boy is being used as a means to promote the moral welfare of others.

Ultimately, even the 'vale of soul-making' theodicy leaves many questions unanswered. Why is it that some people have such easy lives while others suffer so terribly? Is it really necessary for there to be *so* much suffering in the world? Couldn't human beings exercise free will and live morally rich lives in a world where there was less misery? The theodicy in question may offer a decent explanation for why we do not live in a vale of contentment; but it does not explain why God could not eliminate what appears to be gratuitous suffering and still achieve his ends. Of course, the believer can always fall back on that old saw, 'God moves in mysterious ways.' And in fact most theodicies, when pressed, do tend to fall back to this last line of defence. They set about trying to understand and explain why an omnipotent, omniscient, omnibenevolent God would allow us to suffer. Couched in these terms, the problem is general – Why is there suffering? – rather than specific – Why is this six-year-old thrown to the dogs? And the explanations offered also operate at a high level of generality, appealing to notions like the unreality of evil, original sin, cosmic harmony or the need for 'soul-making'.

Such ideas offer blanket solutions. But for that very reason there are many specific cases of individual suffering that they do not seem able to explain or justify. Confronted with such cases, the theodician inevitably appeals to the idea that since our understanding is finite we cannot hope to fathom God's methods and motives completely. To the critic of religion, however, this move is a cop out. Suppose a scientist were to advance a general hypothesis in order to explain various phenomena, but was then confronted by a very large number of apparent counter-instances – specific cases that the hypothesis could not account for and that actually called it into question. Would we allow the scientist to deal with these anomalies by saying that the universe is mysterious and cannot be fully understood by the human mind? Or would we say that such a response represents the abandonment of the attempt to use reason to understand the world?

In the same way, any move by theologians to invoke the mysteriousness and unfathomability of God, especially when this comes at the point where their argument is under the greatest stress, leaves them vulnerable to the charge that they are not genuinely willing to subject their views to rational criticism. When the going gets tough, they abandon reason and appeal to faith.

Can religious faith be rational?

Why should believers be answerable to the tribunal of reason anyway?
Isn't religious faith, by its very nature, essentially non-rational?

This is the view of the great Danish thinker Sören Kierkegaard, himself a deeply committed Christian. He argued that the whole point about a religion like Christianity is that it contradicts reason and therefore requires faith. After all, if it were perfectly sensible everyone would accept it and there would be no particular merit in having faith. But this is very much a modern view. Earlier philosophers usually saw the relation between faith and reason rather differently. Descartes, for instance, argued that reason can provide a solid foundation for faith. Aquinas held that faith supplements reason, enabling us to embrace religious doctrines that lie beyond rational proof and that must therefore be the subject of revelation (for example, the mystery of the trinity). And Hegel viewed faith and reason as complementary, providing two routes to the same underlying truth. Clearly, the relation between reason and faith is a complex issue.

Let us start by clarifying what we mean by 'faith'. The concept of faith is clearly different from the concept of knowledge. If I say I 'know' something, that implies that the belief in question is true. But if I say I have 'faith' that something is the case, there is no such implication. Faith, unlike knowledge, can be mistaken. This difference has nothing to do with how certain I am about the truth of my belief. Religious believers can be every bit as certain about the truth of their faith as scientists are about the truth of their observations. The difference has more to do with the *grounds* for holding the beliefs in question. Compare the belief that the earth is round with the belief that there is an afterlife. The first belief is one we think of as being both true and well-supported by a mass of empirical evidence. That is why it is taken to constitute knowledge. The belief in an afterlife, by contrast, is unsupported by this sort of evidence; it is thus an instance not of knowledge but of faith.

It would be nice if the distinction between knowledge and faith could be drawn as clearly and simply as this. Unfortunately, things are rarely so clear cut. Those who believe in an afterlife might plausibly argue that their belief is not without grounds or empirical support. They might, for instance, point to the many accounts people have given of near-death experiences that exhibit a significant degree of similarity; these experiences often convince those who have them that there really is some sort of continued personal existence after bodily death. Similarly, it could be argued that the testimony of thousands of people who claim to have witnessed miracles constitutes empirical evidence for the religious beliefs that rest on such testimony. We thus have a new problem: What counts as good evidence or rational support for a belief? More specifically, what is the difference, if any, between the kind of evidence that supports scientific beliefs and the kind of evidence on which religious beliefs rest?

This is a very difficult question, to which there may be no clear-cut answer. Certainly, there seem to be some prima facie differences between a straightforward empirical statement like 'The world is round' and claims such as 'God loves me' or 'Every human being has an immortal soul'. 'The world is round' rests on observations that are both public and repeatable; evidence that does not satisfy these requirements is not accepted by the scientific community. In many cases, the 'evidence' that supports an individual's religious beliefs – for instance, a mystical experience, or a prayer being 'answered' – fails to meet one or both of these conditions.

However, some of the experiences that support religious beliefs arguably are public and repeatable. Cases of faith healing are an obvious example. Moreover, there are difficulties with maintaining that all scientifically respectable beliefs rest on evidence that is public and repeatable. Some may be principles we hold to be true a priori or, as Hume argued, simply accept through habit. Thus, while the concepts of faith and knowledge are distinct, and while in some cases we can distinguish between them according to the kind of rational or evidential support they enjoy, it is not always easy to draw this distinction in practice.

Is religious belief necessarily unscientific?

It may be tricky in some cases to know whether a particular belief should be classified as an item of knowledge or an item of faith. But the general distinction still seems to be important and valid. After all, science and religion are very different. And when we say faith is not rational, what we mean is that it is unscientific.

This could be a useful lead. But it raises a problem: What do we mean when we say that religious beliefs are unscientific? There are at least three possibilities here:

1. Religious beliefs contradict scientific findings.
2. Religious beliefs are held in an unscientific way (dogmatically, for instance).
3. Religious beliefs go beyond science.

The first of these is fairly straightforward. If it is reasonable to accept the findings of science – at least where these are well established and accepted by the vast majority of scientists today – then it is unreasonable to believe things that science declares to be false or impossible. For example, to believe that the world is only a few thousand years old (as implied by Genesis) contradicts the findings of geology. Or to believe that a person could die (*really* dic, that is, as opposed to being in a deep coma) and then come back to life several days later is incompatible with biological science. Such beliefs may be declared unreasonable on this count.

Yet even here a qualification is in order. In some cases, such as the question of the earth's age, we have positive evidence that the traditional Judaeo-Christian view is false. In cases such as Jesus's immaculate conception or Aaron's rod turning into a serpent, science provides no *direct* evidence that these events did not occur. But to believe that they did occur is to reject a fundamental assumption of most science: namely, that nature operates in a uniform way. If we accept this principle, then we cannot reasonably believe in miracles which, by definition, violate what we take to be laws of nature. We might object that there is good empirical evidence for the occurrence of some miracles, and a reasonable person should respect this evidence. But Hume expressed the attitude of science well when he argued that it is always more reasonable to assume that the report of the miracle is mistaken than to believe that the laws of nature momentarily ceased to operate.

The second way faith can be unscientific is in being adhered to dogmatically. I hold a belief dogmatically if I refuse to recognize the possibility that it could be false or refuse to allow anything to count as possible evidence against it. In the jargon used by philosophers of science, dogmas are *unfalsifiable*. It seems clear that people often hold religious beliefs in this manner. For example, many people believe that God loves them, and nothing is allowed to count as evidence against this belief. If they pray for something and it comes about, this reinforces their faith. But if what they prayed for does not happen, that does not raise any doubts – perhaps they did not deserve it, or it would not have been in their best interests. Whatever the reason, it could not be that God either does not exist or does not care. Similarly, a believing parent whose child survives an accident in which many others die sees this as evidence of God's protection; but if the child had died then they would have said that God has 'taken' the child.

Now, it is certainly true that scientists also work with certain basic assumptions that they may never question: for example, that every event is caused, that the laws of nature operate in a uniform way, that all causes are material (as opposed to mental or spiritual). But it is a distinguishing feature of the scientific attitude that every belief is, *in principle*, open to question and, if necessary, to revision. Thus, even basic assumptions, such as the Newtonian view of space and time or the principle that every event is predictable to someone with sufficient information, have been challenged and ultimately rejected. This ever present possibility of rejecting any particular belief within one's belief system thus seems to be something that distinguishes the scientific attitude from the attitude of faith.

Many believers would accept this point, however, without accepting the inference that faith is thereby shown to be fundamentally irrational:

> *Faith is not simply a matter of holding certain beliefs to be true. At its deepest level it is about participating in a certain kind of relationship – namely, a relationship with God. A prerequisite of this relationship is that one bring to it hope, love and trust. Because the context is that of a personal relationship rather than that of scientific enquiry, the hyper-critical, hyper-rational stance of the scientist would be inappropriate here. The scientific attitude is necessary when one is doing science; but it is out of place at other times.*

As an example of this position, suppose a scientist receives a phone call from her spouse. He tells her he is at a conference and not at the casino. She has no particular reason to disbelieve him; he has no track record of visiting casinos; the sound of slot machines cannot be heard in the background. Should she insist on further corroborating evidence to bear out his claim? Surely not – at least not if she wishes their relationship to continue as one based on mutual love and trust. If she tried to introduce scientific standards of justification into this quite different context she would not be demonstrating her commitment to rationality; on the contrary, she would be showing herself to be obtuse.

This brings us to the third way that faith might be thought unreasonable because unscientific: it involves speculations about matters that lie beyond what we can know by scientific means. Moreover, these speculative beliefs seem to be influenced by a person's wishes, hopes and fears; but to allow this to happen is contrary to the ideal of objectivity that is central to science and also important in everyday life. As so many of its critics have pointed out, religion invariably involves an element of wishful thinking, and this discredits whatever claims it makes to being a rationally respectable system of belief.

Now, one response to this criticism is simply to deny that religion rests on wishful thinking. After all, it could be argued that people who take religion seriously have more to worry about and are likely to impose more constraints on their own worldly pleasures than those without any faith. Interestingly, though, a number of philosophers have responded in a different way. They defend what is sometimes called **voluntarism** – the view that it can be legitimate to believe something because you *want* it to be true. Let us consider two well-known defences of this doctrine.

Pascal's wager

Blaise Pascal (1623–1662) was a brilliant mathematician as well an original philosopher, and his pioneering work on probability theory no doubt informed the following argument in favour of embracing Christianity. I have two basic options regarding the Christian faith: I can either believe or not believe. And in either case the position I adopt may be either true or false. This yields four possible cases, and four possible outcomes, as shown in the table.

	God exists	*God does not exist*
I believe in God	eternal happiness	small loss of worldly pleasure
I don't believe in God	eternal damnation	small gain in worldly pleasure

Embracing faith and the lifestyle that goes with it may mean that one has to sacrifice various pleasures in this life, either because of moral constraints imposed by religion or because of the need to spend time engaging in acts of worship. But in return for this relatively small stake one stands to gain an incalculably huge reward. Refusing to make this sacrifice, on the other hand, means risking absolute catastrophe for the sake of a small short-term benefit. If one assumes that God's existence or non-existence are more or less equally probable, then, Pascal argues, the rational course of action is clearly to embrace faith. It is analogous to buying a lottery ticket for ten pence where the potential prize is a billion pounds and where, moreover, the stake also buys you a comprehensive insurance policy against various calamities.

One objection to Pascal's wager is that it presupposes that one can choose to believe in God by an act of will. But this presupposition is false. We cannot simply *choose* to believe that God exists any more than we can choose to believe that the world is flat or that triangles have three sides. Beliefs are determined by many things: for instance, personal experience, evidence, upbringing, education and reasoning. My personal interests, hopes and wishes may also play a role, but I cannot just decide to let them override these other factors. Pascal himself acknowledges the force of this point, but he argues that one can nevertheless choose to move oneself towards faith through practical participation in the daily rituals of the Church. In his view, this is one of the main functions of the Church: to provide means through which doubters can 'deaden their acuteness' and so attain faith.

Another objection to the wager, voiced by many, is that it makes faith a matter of self-interested calculation – the very opposite of the kind of faith that God requires of us. What God requires, say the critics, is a faith based on trust and love, where the left hand does not know what the right hand is doing. In Pascal's defence, it may be said that the wager he imagines is not an attempt to *describe* religious faith. All he is trying to do is show that in this case it is both legitimate to allow one's hopes and fears to affect one's beliefs, and more reasonable to embrace the Christian faith than to reject it.

William James's 'will to believe'

William James (1842–1910) was unimpressed with Pascal's argument. He thought it rests on a misguided conception of faith, one that robs it of any vitality. But James agrees with the voluntarist thesis that there are times when we may legitimately allow our will or, more generally, what he calls our 'passional nature' – that is, the total complex of our needs, interests, feelings, and desires – to influence what we believe. This is the thesis he defends in his famous essay 'The Will to Believe'.

As James sees it, the success of science has bred scientism – the view that the scientific method is the only legitimate method for discovering truth and that science exhausts our knowledge of reality. But should the scientific way of thinking be the only approach we accept as legitimate? Or may we still respect other grounds for our beliefs as well as the beliefs that these alternative modes of learning support?

James was himself a scientist, trained in medicine and a pioneer of modern psychology. But he rejects scientism, seeing it as a form of dogmatism that arises out of an almost neurotic fear of being mistaken. Extreme epistemic caution, and an unswerving commitment to the ideals of objectivity and neutrality, may be important virtues inside the scientific laboratory. But we do not live our entire lives in a laboratory. As we noted earlier, there are times and contexts when the scientific attitude is inappropriate, even detrimental to our real interests. For example, a person who is sick may have a better chance of recovering if he believes he will recover. This belief may not be justified by the statistical data; but it nevertheless makes sense for him to hold to it since by doing so he makes it more likely to be true. Another example, one of James's favourites, is that of an alpine mountaineer who has to jump across an abyss. Since confidence is needed for a successful leap, the mountaineer has an interest in believing she can do it; by allowing this interest to influence what she believes, she helps to make the belief in question true.

To be sure, these examples describe unusual circumstances. But they suffice to demonstrate the general principle that there are times when it is rational, and therefore legitimate, to allow my interests, wishes, hopes and fears to influence what I choose to believe. According to James, this is the case whenever I find myself faced with a choice between options that are *live* and where the choice is both *forced* and *momentous*.

To say that the options are 'live' means that they must all represent genuine possibilities for me. Embracing the religion of ancient Athens, or believing the earth is flat, for instance, are no longer live options for most people today; embracing Catholicism or *laissez faire* economic theory may be, at least for some. A choice is 'forced' where it is unavoidable: for example, I cannot avoid choosing between either smoking or not smoking, getting married or not getting married (although I can postpone making a decision for a time). Choices are momentous if they can be expected to make a great difference to one's life – because they have such profound long-term consequences, or because the opportunity to make them arises so rarely, or because the decision, once made, is irrevocable. Deciding to specialize in a certain field, to emigrate, to become politically active, to marry, to have children, or to break off a relationship could all fall into the category of momentous decisions.

James views the decision over whether or not to embrace some form of religious belief as forced. Given that it concerns one's overarching view of and attitude towards the world as a whole, it surely counts as momentous. And for some people, at least, the religious hypothesis is indisputably a live option. Therefore, according to James, such people may legitimately, and without falling into any kind of irrationalism or mere wishful thinking, allow their 'passional nature' to influence what they choose to believe. In this sense, and to this extent, religious faith may be considered reasonable.

Needless to say, James's argument does not command universal assent. Probably the most common objection is that it provides a licence for wishful thinking. As one wag put it, instead of 'The Will to Believe', James's essay would be more aptly titled 'The Will to Make-believe'. But it is important to keep in mind the constraints James imposes on faith if it is to be reasonable. The most important is that the options be 'live'. For most modern intellectuals, this means that the beliefs in question cannot contradict the findings of science.

James later remarked that he ought to have titled his essay 'The *Right* to Believe', since this would better capture the basic idea he is defending – namely, that in the age of science there are still occasions when we are entitled to commit ourselves to beliefs that cannot be supported scientifically. Religious faith represents the most important instance where we exercise this right. And in doing so our thinking, while it goes beyond science, is neither irrational nor arbitrary. In many cases, it is based on and guided by what are called religious experiences: for example, a sense of the close presence of God, or of his protective love. James himself did not have such experiences, but he was greatly interested in them and thought that they were sufficiently common and consistent to deserve being taken seriously. A genuinely scientific attitude to such phenomena, he argues, does not dismiss them as simply the effects of temporary chemical alterations in the brain, but keeps an open mind about the possibility that these moments may be windows through which we apprehend a dimension of reality not accessible to science.

The death of God

James's argument may be sound. But a key premise in the argument is that for faith to be reasonable it must be a 'live' option. During the past few centuries, however, the claims of religion have become increasing difficult to believe for many people, especially members of the intelligentsia. In this sense, aren't religious beliefs destined increasingly to seem – and in fact to be – opposed to reason?

Here we touch on what is perhaps the most difficult of the challenges facing religious belief. Theoretical problems, such as those raised by the attempt to prove God's existence, are certainly serious; but believers always have the option of evading the challenge by arguing that faith does not have to be rationally justified. They can even follow Kierkegaard and argue that faith is not *supposed* to be rational, that faith is indeed absurd, and that they believe precisely *because* it is absurd. However, to embrace – even to celebrate – the irrationality of religious belief in this manner is a desperate remedy: a sign that religion faces a grave crisis.

The crisis has been brought on by the fact that in modern society religion no longer enjoys cultural hegemony. A few centuries ago, in all countries where Christianity was dominant the church (of whatever denomination), its theologians and its ministers were generally respected as authorities on matters scientific, political, artistic, moral and social. Theological arguments concerning the age of the world or the character of the solar system were taken seriously. Many of the greatest artistic works – for example, Michelangelo's paintings, Milton's poetry and Bach's music – drew their primary inspiration from religion. Education was largely run by the church; children learned to read using the Bible; religious instruction was central to the curriculum; and college students were required to study divinity and attend chapel daily. The local church was at the centre of social life in each community; it drew everyone together at the weekly service, and oversaw the major civic festivals as well as the ceremonies that solemnify the decisive events in each individual's life: birth, marriage and death.

Today, things are obviously very different. To be sure, even in technologically advanced societies the majority of people may still think of themselves as religious believers: they check the appropriate box on any questionnaire put before them. But the nature of their belief, and the way it relates to other aspects of their lives, has changed enormously. Religion is no longer the centre of social and psychic gravity that it once was. Education and the arts have been thoroughly secularized. Festivals like Christmas or Easter and ceremonies such as weddings and funerals retain something of the *form* of religion; but they do so largely because people find these forms aesthetically pleasing, not because people remain deeply committed to their religious meaning.

The most dramatic changes have to do with what people actually believe. Not so long ago, the central dogmas of Christianity – Jesus's virgin birth, his miracles, his resurrection, the existence of heaven and hell, and the impending final judgement – were generally accepted as literal truths by all but a few free thinkers. Now, even ordained ministers candidly admit that they don't accept many of these dogmas. In place of such concrete, vivid, easily understood claims, Christianity has drifted

Friedrich Nietzsche (1844–1900)

Friedrich Nietzsche is one of the most original, interesting and influential thinkers of modern times. Born and educated in Germany, he was a brilliant student who at the age of 24 was appointed Professor of Classical Philology (classical languages and literature) at the University of Basle in Switzerland.

Plagued by ill health, Nietzsche resigned from this position after ten years and spent the 1880s living in modest circumstances on a small pension, residing in Switzerland during the summer months and wintering in Northern Italy. During this time he wrote a series of books that attracted virtually no attention at the time but are now reckoned among the world's great literary treasures – among them *The Gay Science*, *Thus Spoke Zarathustra*, *Beyond Good and Evil*, and *On the Genealogy of Morals*. Nietzsche's ill health (probably syphilis) eventually culminated in a complete mental breakdown in 1889. He spent the last years of his life in an asylum.

Nietzsche's writings range over almost every conceivable topic, but he was especially interested in morality, religion and the arts. In investigating morality and religion he does not usually concern himself with the truth of moral and religious claims, since he assumes they are generally false. Instead, he studies them as psychological and cultural phenomena, asking questions like: What psychological type would embrace Christian morality? What historical circumstances would produce Judaism? What motives lie behind some particular set of moral-religious doctrines and practices?

Nietzsche is vehemently critical of Christianity, though he has some respect for Jesus. While he acknowledges that some religions have been integral to great cultures (in ancient Greece and ancient Israel, for instance), he holds that the central doctrines of the Judaeo-Christian religious tradition are no longer intellectually credible. This is the event he calls the 'death of God'. It represents a crisis in Western civilization because the metaphysical doctrines in question formed the basis for an entire world view, including an ethical system and a specific sense of the meaning of life.

> The danger facing Western culture at this juncture is that 'nihilism' – a loss of faith in the value of anything – will become prevalent. But Nietzsche believes the death of God also represents a unique opportunity; for with the decline of the old dogmas we are in a position to propose new values and create new ideals to express a much stronger, healthier, more beautiful and more life-affirming attitude to life than Christianity ever offered.

towards insisting on only a few very general ideas about the existence and nature of God. The same could be said of Judaism. Only the most orthodox Jews now insist that the events described in Exodus and the other books of the Torah all happened exactly as they are written.

The most plausible explanation of this trend is simply that people find it increasingly difficult to believe in the old dogmas. And the reason for this is that many of the old beliefs conflict with modern science. Heaven and hell, for instance were supposed to be geographically locatable beyond the stars and beneath the earth. But astronomers and geologists have constructed models of these realms in which heaven and hell have no place; and now belief in horned devils prancing among the fire and brimstone is on a par with belief in witches or fairies. Three centuries ago, at the dawn of the Enlightenment, scepticism about religion was found primarily among intellectuals. Since then, with the spread of education and literacy, it has trickled down into the general population. Today, research, innovation and discussion in the natural sciences, the social sciences, the arts and philosophy go on with virtually no input from religion whatsoever. This loss of credibility that religion has suffered – especially among the intelligentsia – along with its displacement to the periphery of our culture, is a good part of what Nietzsche was referring to when he made his famous pronouncement that 'God is dead' (see box above).

The upshot of these long-running and profound trends in modern culture is that religion is only able to maintain its claim to reasonableness by continually diluting the content of its doctrines. In effect, it has been forced to back out of the fight with science over any of the issues that science believes lie within its domain – the age of the world, the origin of life, the origin of humanity, the possibility of bodily resurrection, the likelihood of miracles . . . What remains is a family of somewhat vague beliefs about the existence of a reality not accessible to science: a being or a force, perhaps characterized by something analogous to what we call purpose and intelligence, that is the 'ground' of our spatio-temporal reality – sustaining it, guiding it and endowing it (and our own lives) with meaning – and with which we may eventually become united after death.

Of course, many believers would dispute this account of the status of religion in contemporary culture. They will point to the fact that the great majority of people in most societies still view themselves as subscribing to some religion. They could also point to the remarkable religious revivals that occurred in diverse societies around the globe in the latter part of the twentieth century. How one views such phenomena will inevitably depend to some extent on one's general attitude towards religion. Sceptics will be inclined to think that fundamentalist revivals and continued church attendance have only a short-term significance; they indicate that God will die a lingering rather than a sudden death. But the general trend will continue; the stock of religion will continue to fall in the long term, and there is little chance that this trend will be reversed.

Those sympathetic to religion, however, are likely to favour a different interpretation. They will say that after four hundred years of scientific progress, we are beginning to realize that although science can provide answers to many of the questions that human beings have long asked about the world, it cannot answer all our legitimate questions nor satisfy all our genuine needs. The picture that science paints of our universe is impressive, beautiful and fascinating; but it is not and can never be complete. Nor do scientific understanding and technological mastery provide the only important ways in which human beings – as individuals or in groups – relate themselves to the whole of which they are part. A sense of this greater whole to which we belong, a feeling that it is what ultimately confers significance on our lives, and a desire to celebrate the mystery it holds (and continues to hold in spite of all our science): these feelings have always been at the heart of religion. If this view is correct, we can expect religious beliefs and practices to persist for as long as human beings experience such feelings, needs, hopes and desires and seek to give them expression.

Glossary

Act utilitarianism: a version of **utilitarianism** which holds that in any particular situation one should act in such a way as to maximize the happiness of all those affected by the action.

Aesthetics: the philosophical study of art or the way we respond to art. The term also covers the study of beauty in general, both in art and in things which are not art (for example, landscapes) but which provoke similar responses in us.

Analytic statement: a statement that is true or false solely because of the meaning of the words used, for example 'all completely bald men have no hair on their heads' is an analytic truth since 'completely bald' *means* 'no hair on the head'; its denial would thus lead to a contradiction.

A priori/a posteriori: a distinction between two kinds of knowledge. **A priori** truths (for example, 'all triangles have three sides') are known independently of experience; **a posteriori** truths (for example, 'elephants are grey') are known on the basis of experience.

Argument: a line of reasoning consisting of one or more premises and a conclusion which they are intended to support.

Argument from analogy: the attempt to show that because two things are similar in at least one respect, they are also similar in another respect.

Autonomy: being able to decide for oneself what one will believe and do

Categorical imperative: (1) an unqualified command which has the form: 'Do X!'; (2) the fundamental principle of Kant's moral theory: 'Always act so that the principle behind your action could be willed as a universal law.'

Causal principle: the principle that every event has a cause.

Civil disobedience: breaking the law for reasons of conscience, often with a view to bringing about a change in the law or in government policy.

Cognitive relativism: the view that the truth or falsity of a statement is always relative to the theoretical framework of some particular community.

Coherence theory of truth: the view that the truth of a statement consists in its coherence with other statements or beliefs.

Coherentism: the doctrine that a belief constitutes knowledge when it coheres satisfactorily with the rest of one's beliefs.

Conclusion: the statement an argument is intended to support.

Consequentialism: the view that the moral rightness or wrongness of an action is determined by its consequences.

Convention: a way of doing things devised by human beings, usually customary, and perhaps based on some kind of agreement.

Correspondence theory of truth: the view that a statement is true if it corresponds to the facts it describes.

Cosmological argument: an argument that moves from the existence of the world or of something in the world to the existence of a being (typically God) causally responsible for it.

Deduction: a kind of reasoning in which the conclusion is supposed to follow necessarily from the premises.

Deontology: a duty-based approach to ethics which holds that the consequences of an action are morally irrelevant.

Determinism: the view that every event is the necessary effect of prior causes.

Direct realism: the belief that our senses put us in immediate contact with the physical world.

Dualism: (1) in **metaphysics** this is the view that there are two fundamental categories of things in the world, usually identified as the material and the mental; (2) in the philosophy of mind it is the view that human beings are made up of physical bodies and non-physical minds.

Emotivism: the view that ethical utterances are merely expressions of the feelings of the speaker and not statements which can be either true or false.

Empiricism: the view that all knowledge of the world rests on sense-experience.

Epiphenomenalism: a variety of **dualism** that sees mental events as epiphenomena, being caused by physical events such as brain activity but having no causal power themselves.

Epistemology: the theory of knowledge.

Ethical naturalism: the view that our ethical judgements should be grounded in what we know about the ordinary properties of the natural world, which includes the physical and psychological attributes of human beings; also the view that ethical terms like 'good' and 'right' can be analysed in non-ethical terms.

Ethical relativism: the view that the correctness or incorrectness of moral beliefs and practices is relative to the culture in which they occur.

Ethics: the branch of philosophy concerning right, wrong, good, and bad, as well as our beliefs about these matters.

Ethnocentrism: believing that one's own race or culture is superior to others. It can also refer to the tendency to interpret and appraise other cultures by reference to one's own.

Existentialism: an approach to the questions of how to live one's life that starts from the facts of the individual's concrete experience rather than abstract theoretical principles. Existentialists tend to emphasize the importance of being *authentic* (true to oneself); some, though by no means all, stress the importance of freedom for the individual.

Expression: used in this book to mean the quality possessed by at least some works of art of communicating an artist's thoughts or feelings.

Fact/value gap: the logical difference between statements of fact and value judgements which some argue invalidates any attempt to base the latter on the former. See also **Is/ought** problem.

Falsifiability: the property of being refutable by experience (at least in principle). In Karl Popper's philosophy of science, falsifiability is held to be the hallmark of genuinely scientific claims. By contrast, the claims of religion and astrology, are unfalsifiable (and hence unscientific) because nothing is allowed to count as evidence against them.

Fatalism: (1) the idea that there is some supernatural force that controls our destinies; (2) the view that what will happen in the future is fixed no matter what we do.

Formalism: any view that emphasizes form over content. The term is used in this book to denote an aesthetic theory which does this, emphasizing shape, pattern, tone, or colour, for example, rather than **expression** or **mimesis**.

Foundationalism: the view that a belief constitutes knowledge only if it belongs to or can be deduced from a secure foundation of beliefs that are free from sceptical doubt.

Freedom: see **practical freedom, metaphysical freedom, positive freedom,** and **negative freedom.**

Functionalism: in the philosophy of mind, the view that a mental state is the type of mental state that it is in virtue of its functional role. Functionalism typically compares the brain to a computer, viewing the physical organ as like the hardware and the mind (which we describe using mental terms) as comparable to software.

Hard determinism: the doctrine that since determinism is true, all our choices are causally determined and are therefore never free.

Harm principle: the principle that one should be able to do as one likes provided one does not cause harm to others.

Hypothetical imperative: a command that has a conditional form, like a piece of advice: 'If you want x, then do y.'

Hypothetico-deductive method: the method, which some take to be central to science, of constructing a hypothesis, deducing its observable consequences, and then testing for their occurrence.

Idealism: the view that reality is fundamentally mental and that what we call physical reality is either dependent on or a manifestation of minds and their contents.

Identity theory of mind: the view that mental states are identical to certain physical states (usually thought to be brain states).

Indeterminism: the view that at least some events are uncaused. According to some defenders of free will, indeterminism must be true if free will is to be possible.

Induction: a kind of reasoning in which the premises are intended to support the conclusion without logically entailing it.

Instrumental value: the value something has for us if we value it for the sake of some other good we think it will bring about.

Intentionality: the quality that consciousness has of always being directed towards an object. We are not just conscious; we are always conscious *of* something.

Intrinsic value: something has intrinsic value if we value it just for what it is in itself.

Is–ought problem: the problem of whether statements of fact ('is' statements) imply moral statements about what ought to be done ('ought' statements). See also **fact/value gap**.

Liberalism: a political philosophy which sees the liberty of the individual as the highest political good. This liberty is generally conceived in terms of **negative freedom**. Two main varieties are distinguished in this book: **libertarians**, who tend to see the state as the main threat to the liberty of the individual, and **social democrats**, who regard the state as an important means of maximizing equality of opportunity.

Libertarianism: a political philosophy which advocates maximizing each individual's **negative freedom** and rejects any interference by the state except for the purpose of protecting this freedom.

Logical behaviourism: the view that mental language (for example talk about a person's beliefs or desires) is just an economical way of talking about behaviour patterns.

Materialism: the view that reality is essentially material. See also **physicalism.**

Metaphysical freedom: being ultimately responsible for one's own choices (i.e. not having one's actions determined by external causes); also known as *freedom of the will.*

Metaphysics: the branch of philosophy concerned with the most fundamental questions about the nature of reality.

Mimesis: a term used in **aesthetics,** variously rendered as copy, imitation, or representation.

Monism: the doctrine that all of reality consists fundamentally of one kind of thing (for example matter).

Naturalized epistemology: an approach to the theory of knowledge which contents itself with describing the process by which individuals acquire and revise their beliefs, and also of the way different communities apply 'epistemic norms' to determine what counts as 'knowledge' for them. No attempt is made to evaluate these processes or norms.

Negative freedom: freedom from constraint; not being prevented from doing something by other people or by the state.

Non-realism: the view that the only reality we can know must be reality as it is experienced and interpreted by us (as opposed to a reality that exists independently of us).

Normal science: Kuhn's term for what happens when scientists work, as they usually do, at solving well-defined problems within the assumptions of a dominant **paradigm;**

Normative/descriptive: normative statements tell us what we ought to do; **descriptive** statements tell us what is the case.

Normative epistemology: the attempt to determine which, if any, of our beliefs constitute genuine knowledge.

Objective: the property of existing independently of a subject's thoughts or desires.

Occam's razor: a principle of theoretical economy. It says that when we are faced with the choice between two explanations we should always choose the simpler, all other things being equal.

Ontological argument: an attempt to prove that God's existence is entailed by the very concept of God.

Ontology: the philosophical study of Being or existence.

Paradigm: an ideal or exemplary instance of something. In Kuhn's philosophy of science, the term refers to a general set of assumptions and way of viewing things that dominates a scientific field at a particular time.

Paternalism: deciding for other people what is in their best interests.

Perception: awareness or apprehension of the world through the senses.

Phenomenalism: the view that all claims about the world must be understood solely in terms of our actual and possible sense-experiences.

Phenomenology: any study or description of the way things appear to us. More specifically, **phenomenology** is usually identified with a school of philosophy started by Edmund Husserl which sees truth as grounded in our direct awareness of how the world appears to us.

Physicalism: the view that ultimate reality is physical. The term **physicalism** is often preferred to **materialism** nowadays, as it more precisely conveys the view that ultimate reality is composed of interchangeable matter and energy.

Positive freedom: the freedom to achieve full self-realization; this includes freedom from conditions which inhibit or prevent self-realization, such as poverty or ignorance.

Practical freedom: the freedom to do as one wishes.

Preference utilitarianism: a version of utilitarianism which focuses on satisfying the desires of the greatest number of people rather than attempting to calculate amounts of pleasure or happiness.

Premise: a statement intended to support the conclusion of an argument.

Presupposition: something assumed in advance or taken for granted.

Primary and secondary qualities: a distinction made central to **epistemology** by Galileo, Descartes, and Locke. **Primary qualities** (for example shape, quantity, motion) are held really to belong to material objects and are the properties of things that can be described mathematically. The term **secondary qualities** has two meanings: (1) properties such as colour, taste, or smell which we directly perceive and which are 'in' the mind of the perceiving subject; (2) the properties possessed by an object that cause us to have such sensations.

Principle of sufficient reason: the principle that every event or state of affairs has a complete explanation.

Rationalism: the view that we can establish important truths about the world by reason alone, unaided by sense-experience.

Realism: in general, the doctrine that a certain kind of thing (for example physical objects, moral goodness, mathematical entities) exists independently of our beliefs about it or experiences of it. See also **direct realism, representative realism, scientific realism**.

Reductionism: the attempt to explain some complex thing in terms of other supposedly more simple things. Typically, the reductionist says that some X is 'nothing but' Y, thereby reducing X to Y.

Relativism: see **cognitive relativism** and **ethical relativism**

Reliabilism: the theory that a belief constitutes knowledge when it has been arrived at through a process which we have good reason to regard as a reliable method for acquiring true beliefs.

Representative realism: the view that our sense impressions are caused by the properties of independently existing physical entities, and that we can infer things about these entities on the basis of our impressions.

Representative theory of perception: an account of cognition which holds that what we actually perceive are our own subjective sense impressions, from which we make inferences about the existence and nature of things in the material world.

Revolutionary science: Kuhn's term for the kind of science that occurs when accumulated problems ('anomalies') cannot be accommodated within the already existing paradigm and a new paradigm is required in order to resolve the ensuing theoretical crisis.

Right: in political philosophy, a justified fundamental claim to be able to do or have something.

Rule utilitarianism: a version of utilitarianism which holds that in any particular situation we should follow general rules which are thought to promote the general happiness if followed by everyone.

Scepticism: the view that human beings either do not or cannot attain knowledge.

Scientific realism: the view that science provides us with a true picture of an independently existing reality.

Situation ethics: the view that since each situation we find ourselves in is different, our judgements about what is right and wrong can only apply to the particular conditions that characterize that situation.

Slippery slope argument: a form of argument which asserts that if certain things are accepted, then other less desirable things will follow.

Social contract: a supposed agreement between ruler and ruled in a society, entered into for reasons of long term mutual benefit. Social contract theorists like Thomas Hobbes and John Locke use this idea to justify the legitimacy of a state or a ruler.

Social democracy: a form of **liberalism** which tempers the commitment to individual liberty with a concern for other ideals such as equality and justice.

Soft determinism: the view that although determinism is true and our choices are causally determined, we can still be said to act freely when we do what we want to do.

Solipsism: the view that nothing exists except one's own mind and its contents.

Soundness: a property of arguments. A deductive argument is sound if all the premises are true and it is logically valid (i.e. the conclusion follows from the premises).

Straw man argument: a fallacious form of reasoning which involves setting up a distorted version of one's opponent's position and then attacking that instead of their actual position.

Subjectivity: the property of belonging to or being a product of the thinking subject.

Synthetic statement: a statement the truth of which is not determined simply by the meanings of the words used, for example 'The planets are not made of cheese' is a synthetic truth; its denial would not entail a contradiction.

Teleological: having to do with a thing's goal or purpose.

Theodicy: the attempt to reconcile the goodness of God with the existence of evil in the world.

Theology: the theoretical elaboration of the premises of a particular religion.

Truth: see **coherence theory of truth**, **correspondence theory of truth**.

Type/token: different instances of the same kind of thing are called tokens; the thing they are instances of is a type. **Type identity theorists** believe that a particular type of mental state is identical with a particular type of physical(brain) state; **token identity theorists** agree that any mental state is identical to some physical state, but they allow the mental state to be physically realized in various ways.

Utilitarianism: the doctrine that the moral worth of an action is determined by the amount of pleasure or happiness ('utility') it produces. See **act utilitarianism**, **preference utilitarianism**, **rule utilitarianism**.

Validity: a property of arguments. A deductive argument is valid if it is not possible for the premises to be true and the conclusion false.

Voluntarism: in the philosophy of religion, the view that it can be legitimate to believe something because one wants it to be true.

Suggested further reading

Metaphysics

Martin Heidegger, *Basic Writings*, trans. David Farrell Krell, New York: Harper and Row, 1977. Ten essays by one of the twentieth century's most original and influential thinkers. Difficult reading at times, but the essays exemplify an important alternative way of reflecting on metaphysical issues to the approach favoured by most of the other thinkers mentioned here.

Ted Honderich, *How Free Are You?* Oxford: Oxford University Press, 1996. A short, accessible defence of determinism and critique of the belief in free will.

Robert Kane, *The Significance of Free Will*, Oxford: Oxford University Press, 1998. A sophisticated defence of the idea that quantum indeterminacy allows for the possibility of free will and ultimate responsibility. Provides a valuable account of recent debates relating to the free will problem.

Immanuel Kant, *Prolegomena to Any Future Metaphysics*, ed. and trans. Gary Hatfield, Cambridge: Cambridge University Press, 1997. Kant's own attempt to present his metaphysics in an accessible form (which still does not mean it is easy going!).

Plato, *Republic*, trans. G. M. A. Grube, Indianapolis: Hackett, 1992. By common consent, one of the greatest philosophical works ever written. At its heart is a discussion of the distinction between appearance and reality, but it ranges over several areas of philosophy, linking metaphysics to epistemology, ethics, and political theory.

Jean-Paul Sartre, *Existentialism and Humanism*, trans. P. Mairet, London: Methuen,1948. A famous lecture Sartre delivered in 1946 on the nature of human freedom and responsibility.

Richard Taylor, *Metaphysics*, 2nd edn, Upper Saddle River, NJ: Prentice Hall, 1974. Exceptionally readable introductory treatment of a selection of metaphysical issues.

Theory of knowledge

George Berkeley, *Principles of Human Knowledge* and *Three Dialogues between Hylas and Philonous*, London: Penguin, 1988. Berkeley's two main philosophical works offering lively and provocative arguments against materialism and in support of idealism.

Roderick Chisholm, *Theory of Knowledge*, Englewood Cliffs, NJ: Prentice Hall, 1989. A concise, readable introduction to epistemology which exemplifies the approach favoured by many analytic philosophers.

René Descartes, *Meditations on First Philosophy*, trans. Donald Cress, Indianapolis: Hackett, 1980. A seminal text in the history of philosophy in which Descartes seeks to refute skepticism and establish the metaphysical foundations for modern science.

Hilary Putnam, *The Many Faces of Realism*, LaSalle, IL: Open Court, 1991. Four accessible lectures which explore issues in and implications of the realism/non-realism debate.

Richard Rorty, *Objectivity, Relativism, and Truth*, Cambridge: Cambridge University Press, 1991. Lucid but sophisticated contributions to current debates about truth, knowledge, meaning, interpretation, culture, and related topics from what many would call a relativistic point of view.

Philosophy of mind

David Chalmers, *The Conscious Mind: In Search of a Fundamental Theory*, Oxford: Oxford University Press, 1997. A reasonably accessible contemporary defence of dualism which poses challenging questions to all forms of materialism.

Daniel Dennett, *Brainstorms*, Montgomery, VT: Bradford Books, 1978. A collection of essays on the nature of the mind and its activities by one of the most important and controversial contemporary philosophers. Engagingly written but sometimes technically demanding.

Nicholas Humphrey, *A History of the Mind*, New York, Harper, 1992. A fascinating and entertaining attempt to explain the origins of consciousness. Offers a wealth of thought-provoking information about the nature of cognition.

Edmund Husserl, *The Paris Lectures*, trans. Peter Kostenbaum, The Hague: Martinus Nijhoff, 1964. One of the clearer introductions to phenomenology by its leading exponent.

Gilbert Ryle, *The Concept of Mind*, New York: Barnes and Noble, 1949. Probably the most widely read presentation of logical behaviourism.

John Searle, *Minds, Brains, and Science*, Cambridge, MA: Harvard University Press, 1984. Six very readable lectures in which Searle defends a materialist view of the mind while attacking attempts to understand the mind as analogous to a digital computer.

Philosophy of science

Nelson Goodman, *Fact, Fiction and Forecast*, Cambridge, MA: Harvard University Press, 1955. A highly original and thought-provoking discussion of the problem of induction.

Carl G. Hempel, *Philosophy of Natural Science*, Englewood Cliffs, NJ: Prentice Hall, 1966. A short but rigorous introduction to the field by one of its leading figures. Covers issues not dealt with in this book, such as the nature of scientific explanation and the definition of scientific concepts.

David Hume, *An Enquiry Concerning Human Understanding*, ed. Eric Steinberg, Cambridge: Hackett, 1977. Hume's most polished statement of his skeptical philosophy.

Thomas S. Kuhn, *The Structure of Scientific Revolutions*, 2nd edn, Chicago: University of Chicago Press, 1970. A readable, fascinating, and extremely influential account of the nature of scientific activity and scientific progress.

Karl Popper, *The Logic of Scientific Discovery*, London: Hutchinson, 1959. The principal work of one of the twentieth century's most important philosophers of science.

Bas C. Van Fraassen, *The Scientific Image*, Oxford: Clarendon Press, 1980. A challenging critique of scientific realism which also serves to acquaint the reader with related controversies in contemporary philosophy of science.

Ethics

Aristotle, *The Ethics of Aristotle*, trans. J. A. K. Thomson, London: Penguin, 1955. Probably the single most influential work on ethics ever. This is a translation of Aristotle's 'Nichomachean ethics'.

John Finnis, *Fundamentals of Ethics*, Washington, DC: Georgetown University Press, 1983. A stimulating review of the main issues, from a committed perspective.

Immanuel Kant, *Foundations of the Metaphysics of Morals*, trans. Lewis White Beck, New York: Macmillan, 1985. One of Kant's more readable works, and without question one of the most important texts in the history of Western ethics. Although sometimes difficult, it is also remarkably rich in insights into the nature of moral reasoning.

Alasdair MacIntyre, *After Virtue*, London: Duckworth, 1981. A stimulating analysis of how moral philosophy came to be in a state of crisis. This work was one of several that helped revive the Aristotelian tradition of virtue ethics.

John Stuart Mill, *Utilitarianism*, Indianapolis: Hackett, 1979. The classic statement and defence of utilitarianism by one of its early champions.

Friedrich Nietzsche, *On the Genealogy of Morality*, trans. Maudemarie Clark and Alan Swensen, Indianapolis: Hackett, 1998. A radical departure from mainstream ethics, Nietzsche examines moral concepts, attitudes, and institutions with a view to uncovering their original social and psychological functions.

Political philosophy

Hannah Arendt, *Between Past and Future*: *Eight Exercises in Political Thought*, New York: Penguin,1954. Representative essays by a major critic of the excessive individualism that pervades modern political culture and philosophy.

Alan Brown, *Modern Political Philosophy*: *Theories of the Just Society*. London: Penguin, 1986. A clear and stimulating introduction which is also a contribution to the debate.

Robert Dahl, *Democracy and Its Critics*, New Haven: Yale University Press, 1991. Dahl constructs engaging dialogues to discuss some of the most fundamental problems of liberal democratic theory.

John Stuart Mill, *On Liberty*, Indianapolis: Hackett, 1978. This famous defence of individualism and the harm principle remains the starting point for modern liberal political theory.

Robert Nozick, *Anarchy, State and Utopia*, New York: Basic Books, 1984. An imaginative argument in favour of extreme libertarianism.

John Rawls, *A Theory of Justice*, Cambridge, MA: Harvard University Press, 1971. Somewhat dry, and undeniably long, this is nevertheless the most widely discussed work of political philosophy of the last fifty years. Most of the key ideas are presented in the first half of the work where Rawls constructs a novel version of the old idea of the social contract.

Charles Taylor, *The Ethics of Authenticity*, Cambridge, MA: Harvard University Press, 1992. A clear, jargon-free and exciting discussion of the place of the 'authentic self' in modernity.

Philosophy of art

Aristotle, *Poetics*, trans. Richard Janko, Indianapolis: Hackett, 1987. Enormously influential account of the representative and cathartic functions of literary art.

H. Gene Blocker, *Philosophy of Art*, New York: Scribner, 1979. A useful, comprehensive discussion of the major issues and movements in contemporary philosophy of art.

R. G. Collingwood, *The Principles of Art*, Oxford: Oxford University Press, 1938. An influential account of art which views it as the expression of emotion and a means to self-knowledge.

Immanuel Kant, *Critique of Judgement*, trans. Werner Pluhar, Indianapolis: Hackett, 1987. Kant's major work on aesthetics. Difficult but important.

Roger Scruton, *The Aesthetics of Music*, Oxford: Oxford University Press, 1997. Lucid and comprehensive treatment of a quite difficult area.

Anne Sheppard, *Aesthetics: An Introduction to the Philosophy of Art*, Oxford: Oxford University Press, 1987. A concise introduction to the central problems in aesthetics.

Philosophy of religion

Sigmund Freud, *The Future of an Illusion*, trans. and ed. James Strachey, London: W. W. Norton, 1961. A short, readable essay which presents Freud's skeptical, rationalistic view of religion as something that human beings will eventually outgrow.

John H. Hick, *Philosophy of Religion*, Englewood Cliffs, NJ: Prentice Hall, 1963. A balanced discussion of the main issues that have occupied twentieth-century English-speaking philosophers of religion.

William James, *The Will to Believe and Other Essays in Popular Philosophy*, New York: Dover, 1956. A classic selection of essays on reason, faith, and life by one of the leading American pragmatists.

C. S. Lewis, *Mere Christianity*, London: Geoffrey Bles, 1952. An exceptionally lucid defence of some central Christian doctrines.

Friedrich Nietzsche, *The Portable Nietzsche*, ed. and trans. Walter Kaufmann, New York: Penguin, 1976. Contains the full text of five of Nietzsche's books along with excerpts from many others. Nietzsche's ideas about religion appear in many places, particularly in his late work, *The Antichrist*.

Richard Swinburne, *Is There a God?* Oxford: Oxford University Press, 1996. A short, readable, up-to-date defence of theism.

Index

absolute idealism: Fichte 26
absolutism: ethical 126, 129, 130
act utilitarianism 149, 248
actions: consequences of 141, 142, 147, 149–50; and ethics 119, 124–5, 132; logical behaviourism 80–1; and responsibility 5–6, 152; use of utilitarianism to justify 147–8, 149
advertising 124
aesthetics 1, 248; art as object 213–14; and expressiveness of art 197; form 203, 205; judgements 207–10, 211–14; Kant 207–10; pleasure 186; of religion 244; responses to art 206–7, 213
Africa: indigenous tribal religions 216
afterlife 68, 69–70, 236, 237–8
altruism 167, 168
Americas: indigenous tribal religions 216
analogy see argument from analogy
analytic philosophy 82–3
analytic truths 21, 23–4, 248
anarchy 177, 178, 179
Anaximander of Miletus **18**
Anselm 219
apartheid: South Africa 131
appearance: Kant's transcendental idealism 25; and reality 7, **22**
Aquinas, St Thomas 222, **223–4**, 237
Arabic thought: importance to Western civilization 219
Arendt, Hannah 258
argument 248; **see also** cosmological argument; ontological argument; premises; reasoning
argument from analogy 66–7, **66**, 227, 248
argument from design 225–30
Aristotle 27, 94, 114, **154**, 157, 189, 259; approach to ethics **154**, 155, 156; influence on Thomas Aquinas **223**; physics **95**, 117
art: aesthetic response 206–7, 213; emotional response 195, 199–201, 205, 207, 214; evaluation and re-evaluation of 211–12, 213–14; expression 197–202, 203–4, 204–5,

214; form 202–5, 205–6; imitation 188–90, 193, 196; importance of 214; and interpretation 190–1, 193, 213; pleasure in 186–7, 208; religious 244; and the spectator 193; and subjectivism 211–13, 214; values in 186, 197, 203, 205–6, 214; view of radical conventionalism 192–3; **see also** aesthetics; films; literature; music; visual arts
assisted suicide: controversy 134–6
assumptions: based on past experience 101–2; in liberal ideas of freedom 166, 167; and moral principles 125, 157; and presuppositions 121, 167; provided by dominant paradigm 113, 115; of science 92–3, 94–5, 111, 239–40
astronomy: assumptions according to relativism 55; predictions 93, 94; and rejection of old beliefs 246
atheism 231
atomic theory 19, 114
atomism 17
Augustine of Hippo, St 232, 233
authority: relation with power in society 158, 176–8; of the state 176–81

Babbage, Charles 194
Bach, Johann Sebastian 200, 202, 244
Bacon, Francis (1561–1626) 32, 59–60, 111–12
bacteriology: before Pasteur 114
Balzac, Honoré de: novels 194
beauty: and aesthetic response 209–10; and artistic form 205–6; subjective judgement of 211
Beethoven, Ludwig van 202, 206, 211
begging the question **44**, 101, 102
behaviour: codes of 125; relationship with mind 82, 86–7; and responsibility for actions 13–14; and theories of human nature 167; traditional ethical notions 140
behaviourism 75; **see also** logical behaviourism
beliefs: and certainty 30–2; coherence of 54; connected with literature 194–5; criteria for 29–30, 36; and cultural difference 130, 132;

Page numbers in bold refer to boxes.

B
72
.H67